Cooking
THE COSTCO WAY™

Amber and Jasen's Italian Creme Cake Page 158

Cooking THE COSTCO WAY™

Across the country and around the world

Anita Thompson
Editorial Director

With a foreword by
Kathy Casey

Issaquah, Washington

Publisher:	David W. Fuller
Editorial Director:	Anita Thompson
Art Director:	Doris Winters
Assistant Editor:	Karen Tripson
Contributing Editor:	Pat Volchok
Copy Editor:	Judy Gouldthorpe
Graphic Designers:	Bill Carlson
	Brenda Tradii
Photographers:	Darren Emmens
	Chris McArthur
	Norman Hersom
	Tom Clements
	Devin Seferos
Food Stylists:	Amy Muzyka-McGuire
	Jane Morimoto
	June Schuck
	Joanne Naganawa
Business Manager:	Jane Klein-Shucklin
Advertising Manager:	Steve Trump
Advertising Assistant:	Aliw Moral
Production Manager:	Pam Sather
Production Assistant:	Antolin Matsuda
Color Specialist:	MaryAnne Robbers
Indexer:	Nan Badgett

FIRST EDITION

Photography by Iridio Photography, Seattle
Printed in China by Midas Printing International Ltd.

ISBN 0-9722164-2-1
Library of Congress Control Number: 2003112405
5 4 3 2 1

Grimmway Farms Low-Fat Fresh Orange Compote with Granola
Page 57

Traffic-Light Smoothie from Zespri Kiwifruit and the California Strawberry Commission
Page 78

Marine Harvest
Oriental Grilled Salmon
Page 222

Grandma Spears
Coca-Cola Cake
Page 125

Contents

Foreword

COOKING IS A UNIVERSAL LANGUAGE: everyone speaks it. For centuries, the shared meal has been the medium for connecting with friends and family—enjoying lively conversation, food and drink across the dinner table. Similarly, breaking bread together has built bridges among different peoples since ancient times. *Cooking the Costco Way* enthusiastically demonstrates this cosmopolitan spirit.

In addition to congeniality, food brings out our curiosity. People are always looking for new and exciting flavor sensations. With *Cooking the Costco Way* as your guide, you'll journey to culinary destinations outside your home region and confidently have a go at the cooking innovations found in this impressive array of recipes.

Being a native of the Pacific Northwest, I grew up eating fascinating things. The bounty of our region brought a wealth of interesting tastes and textures, and I have always loved to experiment—even when very young and prompted to eat pickled herring, sea beans and smoked oysters.

When I travel, I love to sample the local cuisine and to try a city's or town's "must have" local favorites. Over the years I've kept notes to document my "foodie finds." *Cooking the Costco Way* is like that—a collection of the best recipes contributed by great cooks and chefs from across our country and around the world. And the photos bring the recipes alive!

This gorgeous book brings together ideas and insights of famed food figures and the beloved recipes of Costco members, vendors and staff. Celebrity chefs and well-known epicures celebrate the foods of their regions. It's all here—the inventive spontaneity of Jeremiah Tower, that icon of California cuisine; Hawaii's Sam Choy "surfin' in" on slow-cooked pork and exotic tropical flavors; Jasper White extolling the famed chowder and lobster of the East Coast; Nathalie Dupree's reclamation of the comfort foods of the South; the heritage cooking of the Midwest detailed by recipe historian Judith Fertig; cowboy chef Grady Spears's chile-laced Southwestern fare; and of course the bright-flavored cuisine from my backyard, inspired by juicy berries, wild mushrooms and luscious Dungeness crab. This beautiful, photo-packed book also opens the door to culinary adventures in international lands, including Mexico, Canada and the UK, and Japan, Korea and Taiwan.

Cooking the Costco Way will make it easy for you to discover new dishes that will please everyone's palate. So get cooking—and set out on your own culinary adventure. Just think, a favorite recipe from someone across the country or in another corner of the globe may just become your favorite, too.

Kathy Casey

A YEAR AGO, when we released Costco's first-ever book, *Entertaining the Costco Way*, we were asked more than once whether Costco was getting into the book publishing business. Our answer then and now is no. But there can be no question as to whether we are in the food business. It is that commitment to offering our members the best possible food values that has resulted in *Cooking the Costco Way*. While our first book organized its recipes in menus tied to seasonal events, *Cooking the Costco Way* celebrates the differences in regional cuisine throughout the United States and in the six other countries in which Costco operates. Each book is meant to complement the other.

Recipes within each regional chapter are organized by meal category—appetizers, salads, side dishes, entrées, desserts, beverages. We open each chapter with an interview with a chef whose work has epitomized a region or who, as in the case of Jeremiah Tower in California or Kathy Casey in the Northwest, has long been at the forefront of bringing the joys of the region's cuisine to audiences around the country or the world.

As before, our vendors have supplied recipes that show off their products to the greatest advantage—not just something from one of their box tops, but something new, exciting or unusually tasty. Please note that each recipe contributed by a vendor has been identified with that vendor's corporate name or product branding. Some branded products may not be sold in your part of the country. In such cases, you should substitute a similar product.

With more than 65,000 copies of *Entertaining the Costco Way* in people's hands, as you can imagine, we have been receiving many new recipes from members. We are pleased to offer a delectable sampling of these in this new volume. A panel of Costco employees and other food professionals cooked and tested each of these and has given them the stamp of approval.

We hope you enjoy this new offering from Costco's vendors, members, employees and culinary friends.

DAVID W. FULLER
PUBLISHER

NOTE ON BRANDS

Many of the recipes in this book were submitted by companies that hold copyrights to the recipes and/or trademark applications/registrations on the brands listed in the recipes. Each of the companies represented in this book asserts its ownership of the trademarks, applications/registrations and copyrights it holds on its company name, brands or recipes. Trademark, application/registration and copyright symbols have been eliminated from the titles and text of the recipes by the publishers for design and readability purposes only.

Cooking
THE COSTCO WAY™

Meet the Costco food team

IN 1987, COSTCO OPENED its first fresh meat, seafood, deli and bakery departments at the Tukwila, Washington, warehouse. It was a bold step, because until then, no other warehouse club had successfully sold fresh food. But the skeptics have been silenced, as today Fresh Foods is a major category copied by others in the industry.

Its success is a measure of not just the quantities sold (150 million pounds of ground beef annually, 125 million muffins and 130 million pounds of bananas), but also the confidence of members and food professionals in the outstanding product quality. This recognition reflects well on the expertise and diligence of the Fresh Foods teams who source, buy and merchandise perishable products in warehouses from Hawaii to New England. Their mantra, as expressed by **Tim Rose**, senior

vice president, is: "We constantly look at every item to see what we can do to make it a better value for our member."

Under Tim's leadership Costco's Foods and Fresh Foods departments have added numerous innovations in product development, buying and distribution. The key to these successes is the close working relationships with suppliers.

Costco's meat department, under the direction of **Charlie Winters**, has become legendary for its consistent high quality and great prices. Professional meat cutters on-site closely trim off extra fat and gristle. No summer barbecue is complete without T-bones or rib-eyes from Costco.

The hard work of the meat department, including buyers Doug Holbrook and Chris Ostrander, has paid off. Costco is one of the largest buyers of USDA Choice beef in the United States. "The impact we have made on the industry and the volume

Tim Rose
Senior vice president foods, general merchandise, Foods, Sundries, Fresh Foods

Charlie Winters
Vice president/ director of meat operations

Sue McConnaha
Vice president of bakery operations

of meat we have processed and sold (550 million pounds in 2003 alone) is a true indicator of our success," Charlie says.

Sue McConnaha founded Costco's bakery department in 1987. A self-proclaimed "scratch not technical" baker, Sue instituted hands-on training, coordinated production methods to improve consistency and developed new items. Today she oversees 305 bakeries that create delectable goodies fresh each day. With assistance from Tom Fox and Jean-Yves Mocquet, "we're always looking around the next curve," she says.

But members also love the tried and true. What's a special occasion without a Costco cake? This year Costco bakeries will make more than 165 million servings of cake.

Before **David Andrew** joined Costco in 1998, the company's warehouses were already known as a source of wine values. But through his broadened selection of fine and rare wines at excellent prices, Costco has earned national recognition for its wine program. Sales have increased 400 percent, and Costco is now the biggest wine retailer in the country.

To accomplish this, David travels the world, tasting 5,000 wines per year and searching for the right wines at the right prices. A candidate for the Master of Wine—a position held by fewer than 20 people in the U.S.—David says his philosophy is, "The world's finest wines are available at Costco."

Jeff Lyons is known within Costco for the "salmon story." As he explains, "Five times we upgraded the product by improving the trim and removing the pin bones, among other things. And with volume purchasing we lowered the price each time! It's a classic example of Costco's dedication to value and commitment to our members."

Jeff has also been involved in similar quality improvements of poultry products and in translating some of Costco's most popular Fresh Food items, such as Atlantic salmon fillets and chicken breasts into Kirkland Signature brand frozen products.

Frank Padilla is the ultimate greengrocer, a former produce wholesaler with extensive merchandising experience. Frank and his team coordinate with more than 400 suppliers to assure that produce meets Costco's exacting standards. Unique packaging suitable for businesses or for home use protects fragile fruits and vegetables in transit. More speciality products have been added such as romaine hearts, portobello mushrooms and mangoes, many of which are now available year-round.

You'll find recipes and tips from these experts throughout *Cooking the Costco Way*.

David Andrew
Global wine director

Jeff Lyons
Vice president/senior general merchandise manager of Fresh Foods/ Corporate Foods

Frank Padilla
Assistant general merchandising manager, Fresh Foods

Fish *and* fusion

Far East flavors meld with sumptuous seafood

Kathy Casey

An exuberant champion of Northwest foods, Kathy Casey is always seeking ways to add an unexpected twist to traditional fare. A quick walk through her store, Dish D'Lish in Seattle's Pike Place Market, finds her blueberry lavender chutney sharing space with The Ultimate Macaroni and Cheese and smoked salmon paired with sesame crackers, wasabi cream cheese and ginger pickled onions.

S ILVER-COATED SALMON, *succulent crabs, dew-kissed apples, luscious berries, full-flavored mushrooms and hearty earth-born potatoes and onions hail from this region known as the Northwest.*

It's a land whose culinary underpinnings are such noteworthy Native American dishes as alder-roasted salmon and smoked oysters. Immigrants of European and Asian descent added their own homeland food twists, and a cuisine eventually evolved that truly reflects the melting-pot nature of the United States.

No settlers had a bigger culinary influence on this land of dramatic coastlines, desolate tidelands and snowcapped peaks than those arriving from the Pacific Rim, most specifically China, Japan, the Philippines, Korea, Thailand and India. Quick to appreciate the vast abundance of seasonal fare provided by the land and seas of Oregon, Washington and Alaska, they began to fuse local ingredients with their traditional cooking techniques and flavors. This cuisine, called Pacific Rim or Pan-Asian, is now embraced by fine regional restaurants as well as home cooks. Today one needs only to open a menu or visit a friend for dinner in the Northwest

to enjoy grilled teriyaki salmon with Asian noodles, coconut curry crab, shrimp dumplings with sweet ginger sauce, black cod with wasabi paste or ginger-blueberry sorbet.

Walking the aisles of any Northwest Costco warehouse is an easy way to discover more about the region's grand array of local foods. (See www.costco.com's warehouse locator for information and location of all Northwest Costco warehouses.) At points throughout the year you may find blueberries, blackberries, sweet cherries, stone fruits (peaches, apricots) and apples (Granny Smith, Red and Golden Delicious), Copper River salmon, king crab, clams, mussels, shrimp, sweet yellow onions, asparagus, mushrooms, carrots, stir-fry vegetables, spinach and lettuces.

Kirkland Signature foods are always a standout. They include canned albacore tuna, canned chicken, and fresh meats and seafood such as beef tenderloin, top loin steaks, Atlantic salmon and oxtail. Fruits and vegetables include fabulously fresh basics plus Japanese and Korean mandarins, pummelos (similar to grapefruit), local strawberries, cherries and black-berries, Walla Walla sweet onions and Idaho peaches.

The delis and food courts abound with comfort food such as chicken potpies and chicken enchiladas, as well as chicken bakes and Costco hot dogs. And as elsewhere across the nation, Costco bakeries showcase bagels, variety muffins, butter croissants, gourmet cookies and sheet cakes.

Regional favorites include pilot bread—which has a shelf life of two years—in Alaska warehouses, huckleberry jam in Montana and old-fashioned Grandma Sycamore bread in Utah. Salmon portions, batter halibut, salmon jerky, reindeer sausage, teriyaki chicken, pad thai, yakisoba and a variety of rices such as jasmine, basmati and homai can also be found in specific locations.

Seattle native Kathy Casey, named one of Food and Wine magazine's "25 hot new American chefs" when she was only 23, continues to dish out Northwest cuisine with her signature flair as a chef, restaurateur, cookbook author, food writer and consultant. Besides overseeing her new Dish D'Lish takeout food deli at Seattle's Pike Place Market and the Kathy Casey Food Studios (a full-service food and beverage consulting firm), she recently penned Dishing with Kathy Casey: Food, Fun and Cocktails from Seattle's Culinary Diva.

Q: *Describe pure Northwest cuisine.*
A: Northwest cuisine is very bright, fresh and full of flavors that pop. It's not necessarily a particular type of dish but more an attitude and flavor profile that's inspired by the local bounty.

Q: *Can you cite an example of a dish that has evolved as the region matured?*
A: For a long time everybody served oysters smoked or fried or, on the rare occasion, raw with cocktail sauce. Now, instead of breading and frying and covering up their briny fresh flavor, we're throwing oysters on the grill till just popped or slurping them raw with just a splash of lemon. And by the way, a true Northwesterner doesn't use cocktail sauce.

> *"Some chefs say that there is no true Northwest cuisine— they must not be from here."*

Q: *Pacific Rim fare is very popular in the Northwest. What is this cuisine, and why is it such a Northwest natural?*
A: Pacific Rim cuisine is food of the Northwest and West Coast that is inspired by the great flavors of Asia. This is largely due to the huge Asian population that moved here in the early 1900s.

Q: *You're known as a fearless food experimenter. How is the Northwest epicurean scene conducive to your spirit?*
A: The Northwest is open to trying new things and has such a free-spirit attitude. I think it's one of the most creative places in the United States. Just look at

the companies that have come from this region—Costco is one of them.

Q: *It's a Sunday evening in the Northwest. What dishes would you expect to be served at a friend's home?*
A: If it was summer, I'd say definitely something from the grill, most probably super-delicious halibut or Northwest salmon. During the winter it would be a tender pot roast slow braised with plenty of Washington red wine or a juicy roast rack of lamb served with fruit chutney.

Q: *You note in* Dishing with Kathy Casey *that "in cooking it's not just one 'thing' that makes a great dish or meal." What are the components that elevate a dish or meal from mediocrity to greatness?*
A: Accessories make the outfit, and they make the dish, too. It's the details that really count, like the plates, the presentation, the table, the wines, the place cards, the music and the glasses. My philosophy is "give everything a little twist."

Q: *What's the most misunderstood aspect of Northwest cuisine?*
A: Some chefs say that there is no true Northwest cuisine—they must not be from here.

Q: *The Northwest is the birthplace of Costco. How has this company affected the cuisine of this region?*
A: Costco has had a lot to do with new food trends. It brings in a lot of interesting, cutting-edge, high-quality products at reasonable prices. This allows people to experiment without a huge outlay of money.

Q: *If you were given a bag of Costco baking potatoes, what would you prepare?*
A: This would have to be my Blue Cheese Scalloped Potatoes. People just love them.

Q: *What is your dream for American cuisine?*
A: I wish there were a farmer's market and a Costco in every neighborhood and city; that way everyone would have the best of both worlds. 🍽

Jimmy Dean Sausage and Spinach-Stuffed Mushrooms

Jimmy Dean is America's favorite sausage, employing only the freshest cuts of quality pork, seasoned with authentic whole ground herbs and spices.

2 pounds large mushrooms	1/2 cup grated Parmesan cheese
2 10-ounce packages frozen spinach, thawed, drained and squeezed dry	1 teaspoon olive oil
	3 tablespoons Italian-style bread crumbs
16 ounces Jimmy Dean roll sausage, cooked, drained and crumbled	3 tablespoons melted butter

1. Preheat oven to 350°F. Remove stems from mushrooms and place caps upside down in 2 greased 9-by-13-inch baking dishes.

2. Combine spinach, sausage, Parmesan and olive oil.

3. Stuff sausage mixture into mushroom caps. Sprinkle with bread crumbs and drizzle with melted butter. Bake for 30 minutes, or until brown and bubbly. Makes 10-12 servings.

Wallace Farms, Skagit Valley and Valley Pride Stuffed Red Potatoes

6 small Washington red potatoes	1/4 cup shredded Swiss cheese
1/2 cup chopped fresh shiitake mushrooms	2 tablespoons chopped green onion
2 teaspoons butter	1/2 teaspoon dried thyme, crushed
1 tablespoon dry white wine	1/2 teaspoon salt
1 cup chopped cooked chicken breast	1/4 teaspoon ground pepper
1/4 cup marinated sun-dried tomatoes, chopped	

1. Preheat oven to 375°F. Boil potatoes until tender. Cut off the tops. Place in a large pan coated with cooking spray. If necessary, cut a thin slice off the bottom so potatoes will stay upright. Scoop out potatoes, leaving a 1/4- to 1/2-inch shell; reserve 1/2 cup of potato.

2. Cook mushrooms in butter over medium heat for 3 minutes; stir in wine. Add chicken, reserved potato, tomatoes, cheese and green onion. Add thyme, salt and pepper; mix well. Spoon chicken mixture into potatoes. Bake for 15 minutes, or until thoroughly heated. Makes 6 servings.

Mastronardi Produce

Mastronardi Produce in 2003 celebrated its 50th year of growing the safest and finest-quality greenhouse vegetables. Use Sunset brand peppers, seedless cucumbers and Campari tomatoes to make these delicious treats.

Sunset Greenhouse
Cucumber Spring Rolls with Asian Dipping Sauce ▸

3 tablespoons
   rice wine vinegar

1 1/2 tablespoons sugar

1 tablespoon soy sauce

1 tablespoon toasted
   sesame oil

3/4 teaspoon or more
   hot chili-garlic sauce

10 8 1/2-inch
   rice-paper rounds

2 Sunset Greenhouse*
   cucumbers, unpeeled,
   cut in 80 4-inch-long
   matchstick pieces

3 carrots, cut in 40 4-inch-
   long matchstick pieces

2 Sunset sweet red peppers,
   cut in 40 4-inch-long
   matchstick pieces

Fresh cilantro leaves

Fresh chives, blanched
   for 1 minute

1. ASIAN DIPPING SAUCE: Combine vinegar, sugar, soy sauce, sesame oil and chili-garlic sauce in a small bowl. Cover and chill. Taste and adjust seasonings. Makes about 1/3 cup.

2. Quickly dip rice papers in a shallow dish of warm water one at a time, letting excess water drain off. Place in a single layer between damp tea towels; let stand for 10 minutes.

3. For each spring roll, place 8 cucumber, 4 carrot and 4 red pepper sticks on the bottom third of rice paper, 1 inch from edge. Roll up rice paper tightly just far enough to enclose filling. Top with cilantro leaves, then fold two sides of rice paper over cilantro and continue rolling up.

4. Cut rolls in half diagonally. Tie each piece with chives. Cover and chill rolls for up to 4 hours before serving. Serve with Asian Dipping Sauce. Makes 20 pieces.

Brands may vary by region; substitute a similar product.

Sunset Campari Tomato Spuntini ▲

1 teaspoon parsley flakes

1 teaspoon sesame seeds

1/2 cup olive oil

1/2 garlic clove, crushed

12 Sunset Campari*
   tomatoes, sliced

24 crisp wheat crackers
   or round melba toast

1/4 cup grated
   Romano cheese

12 black olives,
   halved and pitted

1. Combine parsley, sesame seeds, olive oil and garlic in a small bowl.

2. Lightly toss tomatoes with dressing. Cover each cracker with sliced tomato; sprinkle with cheese and top with an olive half.

3. Broil for 1 minute, or until cheese has melted. Makes 24 hors d'oeuvres.

Brands may vary by region; substitute a similar product.

Goglanian Bakeries

In a circuitous path from Jerusalem to Chicago and from NASA to Costco, Alexander Goglanian created innovative automation equipment that solved very specific problems for different industries. He got into the bakery business when NASA asked him to design an oven for the space program. A few highly specialized ovens later, Costco wanted pizza dough that combined the perfect bite between crispy and chewy with flavor and tenderness. The Goglanian Bakeries came to the rescue. Today Kirkland Signature pizza crust is created using Goglanian's high-speed, large-volume mixer, which gently prepares dough in two minutes, and then baked in their high-tech oven.

Goglanian Bakeries Kirkland Signature Smoked Salmon Pizza ◀

1 Kirkland Signature 18-inch Cheese Pizza	9 ounces Kirkland Signature smoked salmon, sliced
2 plum tomatoes, sliced thin	3 ounces feta cheese, crumbled
	2 green onions, chopped

1. Preheat oven to 425°F. Arrange tomato slices on the pizza, then salmon slices; top with cheese and onions.

2. Bake for 15 minutes, or until the pizza is heated through and the cheese is melted. Makes 8-10 servings.

Trapper's Creek Smoked Salmon and Cucumber Nests

4 sheets frozen phyllo dough, thawed

1/2 stick butter, melted

1 cucumber, peeled, sliced thin, divided

1/2 cup sour cream

1/2 cup flaked Trapper's Creek* Kippered Wild King Salmon, plus more for garnish

1. Brush the surface of 1 phyllo sheet with melted butter. Lay the next sheet on top and brush with melted butter; continue with the next 2 sheets.

2. Cut into 4-inch squares; place in ungreased muffin cups, forming nests. Bake according to package directions. Cool the nests on a wire rack.

3. Combine half the cucumber, sour cream and 1/2 cup salmon. Fill nests with mixture. Garnish with remaining cucumber slices and smoked salmon. Makes 4 servings.

Brands may vary by region; substitute a similar product.

Frank's Mushroom Tips

Costco produce buyer Frank Padilla offers the following tips for selecting and caring for mushrooms:

Selecting: Look for mushrooms with a fresh, smooth appearance, free of major blemishes, with a dry (not dried) surface. A closed veil (the thin membrane under the cap) indicates a delicate flavor; an open veil means a richer flavor.

Storing: Keep mushrooms refrigerated. They're best when used within several days of purchase. Do not rinse mushrooms until you are ready to use them. To prolong shelf life, store fresh mushrooms in a porous paper bag. Always remove the plastic overlay from packaged mushrooms. Avoid airtight containers—they cause moisture condensation, which speeds spoilage.

Cleaning: Gently wipe mushrooms with a damp cloth or soft brush to remove occasional peat moss particles. Or rinse them with cold water and pat dry with paper towels.

Freezing: Fresh mushrooms don't freeze well. But if it's really necessary to freeze them, first sauté in butter or oil or in a nonstick skillet without fat; cool slightly, then freeze in an airtight container up to one month.

SALAD

Paxton's Asparagus and Shiitakes with Sesame Dressing

Wonderful with asparagus and mushrooms, this garlicky sesame dressing also combines well with shredded cabbage, cold noodles or seafood.

2 tablespoons rice vinegar

2 tablespoons toasted sesame oil

2 tablespoons peanut oil

4 tablespoons soy sauce

2 teaspoons sugar

3 garlic cloves, finely chopped

1 tablespoon grated fresh ginger

1 pound asparagus spears, cut on the diagonal into thirds

8 fresh shiitake mushrooms, stemmed and cut in 1/4-inch strips

1/4 cup sesame seeds, toasted

1. Whisk together vinegar, oils, soy sauce and sugar. Whisk in garlic and ginger.

2. Blanch asparagus in rapidly boiling, salted water for 4 minutes. Drain and refresh in cold water.

3. Toss asparagus and mushrooms with the dressing in a shallow bowl. Sprinkle sesame seeds on top. Makes 4 servings.

Paxton Hunter, Ocean Park, Washington

Diamond Fruit Growers
Pear Couscous Salad

Diamond Fruit Growers, located in the Hood River Valley in Oregon, is the largest supplier of Northwest pears in the United States.

HERB DRESSING:	1 teaspoon lemon juice
1/4 cup white wine vinegar	1 D'Anjou or Bartlett pear, cored and diced
2 tablespoons olive oil	
1 teaspoon Dijon mustard	1/2 cup chopped green bell pepper
1 teaspoon chopped fresh basil	2 tablespoons chopped hazelnuts
1 teaspoon chopped fresh thyme	1 tablespoon chopped parsley
1/2 teaspoon sugar	Salt and pepper to taste
1/4 teaspoon salt	4 lettuce leaves
Pinch of black pepper	1 D'Anjou or Bartlett pear, cored and sliced
PEAR COUSCOUS SALAD:	
3/4 cup chicken broth	4 ounces sliced Jarlsberg or Swiss cheese
1/2 cup uncooked couscous	

1. HERB DRESSING: Combine vinegar, olive oil, mustard, basil, thyme, sugar, salt and pepper; mix well.

2. Bring broth to a boil. Stir in couscous and lemon juice; remove from heat, cover and let stand 5 minutes, or until couscous is tender and all liquid has been absorbed. Toss with 2 tablespoons Herb Dressing and cool.

3. Add diced pear, green pepper, hazelnuts, parsley and additional Herb Dressing to taste. Adjust seasoning with salt and pepper. Place lettuce on plates and top with a scoop of couscous. Surround with pear slices and cheese. Makes 4 servings.

FROM THE
COSTCO
Produce
EXPERT

How to Properly Ripen Pears

Pears are one of the few fruits that do not mature well if allowed to ripen on the tree, according to Costco produce buyer Frank Padilla. A popular misconception is that pears should be placed in the refrigerator when still green. Put only ripe pears in the refrigerator, as cold storage is what keeps them from ripening.

To ripen pears at home, let them stand at room temperature in a covered bowl, brown paper bag or poly produce bag. The ripening process may take a few days or up to a week, depending on the stage of ripeness when purchased. It is difficult to judge whether pears are ripe by skin coloration. However, a simple test will determine when your pears are ready to eat. Gently press your thumb into the neck. If the skin yields to gentle pressure, the pear is ripe. As your pears ripen, put them in the refrigerator until you are ready to use them.

Domex Apple Pecan Salad with Curry Dressing

2 Fuji apples, peeled, cored and diced	1 tablespoon fresh lemon juice
1/2 cup chopped celery	1 pinch curry powder
1/2 cup chopped pecans	1 tablespoon honey
1/2 cup mayonnaise	

1. Combine apples, celery and pecans.

2. Mix mayonnaise, lemon juice, curry powder and honey.

3. Toss apple mixture with the curry dressing. Makes 2 servings.

FROM THE MEMBER'S KITCHEN

Tutka Bay Wilderness Lodge Cook Inlet Chowder

This satisfying chowder served at the Tutka Bay Wilderness Lodge melds the wonderful flavors of seafood harvested from the clean, icy waters of Alaska's Cook Inlet.

1/4 cup cooking oil	4-6 cups seafood, raw
1 cup chopped onion	or cooked (halibut,
1 cup chopped celery	salmon and cod chunks,
1/2 teaspoon garlic salt	smoked salmon, minced
1 teaspoon dried dill weed	clams, shrimp, crab and
	ground octopus)
2 cups diced potatoes	2 cups evaporated milk
2 cups sliced carrots	1 15-ounce can cream-style
4 cups water	corn, optional
4 chicken bouillon cubes	Fresh dill sprigs
	Fish-shaped crackers

1. Heat oil in a 6-quart soup pot over medium heat and cook onion and celery until soft.

2. Sprinkle with garlic salt and dill weed. Add potatoes and carrots and cook for 10 more minutes, stirring frequently.

3. Add water and bouillon cubes, cover and simmer for 20 minutes, stirring occasionally, or until potatoes and carrots are tender.

4. Add raw seafood and simmer 2-3 minutes. Add cooked seafood. When heated through, add evaporated milk and corn. Heat, but do not boil again.

5. Garnish servings with dill sprigs and fish-shaped crackers. Makes 6-8 servings.

Nelda Osgood, Tutka Bay, Alaska

Dean Specialty Foods
Farman's Sauerkraut Gazpacho

This was the winner of the annual Dean Specialty Foods sauerkraut recipe contest in 1999.

3 ounces garlic- and	1 pound ripe fresh
herb-flavored croutons	tomatoes, peeled
1 cup cold water	and chopped
for soaking	1/4 teaspoon
2 cups Farman's* sauerkraut	hot pepper sauce
1 large red bell pepper,	Snipped chives
roasted, cored, seeded	Chopped parsley
and peeled	

1. Soak croutons in cold water until soft. Puree with sauerkraut, bell pepper, tomatoes and hot pepper sauce in a blender in batches or in a food processor.

2. Pour into a large bowl and refrigerate until the soup is well chilled. If too thick, the soup can be thinned with crushed ice. Serve cold in soup plates, garnished with chives and parsley. Makes 4-6 servings.

Brands may vary by region; substitute a similar product.

Bear Creek Scalloped Potatoes

4 cups Bear Creek Chunky
Potato Soup Mix

6-8 medium potatoes

1 cup fresh bread crumbs

1 cup grated Swiss cheese

Salt and pepper

Bacon bits

1. Preheat oven to 350°F. Prepare soup mix according to package directions.

2. Peel and slice potatoes and layer in a large greased casserole. Cover potatoes with prepared soup. Garnish top with bread crumbs and grated cheese.

3. Cook for 1 hour, or until potatoes are tender. Season to taste with salt and pepper. Sprinkle with bacon bits. Makes 8 servings.

Basin Gold Twice-Baked Potatoes

Basin Gold Cooperative handles the marketing of fresh potatoes and onions for eight produce companies throughout Eastern Washington and Oregon, where the rich soil yields superior vegetables.

4 large Basin Gold
russet potatoes

1/2 cup light sour cream

1/4 cup butter, cut in pats

2 ounces Cheddar
cheese, shredded

2 ounces mozzarella
cheese, shredded

1/2 teaspoon salt

1/2 teaspoon freshly
ground pepper

6 green onions, chopped

1. Preheat oven to 400°F. Wash potatoes and prick with a fork in several places. Bake for 60 minutes, or until tender.

2. Reduce heat to 325°F. Cut potatoes in half lengthwise; scoop out insides, leaving a 1/4-inch shell, and mash with a fork until smooth. With an electric mixer, beat in sour cream and butter until smooth. Stir in cheeses, salt and pepper.

3. Stuff potato shells with mixture, dividing evenly. Bake for 25 minutes, or until hot. Sprinkle onions on top. Makes 8 servings.

Tip: For Northwest flair, add 6 ounces of fresh lump crabmeat to the potato mixture.

Fresh Network
Crispy Herbed Potatoes

2 large russet potatoes,
about 14 ounces each,
peeled and sliced thin

6 tablespoons olive oil

2 red onions, sliced thin

1/2 cup grated
Gruyere cheese or
crumbled Stilton

2 tablespoons chopped
fresh basil

1. Soak potato slices in a large bowl of cold water for 10 minutes; drain and dry on paper or kitchen towel.

2. Heat oil in a large frying pan over medium heat. Add onions and cook for 2 minutes, stirring frequently. Add potatoes and cook for 10-15 minutes, turning frequently, until potatoes are tender and golden.

3. Sprinkle potatoes with cheese and cook for 2 minutes without stirring, until the cheese melts. Sprinkle basil on top. Makes 4-6 servings.

Kathy's Ellensburg Rodeo Beans

Washington State's Ellensburg Rodeo, held on Labor Day weekend, turned 80 years old in 2003. This recipe has been a favorite at a family reunion held for many years at the rodeo. It can be made in advance and put in a slow-cooker while everyone is at the rodeo. Serve it with a salad, rolls and barbecued meat.

1 pound hamburger	1 15-ounce can butter beans, drained
1/2 pound bacon, cut in 1-inch pieces	1/2 cup brown sugar
1 cup chopped onion	1/2 cup white sugar
1 15-ounce can red kidney beans, drained	1 tablespoon vinegar
	1 teaspoon dry mustard
1 15-ounce can pork and beans	1/2 cup ketchup
	Salt and pepper

1. Preheat oven to 350°F. In a large skillet over medium heat, cook hamburger, bacon and onion. Pour off grease and add beans, sugar, vinegar, mustard and ketchup. Season to taste with salt and pepper and adjust the seasonings.

2. Bake in a medium-sized covered casserole for 40 minutes, or for 4 hours in a slow-cooker. Makes 8-10 servings.

Kathy Harris, Ellensburg, Washington

Top Brass Grandma Vignolo's Sour Cream Potato Salad

2 cups mayonnaise	1 1/2 cups minced fresh parsley
2 cups sour cream	8 Top Brass* red or white potatoes
Hot pepper sauce to taste	2 teaspoons salt
Fresh onion juice to taste	

1. Combine mayonnaise, sour cream, hot pepper sauce, onion juice and parsley.

2. Place potatoes in a large saucepan, cover with water and bring to a boil; add salt, lower heat and boil gently about 25 minutes, or until tender when pierced with a fork. Drain and cut into cubes.

3. In a large bowl, make a layer of cubed potatoes. Spread dressing on potatoes. Repeat with remaining potatoes. Do not stir.

4. Refrigerate overnight. Stir before serving and add more dressing if necessary. Serves 12.

Brands may vary by region; substitute a similar product.

BC Hot House Beefsteak Tomatoes and Sweet Bell Pepper Roast Chicken

1 roasting chicken, 4 pounds	6 large garlic cloves, finely chopped
2 tablespoons olive oil, plus more for rubbing chicken	4 extra-large BC Hot House* beefsteak tomatoes, coarsely chopped
Salt and freshly ground pepper	1/2 cup dry white wine
4 BC Hot House* bell peppers: 2 red, 1 yellow and 1 orange, thinly sliced	Cooked rice
	French bread
1 medium onion, thinly sliced	

1. Preheat oven to 350°F. Rub chicken with a little olive oil. Sprinkle with salt and pepper and roast for about 90 minutes, or until tender. Remove skin and cut chicken into large serving pieces.

2. Heat olive oil in a heavy skillet; add peppers, onions and garlic. Cook for a few minutes over medium-high heat, then add tomatoes, salt and pepper to taste, and wine. Simmer 20-25 minutes, or until the sauce thickens. Add chicken pieces and simmer for a few more minutes.

3. Serve with rice and plenty of French bread to soak up the tomato juices. Makes 6 servings.

Brands may vary by region; substitute a similar product.

BC Hot House

BC Hot House tomatoes are grown hydroponically in ideal conditions for a healthy tomato. The produce is not genetically modified. The carefully controlled environment eliminates the need for herbicides and reduces the need for pesticides.

BC Hot House tomatoes ripen naturally on the vine. They are not sprayed to make them red—red is their natural color. When the time is right, the tomatoes, still attached to their clusters, are picked by hand to prevent bruising and delivered to state-of-the-art packing and grading facilities.

These recipes were proudly selected by BC Hot House to showcase the beauty and flavor of their special produce.

BC Hot House Fresh Roma Tomato Sauce

3 tablespoons extra-virgin olive oil	2 stems fresh oregano, leaves chopped, or 2 teaspoons dried oregano
1 red onion, finely chopped	1/4 teaspoon sugar
2-3 garlic cloves, finely chopped	1 teaspoon red wine vinegar
2 pounds BC Hot House* Roma tomatoes, peeled and roughly chopped	1/2 teaspoon salt
	1/4 teaspoon freshly ground black pepper
	Cooked pasta

1. Heat the oil over medium heat in a large pan. Cook onion and garlic for about 5 minutes, until soft.

2. Add tomatoes and slowly bring to a boil. Cover and simmer for about 8 minutes.

3. Add oregano, sugar, vinegar, salt and pepper. Simmer 2 minutes more.

4. Serve with pasta. Makes 4 servings.

Brands may vary by region; substitute a similar product.

BC Hot House Campari Tomato and Long English Cucumber Chef's Salad with Soy-Mustard Dressing ▲

1 teaspoon minced garlic	2 tablespoons light oil
1 tablespoon rice vinegar	Salt and black pepper
1 tablespoon sweet soy sauce	2 pounds BC Hot House* Campari tomatoes
1 tablespoon mustard	1 BC Hot House* long English cucumber
1 tablespoon water	1 tablespoon toasted sesame seeds
1 teaspoon toasted sesame oil	

1. Place garlic, vinegar, soy sauce, mustard, water and sesame oil in a mixing bowl. Drizzle in the oil, whisking constantly until smooth and thick. Season to taste with salt and pepper.

2. Slice tomatoes and set aside. Slice cucumber into rounds. Overlap the cucumber and tomato slices on a platter or plate. Season well with salt and pepper.

3. Drizzle the dressing over the vegetable slices. Garnish with a sprinkling of sesame seeds. Makes 4 servings.

Brands may vary by region; substitute a similar product.
Recipe reprinted with permission from Chef's Salad by Bill Jones.

Wild Bill's Mushroom Tart with **Norco Ranch** Eggs ▼

Suezy Proctor created this for her dad, Wild Bill.

1 cup apple juice	1/3 cup applejack brandy
3/4 cup dried porcini or morel mushrooms	1 cup heavy cream
9-inch piecrust	1 cup grated Asiago cheese
1/2 cup chopped scallions	4 Norco Ranch* eggs, beaten
1/3 cup olive oil	1/2 cup chopped parsley
1 pound fresh mushrooms, sliced thin (portobellos, morels, shiitakes or white)	Salt and pepper
	Sprinkle of freshly grated nutmeg

1. Bring apple juice to a boil and pour over dried mushrooms, allowing them to plump up for at least an hour.

2. Preheat oven to 375°F. Bake piecrust for 20 minutes; remove from oven. Reduce heat to 325°F.

3. Cook scallions in olive oil over medium heat in a large skillet. Add fresh mushrooms to the scallions and cook for a few minutes until they release their liquid. Add reconstituted mushrooms with the juice and brandy, and cook, stirring occasionally, over low heat until liquid is absorbed but the mixture is not dry.

4. Add cream and bring to a simmer, stirring. Turn off the heat and stir in cheese, eggs and parsley. Season to taste with salt, pepper and nutmeg. Pour into piecrust and bake for 30 minutes, or until firm. Makes 6-8 servings.

Brands may vary by region; substitute a similar product.

Suezy Proctor, Tacoma, Washington

Mercer Ranch Zesty Roasted Carrots

1/4 cup extra-virgin olive oil	1 teaspoon salt
2 tablespoons no-salt chicken broth	1/4 teaspoon paprika
2 garlic cloves, minced	1/4 teaspoon black pepper
	2 pounds Mercer Ranch baby carrots

1. Preheat oven to 400°F. Combine oil, broth, garlic, salt, paprika and pepper in a large bowl. Toss carrots in mixture to coat.

2. Spread carrots in a large roasting pan. Bake for 40 minutes, shaking the pan or turning the carrots every 15 minutes, until brown and tender. Makes 6-8 servings.

Brands may vary by region; substitute a similar product.

Kathy Casey

Halibut meat is low in fat, white and firm, with a mild flavor. The fish's ability to hold together well makes it suitable for most manners of preparation, especially since the bones are easy to spot and remove. Adding a vinaigrette made with a full-flavored Washington State apple such as a Gala or Braeburn helps create the perfect marriage of land and sea. Experiment with substituting toasted almonds, walnuts or pecans in place of the hazelnuts.

Washington Blue Cheese Potatoes are the perfect buffet dish. You can also serve these potatoes as showstopping individual round towers for a sit-down dinner or a more formal party. Cut the chilled, cooked dish into 12 rounds using a 2 1/2-inch cookie cutter. Place the rounds on a parchment-lined baking sheet and refrigerate until needed. Reheat them in a 400°F oven until warmed thoroughly and browned. They also make the perfect accompaniment for the Hazelnut-Crusted Halibut with Apple Thyme Vinaigrette.

Hazelnut-Crusted Halibut with Apple Thyme Vinaigrette

Big-flavored Washington apples such as Gala or Braeburn are excellent in this dish.

VINAIGRETTE	HAZELNUT CRUST
1 red apple, cored, halved, divided	1 1/2 cups hazelnuts, lightly toasted and skin rubbed off
3 tablespoons hazelnut oil or olive oil	Pinch of dry mustard
2 teaspoons minced shallots	1 1/4 teaspoons salt
2 teaspoons sugar	1/4 teaspoon cayenne pepper
1/4 cup fresh lemon juice	1 tablespoon grated lemon peel
2 teaspoons Dijon-style mustard	1 teaspoon dried whole thyme
1/2 cup vegetable oil	1 1/4 pounds skinned halibut fillet, cut on a bias into 4 pieces, 1/2 inch thick
1 1/2 teaspoons fresh thyme	
1/4 teaspoon salt	4 tablespoons butter, melted
Pinch of cayenne pepper	1 tablespoon vegetable oil
1 tablespoon water	Fresh thyme sprigs

1. VINAIGRETTE: Chop 1/2 of the apple, reserving the other half.

2. Heat hazelnut oil in a small skillet over medium-low heat and add the chopped apple. Cook 1 minute, then add shallots and sugar. Continue cooking till apple is soft, about 1 minute. Add lemon juice. Cool; puree in a blender till smooth.

3. Pour pureed mixture in a medium bowl, add mustard, and slowly whisk in vegetable oil. Add thyme, salt and cayenne pepper. Stir in water to thin slightly. Cut the remaining half apple in 1/4-inch dice, and toss with the dressing. Refrigerate till needed.

4. HAZELNUT CRUST: Place hazelnuts, dry mustard, salt, cayenne, lemon peel and thyme in a food processor. Pulse till finely chopped but not mealy. Place in a large shallow dish.

5. Preheat oven to 425°F. Dip each halibut fillet in the melted butter, coating well. Immediately press each fish piece firmly into the nut crust mixture, turning and coating all sides well. Place coated halibut pieces on a baking sheet brushed with vegetable oil. Bake for about 6 minutes, or until just cooked through.

6. Carefully remove fish to individual plates and drizzle with vinaigrette. Garnish with fresh thyme sprigs. Pass extra vinaigrette. Makes 4 servings.

Washington Blue Cheese and Rosemary Scalloped Potatoes

This recipe makes a lot—once you've tasted it, you'll be glad it does. These potatoes are fabulous to have around as leftovers!

5 pounds russet potatoes	3/4 cup grated Parmesan cheese
2 teaspoons salt	1 cup sour cream
1/2 teaspoon black pepper	2 cups heavy cream
1 1/2 teaspoons minced fresh rosemary	1 teaspoon salt
3/4 cup crumbled blue cheese	

1. Preheat oven to 350°F. Peel and slice potatoes into 1/4-inch slices. Toss them in a large bowl with salt, pepper and rosemary. In a small bowl toss together cheeses.

2. Layer half the potatoes in a buttered 9-by-13-inch glass baking dish. Sprinkle with half the cheese mixture and top with remaining potatoes.

3. In a bowl, whisk together sour cream, heavy cream and salt; pour over potatoes. Tap the baking dish on the counter to spread out the sauce and help release any air bubbles. Sprinkle with remaining cheese mixture.

4. Bake potatoes for about 1 hour and 15 minutes, or until browned and completely tender all the way through when poked with a knife.

5. Serve immediately. You can also make these in advance and store, covered and refrigerated, for 4-5 days. Bring to room temperature, then reheat in a 350°F oven until hot. Makes 8-12 servings.

Global Fishing

Called the king for good reason, genus Paralithodes *is* indeed a very large crab, with records noting 10-foot extensions from claw to claw and weights of up to 25 pounds.

The crabs, sometimes known as Alaskan king crab, are harvested in the icy waters from Alaska to Japan and are immediately frozen to retain flavor and freshness. The large pieces of white meat tinged with red found in the spiny legs are very popular, as are the enormous claws.

Low in fat and calories and an excellent source of protein, this king of crabs is available year-round, especially through Costco's seafood roadshows.

Global Fishing Red King Crab Italian Style ▶

1 14.5-ounce can Italian-style tomato sauce	1/2 cup Italian-style bread crumbs
1 tablespoon lemon juice	Lemon wedges
1/4 teaspoon cayenne pepper	Hot bread
2 pounds cooked Global Fishing king crab legs in shell, thawed if frozen and shells split lengthwise	

1. Preheat oven to 350°F. Combine tomato sauce, lemon juice and cayenne in a small bowl.

2. Remove crabmeat from shell, discarding cartilage; cut meat into 1/2-inch pieces. Arrange in a buttered baking dish. Pour tomato sauce over crab.

3. Sprinkle with bread crumbs. Bake for 15-20 minutes, until just heated through. Serve immediately with lemon wedges on the side and hot bread. Makes 4 servings.

Steaming King Crab: Put 2 inches of water in a large covered roasting pan and bring to a boil. Place the crab on a rack in the pan so it is not touching water. Cover and steam for 10 minutes if crab is defrosted and 15 minutes if frozen. Serve with drawn (clarified) butter.

Trident Seafoods Grilled Kalbi Alaskan Cod

"Kalbi" means Korean teriyaki and is a delicious flavoring for cod.

2/3 cup soy sauce	2 garlic cloves, crushed
3 tablespoons water	5 tablespoons chopped green onions
2 tablespoons honey	
3 tablespoons sugar	32 ounces Trident Seafoods Premium Alaskan cod fillets
1 tablespoon sesame seeds	
2 tablespoons sesame oil	

1. Combine soy sauce, water, honey, sugar, sesame seeds, sesame oil, garlic and green onions. Pour over the cod in a glass dish or resealable plastic bag. Marinate cod for 4 hours in the refrigerator.

2. Grill or broil fish on low heat until it flakes easily with a fork or reaches an internal temperature of 145°F. Makes 6 servings.

Unique Regional Fish Values

Costco aims to offer local fish in every region, notes Jeff Lyons, Costco's seafood expert. For example, fresh Copper River salmon is sold only in the Northwest region and halibut only in the West Coast regions. Enjoy the fresh sea flavors that need little more than a squeeze of lemon or a dollop of fresh salsa. For best results cook quickly and serve simply.

In 10 minutes or less you can:
- Grill salmon fillets
- Pan-roast halibut

Choose the best fish for grilling:
- Salmon, tuna, mackerel or other fish with a high natural oil content
- Fillets or steaks at least 1/2 inch thick
- Jumbo U-15 prawns (15 or fewer per pound)

Prawn-grilling tip: *Peel and marinate in Italian salad dressing for 30 minutes; skewer and grill, basting with melted butter, about 3 minutes on each side, or until pink and firm.*

Chef John's
Cedar Plank Roasted Salmon

Chef John Howie is the owner of the Seastar Restaurant & Raw Bar in Bellevue, Washington, and Plankcooking.com, a resource for supplies, recipes and ingredients for easy plank cooking.

2 teaspoons lemon pepper	1 tablespoon paprika
1 teaspoon granulated garlic	1 tablespoon kosher salt
1 teaspoon dried whole tarragon	2 teaspoons light brown sugar
	4 7-ounce salmon fillets
1 teaspoon dried whole basil	4 lemon wedges

1. Prepare dry rub by placing lemon pepper, garlic, tarragon, basil, paprika, salt and brown sugar in a food processor; pulse several times until well blended. Wrap tightly and store at room temperature. Makes 1/4 cup, or 8 servings.

2. Place salmon on waxed paper. Sprinkle each fillet with 1 1/2 teaspoons of dry rub, spreading it evenly on both sides and pressing the seasonings into the flesh. Refrigerate, uncovered, for at least 2 hours and up to 12 hours.

3. Preheat oven to 375°F. Place salmon on the center of a cedar plank. Squeeze lemon over the salmon.

4. Bake for 12-15 minutes; turn the salmon over and cook for an additional 12-15 minutes, until the internal temperature is 120°F. Makes 4 servings.

Tip: Perfect planked salmon is lightly browned and firm to the touch, but still springy, not solid. It should be very juicy, with a light pink edge and a darker pink or red center.

Temperature is the best way to determine the preferred doneness for salmon: medium-rare, 110-115°F; medium, 120°F; medium-well, 130°F.

Chef John Howie, Seastar Restaurant, Bellevue, Washington

FROM THE
COSTCO
Seafood
EXPERT

Plank Cooking

Plank cooking is part of the Pacific Northwest's heritage from Native Americans, who discovered that the flavor of salmon was enhanced by cooking the fish on wood planks from alder and cedar trees. Cooking over certain woods imbues a desirable smoky spice inside and outside food, as contemporary barbecue enthusiasts will attest. It's seasoning made simple.

The traditional art is revived with modern cedar and alder planks that are kiln dried and ready for use in the oven or on an outdoor grill, gas or charcoal. Soak the planks in water for 1 hour before use. No extra oil is required to prevent sticking. Planks designed for ovens last for several years; grill planks are intended for one use only.

Francine's Baked Salmon with Spinach Parmesan and Artichoke Dip

Here's how Francine, from Costco's research and development group, cooks salmon at home.

1 fresh fillet of salmon, approximately 2 pounds

Salt and black pepper

1 pound spinach artichoke dip

3 tablespoons minced garlic

1/2 cup shredded imported Parmesan cheese

1/2 cup Italian-style bread crumbs

1. Preheat oven to 350°F. Place salmon, skin side down, in a large, shallow ovenproof dish coated with cooking spray. Season with salt and pepper.

2. Mix spinach dip with garlic in a small bowl; spread evenly over the salmon.

3. Mix Parmesan and bread crumbs in a small bowl. Sprinkle over the spinach mixture. The salmon can be prepared 2-3 hours before baking and kept covered in the refrigerator.

4. Bake about 20 minutes, or until salmon registers 145°F in the center. Makes 6-8 servings.

Tip: The cooking temperature and timing is a good rule of thumb for baking fish that's always juicy and perfectly done. Using a thermometer assures best results for fish and meat.

Francine Ades-Weste, Woodinville, Washington

Fletchers Fine Foods Brown Sugar and Maple Glazed Ham

1 Fletchers Fine Foods Semi-Boneless Easy Carve Ham* (about 15 pounds)

1/4 cup Dijon-style or honey mustard

1 cup packed brown sugar

1/4 teaspoon cinnamon

Pinch of ground nutmeg

1/4 teaspoon freshly grated orange peel

2 tablespoons maple syrup

1. Preheat oven to 375°F. Trim ham rind and score the surface in a 1-inch-wide, 1/4-inch-deep diamond pattern.

2. Rub the whole ham with mustard.

3. In a small bowl, mix together brown sugar, spices, grated orange peel and maple syrup. Press mixture onto ham.

4. Bake for 2 1/2 hours, or until dark golden brown and internal temperature is 160°F. Makes 20-22 servings.

Brands may vary by region; substitute a similar product.

Using Leftover Ham

- ✔ Bean soup with ham
- ✔ Chef's salad
- ✔ Deviled ham sandwich
- ✔ Eggs Benedict
- ✔ Grilled ham and cheese sandwich
- ✔ Ham omelet
- ✔ Macaroni and cheese with ham
- ✔ Scalloped potatoes with ham

Holtzinger Fruit Crunchy Apple Salsa with Grilled Chicken

Crisp, fresh, juicy Washington-grown Gala apples are the perfect choice for this delicious recipe. C.M. Holtzinger Fruit Company was founded in the Yakima Valley of Washington State in 1908. For nearly 100 years, it has provided the world with flavorful apples, cherries and pears.

2 cups chopped Holtzinger Fruit* Gala apples	1/4 cup dry white wine
1 Anaheim chile pepper, seeded and chopped	1/4 cup apple juice
	1/2 teaspoon grated lime peel
1/2 cup chopped onion	1/2 teaspoon salt
1/4 cup lime juice	1/8 teaspoon black pepper
Salt and black pepper	2 whole boneless, skinless chicken breasts

1. PREPARE SALSA: In a medium bowl, combine apples, chile pepper, onion, lime juice, and salt and pepper to taste; cover and set aside.

2. PREPARE CHICKEN: In a large bowl, combine wine, apple juice, lime peel, salt and pepper. Add chicken and turn to coat with mixture; cover and refrigerate 30 minutes.

3. Drain chicken and discard marinade. Grill chicken over medium-low coals for about 10 minutes on each side, or until the chicken is tender, with an internal temperature of 160°F. Serve with salsa. Makes 4 servings.

Brands may vary by region; substitute a similar product.

Kirkland Signature/Cibo Naturals Pesto Turkey Roll ▲

2 pounds ground turkey	1/4 teaspoon freshly ground pepper
1 cup chopped yellow onion	
1 cup chopped red bell pepper	3/4 cup tomato sauce
6 garlic cloves, minced	2 eggs, beaten
1 1/4 cups Italian bread crumbs	1 cup Klrkland Signature/ Cibo Naturals Fresh Basil Pesto*
2 tablespoons Italian seasonings	
1/4 teaspoon salt	1/4 pound provolone cheese, thinly sliced, divided

1. Preheat oven to 350°F. Combine turkey, onion, bell pepper, garlic, bread crumbs, Italian seasonings, salt, pepper, tomato sauce and eggs in a large bowl.

2. Spread turkey mixture in a 12-by-15-inch rectangle on a large sheet of plastic wrap or parchment paper. Spread pesto over turkey mixture. Arrange half of cheese on top.

3. Roll up from the short side, peeling back wrap or paper. Place seam side down in a roasting pan. Tent with foil.

4. Bake 1 hour, or until the roll is firm, with an internal temperature of 150°F. Remove foil, place remaining cheese on top and bake 10 minutes more. Makes 6-8 servings.

Brands may vary by region; substitute a similar product.

Foster Farms

Foster Farms invited three of the Pacific Northwest's top chefs to create exciting new ways to prepare chicken. In addition, Deborah Fabricant, former cooking-school owner and food consultant, shares shopping tips for regional products that will enhance your cooking.

Foster Farms Curried Chicken Salad with Washington Apples ▼

Created by Tom Douglas, chef and owner of Etta's, Palace Kitchen and Dahlia Lounge restaurants in Seattle

2 cups diced roasted Foster Farms* chicken meat, chilled, or Foster Farms precooked rotisserie chicken, or Foster Farms cooked chicken strips	3 tablespoons toasted pine nuts
	1/2 cup mayonnaise
	1/2 cup plain yogurt
	1 1/2 teaspoons freshly squeezed lemon juice
2/3 cup diced unpeeled Washington apples	1/2 teaspoon curry powder
1/4 cup diced celery	Kosher salt and freshly ground black pepper
1/4 cup golden raisins	Bibb lettuce leaves

1. Combine chicken, apples, celery, raisins and pine nuts in a large bowl.

2. Whisk together mayonnaise, yogurt, lemon juice and curry powder in a medium bowl.

3. Toss the chicken with enough of the dressing to coat everything well. Season to taste with salt and pepper. Arrange the chicken salad on lettuce leaves. Makes 4 servings.

Brands may vary by region; substitute a similar product.

Foster Farms Chicken with Mushrooms and Smoked Ham

Created by Leif Eric Benson, Executive Chef, Timberline Lodge, Mount Hood, Oregon

1 tablespoon all-purpose flour

1/8 teaspoon salt

1/8 teaspoon pepper

4 fresh Foster Farms* Boneless, Skinless Chicken Breast Fillets, pounded to 1/2-inch thickness

1/2 cup butter

3 ounces shallots, chopped (about 1/2 cup)

6 ounces smoked ham, diced

6 ounces regionally grown chanterelles or other winter mushrooms, quartered

1 cup Riesling

1 cup chicken stock

4 green onions, sliced (about 1/2 cup)

1. Combine flour, salt and pepper in a shallow dish. Coat chicken with flour mixture.

2. Melt butter in a very large skillet over medium heat. Cook chicken for 4-6 minutes, or until brown, turning once. Stir in shallots and ham; cook for 1 minute. Stir in mushrooms; cook for 1 minute.

3. Add wine and chicken stock; cook, stirring occasionally, for 7-10 minutes, or until sauce is slightly thickened.

4. To serve, spoon sauce over chicken and sprinkle with onions. Makes 4 servings.

*Brands may vary by region; substitute a similar product.

Foster Farms Chicken Breasts Baked with Late-Harvest Riesling, Spiced Apples, Cabbage and Parsnips

Created by Cory Schreiber, Executive Chef/Owner, Wildwood Restaurant & Bar, Portland, Oregon

2 tablespoons olive oil

4 fresh Foster Farms* Boneless, Skinless Chicken Breast Fillets

1 1/2 teaspoons salt, divided

1 1/2 teaspoons freshly ground black pepper, divided

1 1/2 cups late-harvest Riesling

3 cups chicken stock (or chicken broth)

2 tablespoons chopped fresh sage

2 locally grown apples, peeled, cored and cut in quarters

2 parsnips, peeled and thinly sliced into rounds

1 small head green cabbage, cored and cut into 8 wedges

1/2 red onion, thinly sliced

1 tablespoon caraway seeds

2 tablespoons unsalted butter

1. Preheat oven to 375°F. Heat olive oil in a large skillet over medium-high heat. Season chicken with 1 teaspoon salt and 1/2 teaspoon pepper. Cook chicken for 3-4 minutes on each side, until browned. Remove chicken from pan. Add wine to pan and simmer for 5 minutes, stirring to scrape up browned bits. Add stock and sage; simmer for 5 minutes.

2. In a 9-by-13-inch baking dish, arrange apples, parsnips, cabbage and red onion in layers. Season with remaining salt and pepper, and caraway seeds. Place chicken on top of apples and vegetables. Bring wine and chicken stock mixture to a boil and carefully pour over chicken. Cover and bake for 35-40 minutes, or until the chicken is opaque throughout and the apples and vegetables are tender.

3. Place chicken, apples and vegetables on 4 plates. Pour the pan liquid into a small saucepan and boil to reduce by half. Stir in butter. Spoon the sauce over the chicken. Makes 4 servings.

*Brands may vary by region; substitute a similar product.

Fresh Tips from Deborah Fabricant, Celebrity Chef

Successful recipes begin with the freshest ingredients. Look for local products and specialties such as San Francisco sourdough, Washington apples, Monterey Jack cheese and Foster Farms chicken. For fresh, tasty meals every time, see page 67 for helpful tips.

Mark Bjorkman, Snohomish, Washington

Suezy's Game and Garden Beer Stew

This recipe was born out of the abundance of game and hearty garden vegetables found in Eastern Washington.

2 pounds bacon, cut in 1-inch pieces	3 pounds stew meat (venison, elk, bear, lamb, pork or beef), cut in pieces
2 large green bell peppers, seeded, sliced and cut in 1-inch pieces	Oil
1 pound fresh morels or other fresh mushrooms	3 bunches of long green onions, trimmed, cut in 1/2-inch slices
2 cups flour	1 cup dark brown sugar
1/4 cup fresh thyme	24 ounces dark beer
3 tablespoons coarsely ground black pepper	Steamed Brussels sprouts and Yukon Gold potatoes

1. Preheat oven to 400°F. Fry bacon until crisp. Drain and place in a roasting pan, leaving grease in sauté pan.

2. Sauté green peppers and mushrooms in the bacon grease over medium heat until not quite soft. Add to the reserved bacon.

3. Combine flour, thyme and black pepper in a shallow dish. Dredge meat in the flour mixture and brown in bacon grease in batches over high heat. Add to the vegetables in the roasting pan. Add more oil to bacon grease if necessary.

4. Reduce heat to medium and cook onions until soft, adding more oil if necessary. Stir in brown sugar and bring to a boil; pour in the beer, stirring frequently to remove any brown bits from the bottom of the pan. Pour over meat, cover and bake for 1 hour, or until meat is tender. Serve with steamed vegetables. Makes 6-8 servings.

Suezy Proctor, Tacoma, Washington

Mark's Gorgonzola Rib-Eye Steak

1 cup olive oil	4 rib-eye steaks, 3/4 inch thick, bone-in or boneless
5 garlic cloves, minced, divided	1 cup butter, at room temperature
3 sprigs rosemary leaves, chopped fine, divided	1 cup crumbled Gorgonzola cheese

1. Mix olive oil with half of the garlic and half of the rosemary; rub on the steaks and marinate overnight.

2. Mix butter, Gorgonzola, and remaining garlic and rosemary until smooth; chill until firm or overnight.

3. Grill steaks over medium heat, turning several times, to an internal temperature of 130°F for medium-rare. Spoon equal amounts of Gorgonzola butter on steaks and serve immediately. Makes 4 servings.

Wine suggestion: Franciscan Merlot 1999

Jon Donaire Desserts
Cheesecake Banana Split

Jon Donaire Desserts combines two American favorites in this recipe: the classic flavors of cheesecake and a banana split.

5 ounces Jon Donaire Baked New York Cheesecake* (1 precut slice)

1/2 banana, peeled and sliced lengthwise into 2 pieces

3 strawberries, hulled and sliced, or 3 tablespoons strawberry sundae sauce

2 tablespoons chocolate fudge sauce

Whipped cream

1 tablespoon chopped nuts (peanuts, walnuts or almonds)

1 long-stem cherry

1. Place cheesecake slice in a parfait cup with the tip facing up.

2. Insert banana slices on each side of cheesecake.

3. Arrange strawberries around the cheesecake.

4. Drizzle fudge sauce over all ingredients. Garnish with whipped cream, nuts and a cherry (optional). Makes 1 serving.

*Brands may vary by region; substitute a similar product.

Diana Parish, Seattle, Washington

FROM THE MEMBER'S KITCHEN

Diana's Summer Berry Tartlets

2 packages frozen puff pastry shells

8 ounces cream cheese, at room temperature

1/2 cup sugar

Grated peel of 1 lemon

1 cup sour cream

2 pints blueberries, halved strawberries or raspberries

Confectioners' sugar

1. Prepare pastry shells according to package directions.

2. Beat together cream cheese, sugar, lemon peel and sour cream.

3. Fill pastry shells with cream cheese mixture. Top with berries and dust with sugar. Makes 12 servings.

Brown & Haley Almond Roca Buttercrunch Coffee Cake

1 cup sugar

1 cup brown sugar

1 stick butter or margarine, in pieces

2 cups flour

1 teaspoon baking soda

1 cup buttermilk

1 egg, beaten

1 teaspoon vanilla extract

3/4 cup crushed Brown & Haley Almond Roca Buttercrunch

1/2 cup almonds, sliced

1. Preheat oven to 350°F. Mix sugars, butter and flour in a large bowl until crumbly; reserve 1/2 cup of crumb mixture for topping.

2. Dissolve baking soda in buttermilk in a bowl. Stir in egg and vanilla. Pour over the crumb mixture and stir until evenly moistened.

3. Spread in a greased 9-by-13-inch pan. Sprinkle with remaining crumb mixture, crushed Almond Roca Buttercrunch and almonds. Bake for 30 minutes, or until a toothpick inserted in the center comes out clean. Makes 12 servings.

DESSERTS

Columbia Marketing International
Washington Apple and Sour Cream Pie

Washington-grown Granny Smith apples, with their tangy, tart flavor and firm texture, are great for pies, salads or eating out of hand.

3/4 cup cream cheese

1/2 cup sugar

1/4 cup flour

1/2 teaspoon cinnamon

1/4 teaspoon salt

3/4 cup sour cream

1/2 teaspoon vanilla

1 egg

5-6 large Granny Smith apples, cored and sliced

1 9-inch piecrust, unbaked

CRUMB TOPPING:

1/4 cup flour

1/4 cup brown sugar

1/4 cup butter

1/4 teaspoon cinnamon

1. Preheat oven to 375°F. Whip cream cheese and sugar in a medium bowl until light. Combine flour, cinnamon and salt; add to cream cheese, mixing well.

2. Stir in sour cream, vanilla and egg; add apples. Pour into piecrust; bake for 30 minutes.

3. CRUMB TOPPING: Mix flour, brown sugar, butter and cinnamon until mixture is grainy. Sprinkle on the pie evenly and bake for 15 minutes more, or until topping is golden and apples are tender. Makes 8 servings.

Columbia Marketing International
Washington State
Cherry Dump Cake

Bake this cake with Washington-grown Bing cherries, a large fruit of finest quality with an exceptionally sweet, vibrant flavor.

5 cups fresh Bing cherries, pitted and crushed for juice	1 16-ounce can crushed pineapple, drained
1 tablespoon cornstarch, dissolved in 1/4 cup water	1 box white cake mix
	1 cup butter, melted
	1 cup chopped walnuts
	1 cup shredded coconut

1. Preheat oven to 350°F. Heat cherries and juice in a saucepan over medium heat; add cornstarch and cook, stirring, until the juice has thickened. Remove from heat and let cool.

2. Pour crushed pineapple into a 9-by-13-inch pan; pour cherries over the pineapple.

3. Sprinkle dry cake mix over the cherries; pour melted butter over cake mix. Bake for 30 minutes.

4. Sprinkle nuts and coconut over cake, return to oven and bake 10 minutes more, or until coconut is golden brown. Makes 12 servings.

Stemilt Growers Cherry Pudding

In 1893, the Mathison family homesteaded land on Stemilt Hill, planting orchards in the rolling high-country near Wenatchee, Washington, where the high-elevation microclimate creates superior growing conditions for cherries. A century later the Mathison family continues to own and operate this family business, growing and packing cherries—and using this old family recipe for cherry pudding.

1/2 cup butter, softened	3 cups pitted Stemilt* sweet cherries
2/3 cup sugar	1/2 cup sugar
2 teaspoons baking powder	2 tablespoons butter
1 1/2 cups flour	2 cups boiling water
1 cup milk	Ice cream or whipped cream

1. Preheat oven to 350°F. Cream butter and sugar. Combine baking powder with flour and beat into butter mixture. Add milk slowly. Mix well.

2. Spread batter in a greased 9-by-13-inch baking dish. Top with cherries. Sprinkle with sugar and dot with butter. Pour boiling water over mixture.

3. Bake for 30 minutes, or until lightly browned. Serve warm with ice cream or whipped cream. Makes 12 servings.

Brands may vary by region; substitute a similar product.

Douglas Fruit Co.
Apple Dessert Salad

Douglas Fruit, located in the rich agricultural area of southeastern Washington, has been Costco's source of fresh apples for many years. Douglas Fruit employees have found real enjoyment from experimenting with newer varieties of apples such as Braeburn, Fuji, Gala and Pink Lady. This recipe is a family favorite of Cyndy Ebberson, a Douglas Fruit employee, who pairs these apples with a favorite local wine.

4 medium to large Douglas Fruit Co.* apples, cut in bite-size chunks	1/4 cup white wine (personal favorite Muscat, or off-dry Gewürztraminer)
1 fresh pear, cut in bite-size chunks, optional	1/4 cup sugar
1 cup seedless grapes, optional	2 tablespoons fresh lemon juice
1 cup dairy sour cream	1/2 to 3/4 teaspoon cinnamon

1. Combine apple with pear and grapes.

2. Stir together sour cream, wine, sugar, lemon juice and cinnamon. Toss dressing together with fruit. Makes 4-8 servings.

Tip: Fruit is best kept chilled. Dressing can be made a day ahead. It can also be used as a dip for fruit.

Brands may vary by region; substitute a similar product.

Wilcox Almond Rice Pudding

3/4 cup light brown sugar	2 cups cooked rice
1 cup sliced, toasted almonds	4 Wilcox* eggs
1/2 cup golden raisins	1 1/2 cups Kirkland Signature milk
Grated peel of 1 lemon	
1/2 teaspoon cinnamon	2 teaspoons fresh lemon juice
1/2 teaspoon nutmeg	1 teaspoon almond extract
1/2 teaspoon salt	

1. Preheat oven to 325°F. Combine sugar, almonds, raisins, lemon peel, cinnamon, nutmeg and salt. Stir into rice.

2. Beat eggs; stir in milk, lemon juice and almond extract. Combine with rice.

3. Pour into a buttered 8-cup baking dish. Bake for 1 hour, or until set.

4. For individual servings, pour into 8 buttered ramekins. Bake in a hot-water bath for 30 minutes, or until set. Serve hot or cold. Makes 8 servings.

Brands may vary by region; substitute a similar product.

Oregon Chai Milkshake

An ancient recipe meets the American palate in a sweet, spicy Oregon Chai Tea Milkshake. Hot or iced, morning or evening, summer or winter—nourish your yin and elevate your yang with this creamy blend of tea, spice and spirit.

3 scoops vanilla ice cream	Chocolate sprinkles, or chocolate-covered espresso beans, or caramel sauce
6 ounces Oregon Chai* Original Chai concentrate	

1. Blend ice cream and chai in a blender.

2. Garnish with sprinkles, espresso beans or a caramel swirl. Makes 2 servings.

Brands may vary by region; substitute a similar product.

Enjoy the perfect cup of coffee at home with Starbucks.

1. **Proper storage will help maintain the freshness and flavor of your coffee.**
   Starbucks FlavorLock bag protects the coffee from air, light and moisture. Once the bag is opened, coffee should be stored in an airtight container in a cool, dry place.

2. **Use fresh, cold water.**
   Water is 98 percent of every cup; for the best results, consider using filtered water or bottled water.

3. **Use 2 tablespoons of ground coffee for each 6 fluid ounces of water.**
   Keep these proportions consistent, regardless of the quantity you make. To moderate your coffee's strength, simply add hot water after brewing.

4. **Use the correct grind for your coffeemaker.**
   Too fine a grind will cause bitter-tasting coffee or clog your brewer. Too coarse a grind will cause watery coffee. For drip brewers, the appropriate grind should allow the coffee to finish dripping in several minutes. Coffee presses require a coarse grind; espresso machines require a very fine grind.

5. **Boiling causes bitterness, so never boil coffee.**
   It should be brewed between 195°F and 205°F to extract the coffee's full range of flavors.

6. **Coffee can be kept warm over a burner for only about 20 minutes.**
   A thermal carafe will keep coffee hot and delicious for much longer periods of time.

7. **Do not reheat coffee.**
   Make it fresh each time you serve it, and make only as much as you plan to drink. Coffee holds its flavor best at 186°F.

With the right coffee and the proper techniques, you're on your way to brewing the perfect cup.

Fruits of nature

Californians create innovative cuisine

C ALIFORNIA, WITH ITS FERTILE *farmlands stretching through the Sacramento, San Joaquin, Imperial, San Fernando, Salinas and Santa Clara valleys, has long been considered the nation's salad bowl. Whether one seeks nectarines, pomegranates, grapes, strawberries, cantaloupes, avocados, Valencia oranges, lemons, kiwis, tomatoes, cauliflower, purple asparagus, artichokes, sweet corn, baby greens or eggplant, all are grown in California.*

Historically, the region has been a major gateway for world explorers and Spanish, Mexican, Italian, Asian and Northern European immigrants. To this day, these various nationalities continue to blend their homeland cuisines with the area's locally grown products. Notables include such favorites as California sushi roll (rice, avocado and mock or true crab legs), San Francisco sourdough bread, chop suey (a variation of Chinese chow mein), French dip sandwich, Cobb salad (chicken, bacon, hard-boiled eggs, avocado, blue cheese and tomato over romaine lettuce), green

Jeremiah Tower

Jeremiah Tower, the father of California cuisine, believes there are no wrong turns in cooking. "If a soufflé falls, turn it into a pudding," he says. It is this spirit of adventure that vaulted him from regional fame to national acclaim and in the process established a cuisine that is embraced around the world.

goddess dressing (mayonnaise, anchovies, tarragon, chives and parsley) and hearty Monterey-style pasta.

Costco mirrors California food trends, with top consideration centered on fresh, seasonal products and healthy eating options. (See www.costco.com's warehouse locator for information and location of all California Costco warehouses.) Expect to find pomegranates, pluots (a cross between a plum and an apricot), kiwis, Hass avocados, Campari tomatoes, fresh figs (Calimyrna, Black Mission, Brown Turkey), donut peaches, Brentwood corn, Crenshaw and casaba melons, Kirkland Signature tripe, beef tongue, flap meat (a Hispanic item that's perfect for carne asada and fajitas), beef brisket, tri-tip steak, pork back ribs, Atlantic salmon and much more.

Regionally, the southern California warehouses focus on healthy alternatives such as organic and soy products, nutrition bars, nuts and jerky, natural cereals, olive oil, soy milk (refrigerated and shelf stable) and low-fat products, as well as items for Mexican and Asian cuisines such as noodle bowls, beef and pork chorizo, uncooked tortillas and tamales. Los Angeles warehouses offer an even greater array of health foods and Mexican-related culinary products, while the Bay Area is of course well stocked with wines from Napa, Sonoma, Livermore Valley, Monterey, Santa Cruz and the Sierra Foothills, as well as other fine local products such as dried fruits, sparkling cider, pastas and world-famous Jelly Bellies.

Chef Jeremiah Tower changed the face of American cooking in the 1970s, when he began applying his commonsense cooking style to California-grown ingredients. In the process he elevated food from the simple to the sublime, becoming one of the country's greatest chefs and a crusader for California Cuisine. He has received many accolades, including the Outstanding Chef Award from the James Beard Foundation. His most recent cookbooks include Jeremiah Tower Cooks and California Dish.

Q: *What are the most distinguishing characteristics of California cuisine?*

A: California cuisine is really a celebration of the region and climate and not a kind of food or a list of recipes. It is a very informal, spontaneous, free-flowing style of cooking that allows perfect, fresh ingredients to speak for themselves.

Q: *In* Jeremiah Tower Cooks *you coin the phrase "new-old" food. What does this mean?*

A: It means pushing the new-ingredient frontier while adhering to historic techniques and cooking principles. For instance, at Stars [he opened the first Stars restaurant in San Francisco in 1984] we introduced beef cheeks, prepared in a very traditional braising method.

Q: *James Beard noted that you are able to catch the spirit of the time. What's special about today's California food spirit as compared to nearly 30 years ago, when the California-cuisine movement started?*

A: When I started I had to almost invent ingredients or wish them out of the ground. There were no fresh truffles, mascarpone, balsamic vinegar, goat cheese or extra-virgin olive oil—nothing. And fresh herbs did not exist in any supermarket across America. Now they're all everywhere.

Q: *What's the most misunderstood aspect of California cuisine?*

A: This cuisine is not a list of recipes; it's letting the ingredients make the call.

Q: *No matter where you live, what California food items can always be found in your pantry?*

A: Avocados for sure, chiles, artichokes, olive oil, olives, Meyer lemons and all the amazing citrus from California, wine of course, and I wish, though it's not true, that I could get fresh abalone—but you just can't get it anymore.

Q: *And your California signature dish would be?*

A: Plate-cooked fish. It's just such in the spirit of California: easy to do, fast and glamorous.

Q: *What are some of the distinctions between today's northern and southern California-style cooking?*
A: In southern California, it is a cuisine of the sun, with a lot of Mexican and Asian influence. The north has a much cooler climate and can occasionally focus on dishes such as braised meats.

Q: *What are some easy ways for home cooks to preserve the essence of a California summer?*
A: Buy tomatoes at their absolute peak and freeze them whole in plastic zip bags. To use, just throw them in the microwave for a bit or let them thaw naturally. I also freeze Meyer lemons whole or preserve them in salt.

> *"California cuisine…*
> *allows perfect, fresh ingredients*
> *to speak for themselves."*

Q: *What's the greatest culinary lesson gained from this region?*
A: All menu decisions should be made by your eyes, hands and nose. Let the ingredients tell you what you should be cooking.

Q: *If you were given a bag of Costco baking potatoes, what would you prepare?*
A: I'd bake them first, puree the potato to make mashed potato, put the mixture back in the skins and heat them up. On top, I'd add a salad of avocado, salsa, lump crabmeat and ancho chile sour cream. The key is the hot potato versus the room-temperature topping.

Q: *You and many other respected chefs across the country continue to build a new American culinary tradition. What do you foresee when you peer into this land's epicurean crystal ball?*
A: I see the cuisines of South Africa and Australia as the next big influences on American food. These two lands took a look at California cuisine and then notched everything up. 🍽

California Grapes

Goodness Grapecious

Color, taste, texture and nutrition. Grapes have a reputation for being a good snack food, eaten by the handful, with no preparation necessary. But they are surprisingly flexible in recipes, holding their own raw or cooked. They add a sweetness and gentle acidity that highlights other flavors much as a squeeze of fresh lemon brightens almost any food.

It's the vibrant green, red or blue-black color that signals the presence of the health benefits of phyto-nutrients, the natural defenders against disease.

- ✔ 60 calories in 1 cup
- ✔ Saturated fat free
- ✔ Cholesterol free
- ✔ High in antioxidant vitamin C

Easy to Buy and Store

Look for plump grapes, with rich color, firmly attached to the stem. Don't mind a little dust. It's actually "bloom," a natural protection against decay and loss of moisture.

Grapes are picked ripe and will not ripen any further, so store them in the refrigerator and they will keep for a week or so. Don't wash them until you're ready to eat them.

Here are a few of the more than 50 varieties of California table grapes available at different times from May through February.

Green Varieties

- ✔ Thompson seedless
- ✔ Perlette

Red Varieties

- ✔ Flame seedless
- ✔ Red globe

Blue-Black Varieties

- ✔ Beauty seedless
- ✔ Ribier

The California Grape Growers: Delano Farms, Fowler Packing, Kirschenman, Four Star Fruit, Stevco

California Grapes Tomato Napoleon with Goat Cheese, Basil and Grape Vinaigrette ◀

Recipe developed for California Grape Growers by Chef David Vartanian, The Vintage Press Restaurante, Visalia, California.

6 vine-ripe tomatoes

Hot oil for frying

12 ounces goat cheese

Coarse salt and freshly ground pepper

1 bunch basil, stemmed

Fried tomato skins, optional

2 cups sliced red, green, black or a combination of California seedless grapes*

1 cup whole red, green, black or a combination of California seedless grapes

1 teaspoon green peppercorns

1/2 cup extra-virgin olive oil

Juice of 1 lemon

Salt

1. Peel tomatoes and fry the skins in hot oil to use as a garnish if desired. Slice each tomato horizontally into 4 slices, keeping each tomato separate.

2. Slice cheese into 18 thin pieces. Reassemble each tomato on a chilled plate, inserting a piece of cheese between each tomato slice. Season to taste with salt and pepper. Arrange basil leaves around each tomato and scatter fried tomato skins and sliced grapes on top of the basil.

3. Puree whole grapes and peppercorns in a blender. With the blender running, slowly add olive oil. Season with lemon juice and salt to taste. Drizzle vinaigrette over the tomatoes and basil. Makes 6 servings.

Tip: To peel tomatoes easily, submerge whole tomato in boiling water for 15-30 seconds. Remove with a slotted spoon. Score the skin with a knife from top to bottom in 4 places. Peel the skin off in 4 pieces.

*1 pound of California grapes is approximately 3 cups.

Lindsay Olive and Brie Pizza Pie ◄

1 9-inch refrigerated piecrust, at room temperature

2 tablespoons Dijon-style mustard

8 ounces Brie cheese, rind removed, cut in 1/2-inch pieces, divided

3 plum tomatoes, halved crosswise, seeded and thinly sliced

2/3 cup Lindsay* pitted ripe olives, drained and halved

3 tablespoons thinly sliced green onion

2 teaspoons chopped fresh oregano, or 3/4 teaspoon dried

1/2 cup coarsely grated Parmesan cheese

1. Preheat oven to 400°F. Place crust on a lightly floured baking sheet. Fold in edges of crust 1/2 inch around, pressing down to form a rim.

2. Spread mustard over the crust; top with half of the Brie, tomatoes, olives and green onion. Top that layer with remaining Brie, oregano and Parmesan.

3. Bake 20 minutes, or until crust is crisp and golden brown. Let stand 10 minutes before serving. Serve warm or at room temperature. Makes 6 servings.

Brands may vary by region; substitute a similar product.

Dare Foods Caesar Savories ►

1/2 cup purchased Caesar dressing

1/2 cup whipped cream cheese

Freshly ground black pepper

Cabaret or Breton* crackers

1 head romaine lettuce, cut in 1 1/2-inch slices

12 cherry tomatoes, halved

Parmesan shavings for garnish

1. In a small bowl, blend Caesar dressing, cream cheese and black pepper to taste. Add more dressing if the mixture is too thick.

2. Spread crackers with mixture. Top with a slice of lettuce, a tomato half and Parmesan. Makes 24 servings.

Tip: Make hearty appetizers by adding grilled chicken or shrimp topped with a splash of fresh lemon juice.

Brands may vary by region; substitute a similar product.

Monterey Mushrooms Spinach, Mushroom and Mozzarella Wraps ▲

Enhance your meals with a selection of fresh, flavorful mushrooms from one of Monterey's nine growing facilities. Monterey provides a full product line of Clean N Ready White, Portabella/ Browns and Specialty Mushrooms.

1 tablespoon olive oil

8 ounces Monterey Clean N Ready Sliced White Mushrooms (about 2 1/2 cups)

1 teaspoon minced garlic

2 10-inch flour tortillas

1/2 pound fresh spinach or arugula

1 plum tomato, diced

1/2 cup (2 ounces) shredded part-skim mozzarella cheese

1. Preheat oven to 350°F. Heat oil in a large skillet over medium-high heat. Add mushrooms and garlic; cook, stirring, until the mushroom liquid has evaporated, about 5 minutes.

2. On each tortilla arrange layers of spinach, tomato, mozzarella and cooked mushrooms. Roll up and place seam-side down in a lightly oiled baking dish.

3. Bake, uncovered, until hot and cheese is melted, about 10 minutes.

4. Cut each tortilla crosswise into quarters. Serve hot or at room temperature. Makes 2 servings.

Sunny Cove Spicy Orange and Shrimp Kebabs ▼

1 cup orange juice

1/4 cup soy sauce

1 tablespoon brown sugar

1 chipotle chile in adobo sauce, diced

1 tablespoon adobo sauce

1/2 teaspoon salt

1 pound 21/25-count raw shrimp, peeled

2 Sunny Cove* oranges, peeled and sliced into 12 sections

Bamboo skewers, soaked in water for 30 minutes

1. Combine orange juice, soy, sugar, chile, adobo sauce and salt in a large bowl. Toss with shrimp and marinate for up to 1 hour in the refrigerator.

2. Thread shrimp and orange sections on skewers. Simmer marinade for 5 minutes.

3. Grill kebabs over medium heat 2-3 minutes on each side, or until shrimp are pink and firm. Serve with hot marinade for dipping. Makes 4 servings.

Brands may vary by region; substitute a similar product.

Borges USA Kirkland Signature Quick Artichoke Dip ▲

13 ounces Kirkland Signature by Cara Mia Marinated Artichoke Hearts

12 ounces light cream cheese spread

1/3 cup sun-dried tomatoes

2 tablespoons chopped parsley

1 tablespoon Star capers, rinsed and drained

Salt and pepper

Assorted vegetable crudités and/or crackers

1. In a food processor, combine artichoke hearts with marinade, cream cheese spread and tomatoes. Process with on-off pulses until blended and artichokes and tomatoes are finely chopped.

2. Transfer to a bowl and stir in parsley and capers. Season to taste with salt and pepper.

3. Serve surrounded with crudités and/or crackers for dipping. Makes 10-12 servings.

Nancy's Specialty Foods
Top-and-Serve Ideas for Lorraine and Florentine Quiche

Try Nancy's Quiche again for the first time. Creamy Quiche Lorraine is dotted with Swiss cheese and smoky bacon, and Florentine is filled with Swiss cheese and spinach. These tasty morsels are ready in minutes for snacks, lunch, dinner and anytime you want to celebrate. Serve them as is, or create your own signature combinations by topping the baked quiches with any of the following ingredients:

✔ Olive slices and a sprig of parsley

✔ Thin slices of red and green bell pepper

✔ Tiny dollops of pesto, purchased or homemade

✔ Slivered prosciutto

✔ Tiny dollops of herbed cream cheese, purchased or homemade

✔ Drained sun-dried tomatoes, chopped, and a sprig of parsley

Hellmann's/Bestfoods
Easy Cheesy Artichoke Bread ▶

1 14-ounce can
artichoke hearts,
drained and chopped

1 cup Hellmann's*
or Bestfoods*
Real Mayonnaise

1 cup (about 4 ounces)
grated Parmesan cheese

1 garlic clove, finely
chopped, or 1/4 teaspoon
Lawry's Garlic Powder
with Parsley, optional

1 loaf French or Italian
bread (about 16 inches
long), halved lengthwise

1. Preheat oven to 350°F. In a small bowl, combine artichokes, mayonnaise, Parmesan and garlic; spread evenly on the bread.

2. Bake for 12 minutes, or until golden and heated through. Makes 8 servings.

Brands may vary by region; substitute a similar product.

Carolyn's Parmigiano-Reggiano "Cannoli" ◀

1 1/2 cups grated
Parmigiano-
Reggiano cheese

1 pound ricotta cheese

2 teaspoons fresh
lemon juice

Salt

Ground white pepper

2 tablespoons finely
chopped dry sun-dried
tomatoes (not oil-packed)

2 tablespoons finely
chopped fresh chives

1. Drop 2 tablespoons Parmigiano-Reggiano into a hot nonstick skillet over medium heat. Cook until brown and bubbly. Remove from the pan and wrap onto a cannoli form. Let it cool slightly and then slide it off the form. Repeat with remaining Parmigiano-Reggiano.

2. Mix ricotta cheese and lemon juice in a bowl. Season to taste with salt and pepper. Place in a pastry bag with a star tip. Pipe the ricotta mixture into the "cannoli" shells.

3. Sprinkle one end of the cannoli with sun-dried tomatoes and the other end with chives. Serve immediately. Makes 10 servings.

Carolyn Foster, Pleasant Hill, California

Prime Time International
Grilled Red Pepper Salsa ▶

Prime Time peppers are grown throughout North America and are available 365 days a year. Although naturally sweet, bell peppers develop a delicious smoky caramelized flavor when they are roasted.

3 Prime Time* red bell peppers	1 1/2 teaspoons fresh lemon juice
1/4 cup chopped black olives	1 garlic clove, crushed
2 tablespoons extra-virgin olive oil	1/4 to 1/2 teaspoon crushed red pepper
2 tablespoons capers, drained	1/8 teaspoon salt
2 tablespoons chopped Italian parsley	

1. Prepare a hot fire. Grill peppers, turning frequently, until skin is blackened all over, 10-15 minutes. Immediately seal peppers in a plastic or brown paper bag and let stand for 10 minutes.

2. Rub peppers under cold running water to remove charred skin. Remove and discard stems and seeds. Finely chop peppers and place in a small bowl.

3. Add olives, olive oil, capers, parsley, lemon juice, garlic, red pepper and salt. Stir to blend well. Let stand at room temperature for up to 3 hours, or cover and refrigerate for up to 3 days. Makes 6-8 servings.

*Brands may vary by region; substitute a similar product.

Christopher Ranch Roasted Garlic ◀

Christopher Ranch Garlic bulbs	Freshly ground black pepper
Olive oil	Water or chicken broth
Salt	French bread
	Sun-dried tomatoes

1. Preheat oven to 450°F. Gently remove the outer layers of skin from several whole garlic bulbs, slightly exposing the individual unpeeled cloves but leaving the bulbs intact. Cut the tip off each bulb and place in a baking pan.

2. Drizzle with olive oil and sprinkle with salt and pepper.

3. Fill the baking pan with enough water or chicken broth to cover the bottom.

4. Seal the pan with aluminum foil and bake for approximately 1 hour, or until garlic cloves are soft.

5. To serve, break the garlic cloves off the bulbs and squeeze the pulp onto slices of French bread. Top each with a slice of sun-dried tomato and enjoy. Makes 2-3 servings per bulb.

Don Miguel Mexican Foods
Cilantro Cream Dip ▼

Try this delicious dip with any Don Miguel Mexican Foods appetizer, such as Chicken Chipotle Flautas or Beef Tamales. It can be served with hot or cold items, which makes it perfect for any kind of gathering.

1 8-ounce package cream cheese, softened	2 teaspoons garlic powder
1 tablespoon sour cream	1 bunch fresh cilantro, chopped
1 7-ounce can tomatillo salsa	1 tablespoon fresh lime juice
1 teaspoon freshly ground black pepper	1 jalapeño pepper, seeded and chopped
1 teaspoon celery salt	1 serrano pepper, seeded and chopped
1/2 teaspoon ground cumin	

1. Combine cream cheese, sour cream, salsa, black pepper, celery salt, cumin, garlic powder, cilantro, lime juice, jalapeño pepper and serrano pepper in a blender or food processor. Blend until smooth and creamy.

2. Place in a serving bowl. Makes 2 cups, about 8 servings.

Selecting the Right Avocado

As scientists discover more about the health benefits of fruits and vegetables, research shows that one of the best additions to your diet is the avocado.

Known for their delicious rich flavor, avocados are also loaded with phytochemicals — natural plant chemicals that help protect against a variety of cancers and diseases.

Nutrient-rich avocados are flavorful, versatile and easy to prepare. Consumers can select ripe, ready-to-eat fruit to enjoy immediately, or stock up on unripened hard fruit to serve in a few days' time. Frank Padilla, Costco produce buyer, says the best way to tell if your avocado is ready to eat is to gently squeeze it in the palm of your hand. Ripe fruit will be firm yet will yield to gentle pressure.

Color alone may not tell the whole story. While the popular Hass avocado will turn dark green or black when ripe, the gentle squeeze test is the best indicator of ripeness. Hard fruit can take as long as a week to ripen on its own. To speed the ripening process, simply place the fruit in an ordinary paper bag and store at room temperature until ready to eat (usually 2 to 5 days). Including an apple, banana or citrus in the bag speeds up the process even more.

Once avocados are at a desired stage of ripeness, they can be refrigerated for up to 5 days.

Hass Avocado Ceviche ▲

Avocados are a delicious part of a healthful diet — naturally cholesterol free — containing just five grams of fat per serving and mostly monounsaturated, the "good fat." Avocados are the highest fruit source of vitamin E, and contain lutein, shown to help prevent prostate cancer.

1 1/2 pounds skinless fish fillets, cut in small pieces, or shrimp or other shellfish	2 tomatoes, diced
	2 canned green chiles, cut in 1-inch cubes
1 cup olive oil	2 tablespoons chopped cilantro
1/2 cup white wine	1 garlic clove, minced
1 teaspoon dried oregano	1 onion, finely chopped
1/2 teaspoon dried basil	3-4 Hass avocados, cubed
2 cups lime juice	3 cups cooked rice

1. Place fish in a large bowl. Combine oil, wine, oregano, basil and lime juice; pour over fish. Cover and refrigerate for at least 8 hours.

2. About 4 hours before serving, add tomatoes, chiles, cilantro, garlic and onion to the fish. Return to the refrigerator.

3. Stir in avocado cubes, lift seviche from the marinade with a slotted spoon and serve immediately over rice. Makes 12 appetizer servings.

Presented by the California Avocado Commission, Calavo Growers of California, Comite de Paltas, Giumarra Companies, Index Fresh of California, Mission Produce and West-Pak Avocado.

Bounty Fresh/Legend Produce
Cold Crab and Melon Soup ▶

Recipe created by Chef Allen Susser for Bounty Fresh, Legend Produce and Agrolibano Growers.

1 large ripe cantaloupe, peeled and seeded	8 ounces crabmeat
1 cup orange juice	2 tablespoons grated coconut
1/2 cup coconut milk	2 tablespoons chopped cilantro
2 teaspoons chopped fresh ginger	2 tablespoons chopped green onion
1/2 teaspoon salt	1 teaspoon minced jalapeño pepper

1. Cut 1/2 of the melon into fine pieces. Puree remaining melon with orange juice, coconut milk, ginger and salt. Chill.

2. Combine diced melon, crabmeat, coconut, cilantro, green onion and jalapeño.

3. Pour the soup into 4 chilled bowls. Spoon the crab mixture into the center of each. Makes 4 servings.

Shiitake-Ya
Mushroom Gift Soup Mix ◀

Shiitake-Ya of Southern California has three generations of experience growing mushrooms in a forest setting. Shiitake-Ya mushrooms offer endless nutritional benefits. This make-ahead soup mix can be kept handy in the pantry or given as a gift.

1/4 cup dried lentils	1/2 teaspoon dried basil
1/4 cup pearl barley	1/4 teaspoon dried oregano
1/4 cup dried minced onions	1/4 teaspoon garlic powder
1/4 cup instant chicken bouillon granules	1/4 teaspoon dried rosemary
1/4 cup chopped sun-dried tomatoes	Shiitake-Ya dried mushrooms, broken by hand

1. In a 1-pint mason jar, layer all the ingredients in the order listed, gently pushing down after each ingredient and ending with enough Shiitake-Ya mushrooms to fill to the top of the jar.

2. Close the lid firmly and attach a tag with the following instructions: "Combine jar of soup mix, 8 1/2 cups water and 3 sliced carrots in a large pot. Bring to a boil, cover and simmer for 40 minutes. Add 1 1/2 cups chopped cooked chicken. Makes 6 servings."

Tanimura & Antle Feta and Almond Salad with Balsamic Vinaigrette ▶

Working with the seasons to provide quality produce year-round, the third generation of Tanimura & Antle farms in locations from Salinas, California, to Yuma, Arizona.

1/2 cup balsamic vinegar	1 teaspoon cinnamon
1 cup olive oil	1 head Tanimura & Antle iceberg lettuce
3 tablespoons chopped fresh basil	1 1/2 cups sliced red and yellow bell peppers
4 garlic cloves, chopped	1 cup sliced red onion
1 8-ounce package sliced almonds	6 ounces French feta cheese, crumbled
1/4 cup sugar	

1. Combine vinegar, olive oil, basil and garlic; mix well.

2. Cook almonds, sugar and cinnamon in a nonstick pan over medium heat, stirring, until almonds are lightly browned and sugar dissolves. Be careful not to burn. Let almonds cool.

3. Cut lettuce into 6 wedges and arrange on plates. Drizzle dressing over lettuce. Garnish with almonds, bell peppers, onion and feta. Makes 6 servings.

Balsamic— The Fine Wine of Vinegar

Fine balsamic vinegar is described in terms usually reserved for wine: complex, balanced, fruity, full-bodied, jammy, tart, aromatic and well structured. True balsamic vinegar is dense, with a rich brown color, and tastes sweet and tart. The impostors that depend on caramel for color can easily be spotted with one sniff or sip. Aged balsamic is too precious to be diluted in cooking. It is used as a powerful accent drizzled over fish, fruit, meat, cheese or ice cream.

Kirkland Signature private-reserve balsamic vinegar is crafted in the traditional Italian solera aging process, blending new grape juice into older vintages every year. Over time the vinegar develops complex flavors and color from wood barrels—and a smoothness with no sharp edges—that can come only from aging for as long as 15 years.

Country Gourmet Foods
Pink-and-Yellow Salad ◄

Wolfgang Puck, founder of the celebrated Spago restaurant and author of best-selling cookbooks, creates his hearty soups from real soup stock and the highest-quality ingredients. This is the perfect salad to accompany Wolfgang's Chicken & Egg Noodles Soup.

1 small butter or Boston lettuce, torn in 1-inch squares	1/4 cup heavy cream
	1 tablespoon ketchup
4 radishes, sliced thin	1 teaspoon lemon juice
1 cup shredded white cabbage	1 teaspoon paprika
	1 teaspoon Worcestershire sauce
1/4 cup sweet corn	Hot pepper sauce
2 ounces cream cheese	Salt and pepper

1. Toss lettuce, radishes, cabbage and corn in a bowl; arrange on two plates.

2. Combine cream cheese, cream and ketchup in a small bowl and mix with a fork. Add lemon juice, paprika, Worcestershire sauce and hot pepper sauce to taste. Adjust the seasonings, adding salt and pepper to taste. Serve alongside the salad. Makes 2 servings.

Country Gourmet Foods LLC is the distributor of Wolfgang Puck's Hearty Soups.

Babé Farms *Great Salad Ideas*

Start with a 16-ounce package of Babé Farms Continental Salad Blend.* Select one of the following three variations of ingredients to make a flavorful salad.

- ✔ *1 cup crumbled feta cheese, 1/2 cup glazed walnuts and 1 cup dried, sweetened cranberries.*

- ✔ *1 cup crumbled goat cheese, 1/2 cup pecans and 1 cup mandarin oranges.*

- ✔ *1 cup crumbled blue cheese, 1/2 cup toasted almonds and 1 cup diced green apples.*

- ✔ *Drizzle with a balsamic or raspberry vinaigrette. Toss and serve. Makes 8-10 servings.*

*Brands may vary by region; substitute a similar product.

Mann's Lemon Sugar Snap Pea Salad with Almonds ▶

2 cups sugar snap peas	Pinch of black pepper
1/2 tablespoon grated lemon peel	1/4 teaspoon salt
	2 tablespoons olive oil
1 tablespoon fresh lemon juice	1/4 cup sliced green onion
1 clove garlic, chopped	1/4 cup toasted sliced, almonds
1/8 teaspoon crushed red pepper	

1. Bring 2 quarts of water to a boil. Blanch sugar snap peas in boiling water for 45 seconds. Drain and immediately plunge into ice water for 2 minutes. Drain.

2. Mix lemon peel and juice, garlic, red and black peppers, and salt; whisk in oil.

3. Toss peas, onions and almonds with dressing. Makes 4 servings.

Sun World Grace and Broccoli Salad ◄

Sun World International is a leading innovator in the research, production, distribution and promotion of fresh produce and maintains integrated agricultural operations throughout central and southeastern California. It also operates one of the world's largest table-grape and stone-fruit breeding programs.

4 cups broccoli florets, blanched	3/4 cup purchased low-fat Oriental-style dressing
2 cups Sun World seedless grapes	1/4 cup toasted sliced almonds, optional
1/2 cup sliced red bell pepper	1/4 cup bacon crumbles, optional
1/2 cup thinly sliced red onion	

1. Combine broccoli, grapes, bell pepper and onion in a large bowl.

2. Toss with dressing; sprinkle almonds and bacon crumbles over the top. Makes 6 servings.

Boskovich Farms Spinach Salad ▶

1/4 cup extra-virgin olive oil	1 small red onion, thinly sliced
1 1/2 tablespoons white wine vinegar	4 ounces Brie cheese, diced
Salt and pepper	1/4 cup chopped walnuts
1 pound Boskovich Farms Fresh 'N' Quick* Spinach	

1. Whisk together olive oil and vinegar in a small bowl. Season to taste with salt and pepper.

2. In a large bowl, combine spinach, onion and Brie.

3. Toss salad with dressing and top with chopped walnuts. Makes 6 servings.

Brands may vary by region; substitute a similar product.

Kandy and Trinity Fruit
Great Western Fruit Salad ▼

Fresh fruit and a bright orange dressing make this salad a delicious complement to any summer barbecue.

½ Kandy* cantaloupe, cut in 1-inch cubes	1 cup peeled, sliced Trinity kiwi
½ Kandy honeydew melon, cut in 1-inch cubes	2 cups sliced Trinity nectarines
2 cups Trinity* green grapes	½ cup Grand Marnier or other orange liqueur
2 cups sliced Trinity peaches	½ cup orange juice
	2 tablespoons sugar

1. Combine fruit in a large bowl. Combine Grand Marnier, orange juice and sugar. Pour the mixture over the fruit. Toss to coat.

2. Refrigerate at least 1 hour before serving to blend flavors. Makes 6-8 servings.

Brands may vary by region; substitute a similar product.

Tanimura & Antle
BLT with Roquefort ▲

As innovators and leaders in the produce industry, Tanimura & Antle employ high-technology systems for efficient use of water and fertilizers, but rely on hand packing in the field to protect the quality of each head of lettuce.

1 cup mayonnaise	4 ounces crumbled blue cheese
½ cup plus 2 tablespoons sour cream	1 head Tanimura & Antle iceberg lettuce
½ cup buttermilk	1 cup cooked diced bacon
1 teaspoon Worcestershire sauce	1 cup diced fresh tomato
½ teaspoon white vinegar	¼ cup chopped Italian parsley
Dash of hot pepper sauce	

1. Put mayonnaise, sour cream, buttermilk, Worcestershire sauce, vinegar, hot pepper sauce and blue cheese in a food processor and pulse a few times, being sure to leave some lumps of cheese.

2. Cut lettuce into 6 wedges and arrange on 6 plates.

3. Drizzle with dressing. Sprinkle bacon, tomato and parsley over the lettuce. Makes 6 servings.

Ready Pac Sidewalk Café
Salmon Salad ▲

Elegant meets easy with Ready Pac Grand Parisian salad, complete with white balsamic vinaigrette dressing, almonds, cranberries and feta cheese. A delicious side salad, Grand Parisian makes a stunning entrée when topped by grilled salmon with a simple peppercorn glaze.

2 tablespoons olive oil	1 16-ounce Ready Pac Grand Parisian salad with white balsamic dressing packet
2 teaspoons cracked multi-colored peppercorns	
1 teaspoon honey Dijon-style mustard	4 4-ounce skinned salmon fillets

1. In a small bowl, whisk oil, peppercorns, mustard and 2 tablespoons white balsamic dressing from salad package.

2. In a large bowl, toss remaining balsamic dressing with salad greens; chill.

3. Lightly brush salmon with peppercorn glaze. Grill fillets, turning and brushing with glaze.

4. Divide chilled greens among 4 plates. Top with grilled salmon and equal amounts of frosted almonds, cranberries and feta cheese from the salad package. Makes 4 servings.

Earthbound Farm Mixed Baby Greens with Curry Vinaigrette ◀

Earthbound Farm brings fresh, delicious organic salads from their fields to your fork. This crunchy and delicious salad will charm your taste buds with its spicy simplicity.

2 tablespoons red wine vinegar	8 ounces Earthbound Farm* Organic Mixed Baby Greens
1/2 cup olive oil	1/2 cup whole pecans, toasted and chopped
1 tablespoon Dijon-style mustard	1/3 cup raw pumpkin seeds, toasted
4 teaspoons curry powder	1 Gala apple, diced
1/4 teaspoon salt	1/3 cup raisins

1. Combine vinegar, oil, mustard, curry powder and salt in a jar and shake vigorously to combine.

2. Place greens in a bowl with pecans, pumpkin seeds, apple and raisins. Add about half of the dressing and toss thoroughly. Add more vinaigrette if needed. Makes 6-8 servings.

Brands may vary by region; substitute a similar product.

Cello Genuine Pecorino Romano Caesar Salad ▶

1/4 cup extra-virgin olive oil	3-4 anchovies, chopped
4 garlic cloves, divided	1 head romaine lettuce, torn in small pieces
2 tablespoons Worcestershire sauce	1 cup croutons
1 teaspoon capers	Cracked pepper
1/4 teaspoon dry mustard	1/3 cup grated Cello Genuine Pecorino Romano
Juice of 1/2 large lemon	

1. Place olive oil, 2 garlic cloves, Worcestershire sauce, capers, mustard and lemon juice in a blender or food processor. Pulse a few times to puree ingredients.

2. Rub the inside of a large bowl with anchovies and the remaining garlic cloves.

3. Add lettuce and croutons to the bowl and toss with salad dressing. Season to taste with pepper and sprinkle with Pecorino Romano. Makes 4 servings.

Grimmway Farms
Dilled Honey Mustard Carrots ▼

Grimmway Farms baby carrots are sweet and ready to eat right out of the bag. They add taste, texture and nutrition to any meal. This easy-to-prepare side dish is a dieter's delight, loaded with good nutrition and beta-carotene.

4 cups (16 ounces) Grimmway Farms Cut and Peeled Baby Carrots	1 tablespoon Dijon-style mustard
1/4 cup water	1 teaspoon chopped fresh dill or 1/2 teaspoon dried dill weed
2 tablespoons honey	

1. In a medium saucepan, combine carrots and water; bring to a boil. Reduce heat, cover and simmer until carrots are tender, about 10 minutes. Uncover and cook over medium-high heat until almost all water has evaporated, about 3 minutes.

2. Combine honey, mustard and dill in a small bowl. Pour over the carrots, stirring until well coated and warm. Makes 4 servings.

Grimmway Farms Low-Fat Fresh
Orange Compote with Granola ▲

2 Grimmway Farms oranges, peeled and separated into segments	1 banana, sliced thin
1 apple, cored and sliced thin	2 tablespoons fresh-squeezed orange juice
1/2 cup seedless red or green grapes, halved	1/2 cup fat-free or low-fat granola

1. In a medium bowl, toss together orange segments, apple, grapes, banana and orange juice. Sprinkle granola over mixture; toss lightly.

2. Serve immediately as dessert, or for breakfast topped with low-fat yogurt, or over lettuce as a salad. Makes 6 servings.

Lee Brands Fiery
Grilled Asparagus ▲

2 1/4 pounds Lee Brands* large or jumbo asparagus, trimmed	4 tablespoons rice vinegar
	2 teaspoons sugar
1-4 tablespoons hot chili sesame oil	Salt and pepper
	2 teaspoons sesame seeds, toasted

1. Grill asparagus over high heat, turning frequently, until crisp-tender and lightly charred. Place in a large bowl.

2. In a small bowl, whisk together oil, vinegar and sugar. Pour over asparagus and toss to coat well. Season with salt and pepper.

3. Arrange on a platter and sprinkle with sesame seeds. Serve at room temperature or chilled. Makes 12 servings.

Brands may vary by region; substitute a similar product.

Milton's Healthy Multi-Grain Turkey Surprise ◀

Smoked turkey, apple, bacon and Monterey Jack top spicy peanut butter on Milton's Healthy Multi-Grain Bread.

2 tablespoons crunchy peanut butter	2 ounces smoked turkey breast, sliced
1/2 teaspoon hot chili sauce	2 slices cooked bacon, cut in half
2 slices Milton's Healthy Multi-Grain Bread	2 ounces Monterey Jack cheese, sliced
1/2 Granny Smith or Gala apple, sliced thin	

1. Preheat broiler. Combine peanut butter and hot chili sauce; spread on bread slices. Top each slice with apples, turkey, bacon and cheese.

2. Place on baking sheet. Broil 1 minute, or until cheese is melted.

3. Assemble the two slices and cut on the diagonal to serve. Makes 1 serving.

Artisan Breads

FROM THE COSTCO *Bakery* EXPERT

Tom Fox of Costco's Fresh Foods department has this to say about the quality and preparation of Kirkland Signature Artisan Bread:

Each loaf begins with the simple ingredients of flour, water, salt and a touch of leavening. To create its distinctive line of breads, Artisan adds ingredients such as potatoes, walnuts, pecans, raisins, garlic, olives and herbs.

The distinctive flavor of the bread also comes out through the slow fermentation process, much like wine that is aged in an oak barrel. After the dough has risen, it is divided and molded. Then each loaf is hand scored and loaded into a hearth oven, where steam and high temperatures produce a loaf of bread with a crispy crust and a light and chewy center.

In the Pacific Northwest and the Bay Area, the varieties of bread include potato rosemary, pugliese, garlic and demi baguettes. In the Los Angeles and San Diego regions, members will find roasted garlic, pain rustique and rosemary olive bread along with sourdough and French baguettes. Pan bigio, roasted garlic and multigrain bread are available in all other regions, along with French baguettes.

Kirkland Signature Artisan Bread is best stored at room temperature. If you serve one loaf immediately and want to save the other for later, wrap the second loaf in plastic and pop it in the freezer. To refresh the loaf after freezing, let it thaw and then heat it at 425°F for three to five minutes, or until it reaches the desired crispness.

Gold-N-Soft Lemon Basil Pasta ▼

1/2 cup Gold-N-Soft* Margarine	2 tablespoons chopped fresh parsley
2 garlic cloves, chopped	1/8 teaspoon ground black pepper
1/4 cup Dijon-style mustard	12 ounces linguine, cooked according to package directions
1 tablespoon lemon juice	
2 tablespoons chopped fresh basil, divided	

1. In a large saucepan, cook margarine and garlic over medium heat for 2 minutes, or until garlic is soft. Stir in mustard, lemon juice, 1 tablespoon basil, parsley and pepper and cook until sauce is hot.

2. Add cooked hot pasta to the sauce and mix thoroughly.

3. Garnish with remaining basil; serve immediately. Makes 4 servings.

Brands may vary by region; substitute a similar product. Recipe created by Ventura Foods, Brea, California.

Michael Foods Broccoli, Tomato and Basil Frittata ▲

2 cups Kirkland Signature Egg Starts	1 medium onion, diced
3 tablespoons milk	3 medium tomatoes, peeled, seeded and diced
3 tablespoons grated Parmesan cheese	1 teaspoon dried basil
Freshly ground pepper	1/2 cup sliced mushrooms
3 tablespoons olive oil	1/2 cup chopped broccoli

1. Preheat oven to 325°F. In a large bowl, combine Egg Starts, milk, Parmesan and pepper to taste.

2. Heat olive oil in a large skillet over medium heat; cook onion for 5 minutes, or until soft. Add tomatoes and basil and cook for 10 minutes, stirring frequently. Add mushrooms and broccoli and cook 5 minutes more. Spoon into an oiled 8-by-8-inch baking dish.

3. Pour Egg Starts mixture over vegetables. Bake for 15-17 minutes, or until just set. Do not over-bake. Serve immediately. Makes 4 servings.

Ling Ling Crispy Dumpling Stir-Fry ▲

2 packets Ling Ling Sweet and Sour Sauce (included in Ling Ling Dumplings package)	1/4 cup sugar
	1 tablespoon oil
4 tablespoons vinegar	35 Ling Ling Crispy Chicken Dumplings (1/2 package)
4 tablespoons ketchup	14 ounces frozen stir-fry vegetable blend
Pinch of paprika	Steamed rice

1. In a small bowl, combine sauce packet contents, vinegar, ketchup, paprika and sugar.

2. Heat oil in a 12-inch skillet over high heat for 1-2 minutes. Add dumplings and reduce heat to medium-high. Cook, turning occasionally, for 6 minutes.

3. Mix in vegetables. Cover and reduce heat to medium. Cook, stirring occasionally, 6 minutes more, or until vegetables are crisp-tender.

4. Turn off heat, stir in sauce mixture, cover and let stand 1 minute. Serve over steamed rice. Makes 4 servings.

Thai-style variation: Add 2 tablespoons chili garlic paste and 1 tablespoon chopped fresh basil to the sauce mixture.

Jeremiah Tower

Jeremiah Tower, an icon of California cuisine, reports that the 1976 California Regional Dinner Festival was the tipping point for the California-cooking movement. A crew of chefs was desperately trying to make California ingredients fit a French menu when he suddenly realized that local ingredients could and should stand on their own. Chef Tower decided to put all the California ingredients into one menu and change the language of the menu from French to English. He says they even served fine California wines, of which there were very few at the time, and called the meal the California Regional Dinner. It was met with rave reviews and pushed California cuisine into the national spotlight.

Fast and Easy Plate-Cooked Fish Paillard with Ginger, Garlic and Tomatoes ▼

4 2-ounce slices boneless, skinless fillet of salmon, halibut, grouper, red snapper, sturgeon, sea bass or albacore, no thicker than 1/4 inch

3 tablespoons butter, divided

Salt and freshly ground black pepper

1 cup fish stock

1 2-ounce piece fresh ginger, peeled, finely chopped

3 garlic cloves, finely chopped

2/3 cup chopped tomatoes

12 sprigs fresh cilantro

1. Preheat the broiler or oven. Pound fish slices between pieces of lightly oiled plastic wrap or in resealable bags until evenly 1/8 inch thick. Put 4 heat-resistant plates in the oven until hot. Remove and brush each one with 1/2 teaspoon of butter.

2. Season the paillards of fish with salt and pepper and put one on each heated plate. Mix fish stock, ginger, garlic and tomatoes in a sauté pan. Bring to a boil and cook 2 minutes. Whisk remaining butter into the sauce and pour over the fish. Garnish with cilantro. Makes 4 servings.

Grilled Fish Gazpacho ◄

1 stem fresh basil, coarsely chopped	Salt and freshly ground black pepper
1/2 cup extra-virgin olive oil, divided	1 red bell pepper, stemmed, seeded and diced
8 ounces fresh fish fillet (cod, snapper, halibut, striped bass)	1 yellow bell pepper, stemmed, seeded and diced
2 tablespoons ancho chile puree	1 English cucumber, peeled, seeded and diced
1/2 cup sour cream	3 tablespoons freshly squeezed lemon juice
6 large ripe tomatoes (2 red, 2 yellow, 2 green such as Zebra)	1 tablespoon sesame oil
	12 fresh chive stems, cut in 1-inch lengths

1. Mix basil and 2 tablespoons oil in a bowl; spread on both sides of the fish fillet. Cover and marinate for 1 hour in the refrigerator.

2. Mix ancho chile puree and sour cream together; cover and refrigerate.

3. Peel, seed and puree the tomatoes, one kind at a time, through a food mill. Refrigerate the 3 purees separately.

4. Wipe the marinade off the fish and grill or broil until just cooked, 5-10 minutes, or until the internal temperature is 150°F. Flake the fish in 1/2-inch pieces, removing any bones. Combine with sour cream mixture. Season to taste with salt and pepper.

5. Combine peppers and cucumber in a bowl. Add lemon juice, sesame oil and a pinch each of salt and pepper.

6. Mix a small pinch each of salt and pepper into each of the tomato purees with; whisk 2 tablespoons of the remaining olive oil into each puree.

7. Pour the purees onto chilled large rimmed shallow plates, making whatever pattern you like. Put the fish salad in the center of the plates and scatter the pepper and cucumber mixture around the plates. Sprinkle chives over the fish. Serve immediately. Makes 4 servings.

See Jeremiah Tower's recipe for Warm Fruit Stew on page 73.

Ancho Chile Puree

10 ancho chiles	1 tablespoon red wine vinegar
1 small red onion, cored and coarsely chopped	1 tablespoon salt
2 garlic cloves	1/2 cup fresh peanut oil
2 tablespoons freshly squeezed lime juice	

1. Submerge the chiles overnight in a bowl of water. Reserve the soaking water; remove and discard the stems and seeds. Puree the chiles in a food processor with all the other ingredients except the oil. Use a little of the soaking water if necessary to allow the ingredients to move freely around the processor bowl.

2. Push the puree through a fine sieve into a bowl.

3. Whisk the oil into the puree and add salt to taste. Transfer the puree to a sealed jar and store in the refrigerator for up to 2 weeks. Makes 1 cup.

Mazzetta

Mazzetta Company, LLC believes the preservation of our environment is everyone's responsibility. Their SeaMazz shrimp is farm-raised and harvested without endangering the habitat of the sea turtle or any other marine animal. Here is one of their favorite recipes.

SeaMazz Shrimp de Jonghe ▶

2 pounds SeaMazz raw shrimp, thawed and rinsed

1/2 cup butter

4 garlic cloves, peeled and crushed

Juice of 1 lemon

1 cup dry white wine

1/2 cup seasoned Italian bread crumbs

1 tablespoon minced fresh parsley

Salt and freshly ground pepper

1 cup grated Parmesan cheese

1 pound pasta, cooked according to package directions

1. Preheat oven to 350°F. Place shrimp in a single layer in a large glass baking dish.

2. Melt butter in a large saucepan over low heat; add crushed garlic and cook until garlic turns fragrant, about 1-2 minutes. Add lemon juice, wine, bread crumbs and parsley. Season to taste with salt and pepper.

3. Pour butter mixture over shrimp and sprinkle with grated Parmesan. Cover and bake for 10-12 minutes. Uncover dish and broil on high for 3-5 minutes, or until top turns crisp and crunchy. Serve over pasta. Makes 4-6 servings.

Metz Fresh Quick Spinach, Shrimp and Pasta ◀

1 16-ounce package wide egg noodles	1 teaspoon dried basil
1 tablespoon olive oil	4 cups Metz Fresh pre-washed spinach leaves
1/2 teaspoon minced garlic	
12 ounces medium shrimp, peeled and deveined	Freshly grated Parmesan cheese
1 cup chicken broth	Ground black pepper or crushed red pepper
1 tablespoon cornstarch	

1. Cook noodles according to package directions. Drain. Return to cooking pot.

2. Heat oil in a large skillet and cook garlic over medium-high heat for 15 seconds. Add shrimp; cook, stirring, for 2-3 minutes, or until shrimp are opaque; remove from pan.

3. Combine chicken broth, cornstarch and basil. Add to skillet; cook, stirring, until thickened and bubbly. Add spinach; cook 1-2 minutes more, or until spinach is wilted. Return shrimp to skillet and stir to combine.

4. Add shrimp mixture to noodles and toss to combine. Pass Parmesan and pepper at the table. Makes 4 servings.

Singleton Shrimp and Sweet Pepper Pasta ▶

2 tablespoons butter	1/4 cup minced fresh parsley
2 tablespoons olive oil	1/4 cup grated Parmesan cheese
1 garlic clove, chopped	
2 cups mixed sliced green, red and yellow bell peppers	2 tablespoons fresh lemon juice
	Cooked pasta
1 pound Singleton* raw peeled and deveined Black Tiger Shrimp, thawed	Freshly ground black pepper

1. Heat butter and olive oil in a large skillet over medium-high heat. Cook garlic for 2 minutes. Add bell peppers and cook, stirring, for 1 minute.

2. Add shrimp and cook, stirring, for 3-4 minutes. Add parsley, Parmesan and lemon juice. Mix well.

3. Serve over hot pasta with freshly ground pepper. Makes 3-4 servings.

Brands may vary by region; substitute a similar product.

Lawry's Teriyaki Salmon with Fresh Pineapple Salsa ▲

From seasonings to marinades, sauces and spice blends, Lawry's continues to tantalize millions of taste buds.

1 1/2 cups Lawry's Teriyaki Marinade with Pineapple Juice, divided	1/4 cup finely chopped red onion
1 1/4 pounds salmon fillets or steaks	1 tablespoon chopped fresh cilantro
1 cup diced fresh or canned pineapple, well drained	2 tablespoons diced red bell pepper
	1 tablespoon finely chopped fresh jalapeño pepper

1. Combine 1 cup marinade and salmon in a large resealable plastic bag; refrigerate for 30 minutes or up to several hours.

2. Combine 2 tablespoons marinade, pineapple, onion, cilantro, bell pepper and jalapeño in a small bowl. Let pineapple salsa stand at room temperature for up to 1 hour.

3. Remove salmon from bag, discarding used marinade. Grill salmon over medium-high heat until it begins to flake easily, about 10-12 minutes, brushing often with remaining marinade.

4. Serve with room-temperature salsa on top or on the side. Makes 4 servings.

Hansen's Beverage Spicy Thai Mandarin Lime Salmon ▼

This exotic but easy salmon dish evokes the sweet and spicy flavors of Thailand.

1 cup Hansen's Natural Mandarin Lime Soda	2 teaspoons chopped French basil and/or mint
1/4 cup fish sauce or soy sauce	2 tablespoons canola oil
1 tablespoon chili-garlic sauce, or to taste	2 teaspoons toasted sesame oil
2 teaspoons finely chopped fresh ginger	4 6-ounce salmon fillets, bones removed
2 tablespoons chopped fresh cilantro	1/4 cup grated carrot

1. Whisk together lime soda, fish sauce, chili-garlic sauce, ginger, cilantro and basil. Whisk in oils. Reserve half the lime mixture for dipping. Pour the remainder over salmon fillets in a shallow glass dish. Marinate salmon, covered, in the refrigerator for 30 minutes, turning once.

2. Grill or broil salmon for 5 minutes on each side, or until the internal temperature is 160°F.

3. Divide reserved lime mixture into four small bowls. Arrange salmon fillets on serving plates along with individual bowls of dipping sauce. Top each with grated carrot. Makes 4 servings.

Rio Mar Tilapia Fillets in Dijon Mustard Cream ▲

1 pound Rio Mar* red tilapia fillets	2 tablespoons dry sherry
1/2 cup all-purpose flour, seasoned with salt and pepper	1 cup heavy cream
	1 tablespoon Dijon-style mustard
2 tablespoons butter	Salt and pepper
2 tablespoons finely chopped shallots	2 tablespoons chopped green onions

1. Dust fillets in seasoned flour and cook in butter in a large skillet over medium-high heat until browned on both sides; remove.

2. Add shallots to the pan and cook until soft, stirring occasionally; add sherry and stir rapidly to remove all the brown bits from the bottom of the pan. Stir in cream and cook until it has thickened and coats the back of a spoon, approximately 2 minutes.

3. Remove the pan from the heat, add mustard and stir until smooth. Season to taste with salt and pepper.

4. Place fillets on warmed plates, spoon several tablespoons of sauce over each serving and garnish with green onions. Makes 4 servings.

Brands may vary by region; substitute a similar product.

Darleen's Grilled Mesquite Chicken Salad with Balsamic Vinaigrette ◀

1 cup balsamic vinegar	1/2 pound cherry tomatoes
1/2 cup olive oil	1 pound mesquite-grilled
1/2 cup honey	skinless chicken breast,
8 large garlic cloves, crushed	cut in thin slices
1/2 pound curly pasta	1 11-ounce cans mandarin
cooked al dente	orange segments, drained
1/2 pound mixed baby	4 ounces slivered almonds,
salad greens	lightly toasted with
	4 tablespoons sugar

1. Combine vinegar, oil, honey and garlic in a jar and shake vigorously. Prepare a day in advance and store in the refrigerator.

2. In a medium bowl, toss pasta with 1/2 cup of vinaigrette.

3. In a large bowl, toss greens, cherry tomatoes and chicken with vinaigrette. Add pasta and toss well.

4. Sprinkle salad with mandarin oranges and candied almonds. Makes 6 servings.

Darleen Lau, Mill Valley, California

Safe Seafood at Home

Seafood is a delicious and nutritious choice that should be enjoyed as often as possible. Because it is so perishable, handle it carefully and eat it quickly after purchasing.

- ✔ *Keep seafood cold at all times, as close to 32°F as possible. Store in the coldest part of the refrigerator, close to the back, or in a meat or vegetable compartment.*

- ✔ *Keep frozen fish in the freezer until ready to thaw in the refrigerator. Do not thaw at room temperature or in standing water.*

- ✔ *Fish that will be eaten raw should be frozen for at least 15 hours to kill parasites. For example, sashimi-grade fish is flash frozen.*

- ✔ *Harmful bacteria exist on the exterior of fish, not the interior, and are killed by heat. Clean hands, knives and work surfaces minimize the spread of bacteria from the skin to the flesh of the fish.*

- ✔ *Wash hands frequently—before, during and after food preparation.*

Mariani Mediterranean Chicken Breasts with Dried Apricots ▶

For four generations, the Mariani family has grown, dried, processed and packaged the finest and freshest fruits from prime growing regions around the world.

2 boneless chicken breasts	3/4 cup Mariani-Kirkland
Salt and pepper	Signature Mediterranean
1 teaspoon ground cumin	Apricots, sliced
3 tablespoons olive oil	3/4 cup dry white wine
2 garlic cloves,	1/4 cup low-salt
finely chopped	vegetable broth
	12 pitted green olives

1. Season chicken with salt, pepper and cumin. Heat olive oil in a large skillet over medium heat. Add chicken and cook until browned. Remove chicken.

2. Add garlic to the skillet; cook for 30 seconds. Add apricots, wine, broth and olives; bring to a boil. Reduce heat to medium-low and simmer until sauce is thickened.

3. Return chicken to the skillet and cook until tender. Season to taste with salt and pepper. Makes 2 servings.

Tillamook Chilaquiles ▼

Farmer-owned since 1909, Tillamook has earned a reputation as one of the nation's premier brands of cheese and continues to make quality, naturally aged cheddar using the same 100-year-old recipe. Their chilaquiles recipe features creamy Tillamook Monterey Jack cheese.

2 cups tortilla chips

1 cup shredded cooked skinless chicken breast

1/3 cup chopped onion

1 8-ounce can tomato sauce

1 8-ounce can hot "Mexican-style" tomato sauce

1 cup shredded Tillamook Monterey Jack

Sliced olives or avocado, optional

1. Preheat oven to 350°F. Coat a 9-by-13-inch baking dish with nonstick cooking spray. Cover the bottom of the baking dish with 1 cup tortilla chips. Layer shredded chicken over the chips. Layer onions over the chicken. Top with remaining tortilla chips.

2. In a separate bowl, combine the tomato sauces; spread evenly over the casserole. Sprinkle cheese on top.

3. Bake for 20 minutes, or until hot and bubbly. Garnish with olives or avocado. Makes 4 servings.

Foster Farms Posole ◀

6 dried California chiles (or guajillo or pasilla chiles)

2 tablespoons oil or lard

3-4 pounds fresh Foster Farms chicken thighs and breasts

2 onions, minced

3-4 fresh garlic cloves, chopped

3-4 cups chicken stock

1/2 teaspoon ground cumin

2 teaspoons salt

3 cups fresh hominy

2-3 limes or lemons, cut in wedges

1 small head cabbage, shredded

10 green onions, chopped

1 cup cilantro leaves, chopped

1. Remove seeds and veins from dried chiles. Cover chiles with boiling water and soak for about 20 minutes. Drain and puree in a blender or rub through a sieve.

2. Heat oil in a large pot over medium heat and cook chicken with the skin side down until it doesn't stick; turn and continue cooking for 3 minutes, then remove and set aside.

3. Add onions to the pot and cook, stirring constantly, until translucent (about 5 minutes). Add garlic and cook 2 minutes.

4. Return chicken to pot and cover with chicken stock, bring to a boil and reduce to a simmer. Simmer uncovered for 1 hour. (You can debone chicken at this time if you like.)

5. Add cumin, salt and water if needed. Add hominy and chile puree and continue to cook until hominy pops, about 30 minutes.

6. Serve with lime wedges, shredded cabbage, chopped onion and cilantro. Makes 8-10 servings.

Fresh Tips from Deborah Fabricant

A former restaurateur, Deborah Fabricant owns The Art of Entertaining, a Los Angeles–based business that brings the easy elegance of entertaining to today's busy person. She is also the author of Stacks: The Art of Vertical Food and a spokesperson for Foster Farms.

Successful recipes begin with the freshest ingredients. Look for local products and specialties such as San Francisco sourdough, Washington apples, Monterey Jack cheese and Foster Farms chicken. Try these tips for fresh, tasty meals every time:

✔ For the freshest-tasting chicken, buy locally-grown Foster Farms and use within two days of purchase or wrap well and freeze.

✔ Marinate meats and poultry overnight for optimum flavor. Combine fresh lemon juice, crushed garlic, chopped cilantro and olive oil for a quick, fresh-tasting marinade.

✔ Seek out the freshest local fruits and vegetables. Buy what's in season. Be flexible with your shopping list to include new discoveries: leeks, persimmons, star fruit and pumpkins in fall; Brussels sprouts, cabbages, tangerines and sweet potatoes in winter; asparagus, beets, snap peas and blood oranges in spring; and apricots, corn, okra and eggplant in summer.

✔ When selecting produce, choose vibrant colors—red peppers, yellow squash, orange carrots and green Brussels sprouts—which make for a pretty plate that also packs a nutritional punch. Produce that is rich in color is typically also rich in vitamin content and flavor.

✔ To keep veggies fresh longer, place herbs, with stems submerged, in a container of ice water in the refrigerator; wrap rinsed lettuce leaves loosely in paper towels and store in a resealable plastic bag, squeezing out excess air; store mushrooms in a paper (rather than plastic) bag and do not wash until ready to use.

✔ Fresh herbs will brighten up almost any dish.

✔ Store tomatoes at room temperature to keep their flavor longer.

ConAgra Foods California Steak and Broccoli Pasta Skillet ▲

ConAgra Foods creates a fresh and healthy skillet dish combining the crispiness of sautéed fideo, a very thin vermicelli-style pasta, with tender steak strips, spicy tomatoes and broccoli.

1/4 cup Wesson* Vegetable Oil, divided

1 pound sirloin steak, thinly sliced, seasoned with salt and pepper

8 ounces fideo or angel hair pasta, broken into 1-inch pieces

1/2 tablespoon minced garlic

1 15-ounce can Hunt's* Tomato Sauce

1 10-ounce can Rotel* Original Diced Tomatoes with Green Chilies

3 cups frozen broccoli florets, thawed and drained

1. Heat 1 tablespoon oil in a large skillet over medium-high heat; cook steak until browned, stirring frequently. Remove from pan.

2. Add remaining oil, pasta and garlic. Toss pasta in oil to coat; cook and stir until lightly browned. Stir in tomato sauce and tomatoes. Cover and reduce heat to low. Cook about 10 minutes, or until tender.

3. Stir steak and broccoli into pasta. Cover and cook over low heat until heated through. Makes 4 servings.

*Brands may vary by region; substitute a similar product.

FROM THE COSTCO *Meat* EXPERT

Charlie's Grilled Pork Tenderloin with Port and Dried Cranberry Sauce ▼

1/2 cup olive oil

6 garlic cloves, minced

1 teaspoon black pepper

1 tablespoon fresh thyme or 1 teaspoon dried thyme

1 tablespoon crushed red pepper

2 Kirkland Signature pork tenderloins, about 16 ounces each, cut in two pieces

1. Combine oil, garlic, black pepper, thyme and red pepper in a large resealable bag. Add tenderloins; marinate 4-6 hours or overnight.

2. Grill over medium heat for about 10 minutes, browning on all sides, or until the internal temperature is 150°F. Slice and serve with port sauce. Makes 8 servings.

Port and Dried Cranberry Sauce ▼

1 fifth ruby port

1 pint heavy cream

2 tablespoons minced shallots

1 teaspoon black pepper

1/2 teaspoon fresh thyme or 1/4 teaspoon dried thyme

1/2 cup dried cranberries

In a medium saucepan, reduce port over high heat to 1 cup. Stir in cream, shallots, pepper and thyme; reduce heat to low and cook, stirring occasionally, until the sauce starts to thicken. Add cranberries; stir until the sauce is thickened.

Special Occasion Cuts

Serve something special at home the next time you have a reason to celebrate. Here are some suggestions from Charlie Winters and Doug Holbrook of Costco's meat department on making the best use of larger premium cuts, plus a marinade recipe from Doug's wife, Sherry:

Pork Tenderloin

✔ *This cut is endorsed by the American Heart Association.*

✔ *It's conveniently packed two tenderloins to a bag, two bags to a tray, for 4 to 6 pounds of total weight, which makes 8 to 12 servings.*

✔ *Use one bag and freeze one in the store packaging.*

✔ *Bake or grill tenderloins to 140°F for the juiciest results.*

Beef Tenderloin

✔ *Use tenderloin ends for stir-fry and bake the midsection for tender roast beef.*

✔ *Cut your own premium steaks for grilling.*

✔ *Restaurant menus call steaks from the tenderloin either fillet or filet mignon.*

Tri-Tip Roast

✔ *Marinate tri-tip for an extra layer of flavor.*

✔ *It has become well known as the meat used in fajitas.*

✔ *This well-marbled cut is tender and flavorful.*

Sherry Holbrook's BBQ Tri-Tip Marinade

1/2 cup soy
2 tablespoons honey
2 tablespoons white vinegar
2 1/2 teaspoons garlic powder
1 1/2 teaspoons powdered or less fresh ginger
3/4 cup peanut oil
1/2 cup chopped red onion
1/2 cup pineapple juice

Brawley Beef
Stockmen's Club Prime Rib ▼

Brawley Beef, of Brawley, California, takes advantage of its new state-of-the-art facility, where choice local corn-fed cattle are processed using the most stringent food-safety measures to produce the tastiest and most tender beef.

13-15 pounds choice Brawley Beef* Prime Rib	1 tablespoon black pepper
	2-3 garlic cloves, sliced
1/2 - 3/4 cup vegetable oil	1 yellow onion, sliced
5 tablespoons seasoned salt	

1. Preheat oven to 375°F. Place Brawley Beef Prime Rib in a large roasting pan. Rub oil over entire prime rib. Combine seasoned salt and pepper; rub over meat.

2. Cut 1-inch slits all over the meat; insert garlic slices.

3. Spread sliced onions on top. Bake for 2 1/2 hours, or until the internal temperature is 130-140°, for medium-rare. Makes 15-25 servings.

Brands may vary by region; substitute a similar product.

Hormel Backyard Barbecue Ribs ▲

1 package Hormel* pork loin back ribs	2 tablespoons Worcestershire sauce
3/4 cup cherry cola soft drink	1 teaspoon chili powder
1/2 cup finely chopped onion	1 teaspoon paprika
1/2 cup ketchup	Salt and pepper to taste
2 tablespoons vinegar	

1. Preheat oven to 350°F. Place ribs, bone side down, in a shallow baking pan. Cover and bake 1 hour.

2. In a saucepan, combine remaining ingredients. Simmer 10 minutes. Brush ribs generously with sauce. Cover and bake 30 minutes.

3. Brush ribs with sauce and bake, uncovered, 30-60 minutes longer, basting with additional sauce. Serve with any remaining sauce. Makes 4 servings.

Brands may vary by region; substitute a similar product.

Dole California Crisp ▼

4 Dole* bananas, cut in 1/2-inch slices	3/4 cup rolled oats
3 cups chopped Dole fresh pineapple	1/2 cup flaked coconut
1 cup packed brown sugar, divided	1/2 teaspoon ground nutmeg
1 cup all-purpose flour	1/2 cup margarine, softened

1. Preheat oven to 350°F. Toss bananas and pineapple with 1/4 cup sugar in a 9-inch baking dish.

2. In a bowl, combine remaining sugar, flour, oats, coconut and nutmeg. Cut in margarine with a fork until crumbly. Sprinkle over fruit mixture.

3. Bake for 45-50 minutes, or until topping is crisp and juices are beginning to bubble around the edges. Makes 8 servings.

*Brands may vary by region; substitute a similar product.

Primavera Black Cherry Dessert Cake ▲

Primavera's growers are recognized not only for their experience but also for their proven ability to produce the largest, sweetest and most colorful cherries available. Together, their horticultural practices, technology, packing and marketing expertise create a passionate family of dedicated farmers.

3 eggs	1/2 teaspoon vanilla extract
1 cup sugar	1/4 teaspoon almond extract
1 3/4 cups all-purpose flour	1 1/3 cups pitted Bing cherries, divided
1/8 teaspoon salt	
2 teaspoons baking powder	1/4 cup chopped walnuts
2 tablespoons water	Sweetened whipped cream

1. Preheat oven to 350°F. Beat eggs until light; gradually add sugar, beating until lemon-colored. Sift together flour, salt and baking powder; stir into eggs. Add water, vanilla and almond extract.

2. Pour into 2 greased 8-inch round cake pans. Drop 1 cup cherries over batter. Sprinkle with nuts.

3. Bake for 30 minutes, or until the sides start to pull away from the pan.

4. When cake is still slightly warm, frost with whipped cream. Garnish with remaining cherries. Makes 16 servings.

Big Valley Strawberry Pie with Almond Crust ▼

Big Valley is the premier brand of J.R. Wood, Inc., one of the largest growers and processors of fresh frozen fruit. Enjoy strawberries in an easy press-in crust of graham crackers and almonds. Take pleasure in the taste of spring year-round.

1 cup almonds	3/4 cup sugar
1/2 cup graham cracker crumbs	2 tablespoons cornstarch
	1 1/2 cups water
1/2 cup sugar	1 3-ounce package strawberry-flavored gelatin
6 tablespoons butter, melted	
1/2 5-pound package Big Valley Strawberries, halved, partially thawed	

1. Preheat oven to 350°F. Coarsely chop almonds in a food processor. Add graham cracker crumbs and sugar; process until finely ground. Add butter; process until evenly moistened. Press crumb mixture onto bottom and sides of a greased and floured 9-inch pie pan. Bake for 12 minutes. Cool. Arrange strawberries in the pie shell.

2. Mix sugar, cornstarch and water in a medium saucepan; bring to a boil over high heat, stirring constantly. Reduce heat and cook until thick and clear. Add gelatin and stir until dissolved. Pour gelatin mixture over strawberries. Refrigerate for approximately 2 hours before serving. Makes 6-8 servings.

SunWest Golden Peach Cobbler ▲

SunWest Fruit Company's San Joaquin Valley location, with its hearty soil, very warm days and surprisingly cool evenings, produces the sweetest tree fruit in the marketplace.

2/3 cup sugar, divided	4 tablespoons butter, divided
1 1/4 cups flour, divided	1 tablespoon ground cinnamon
Salt	
5 cups peeled and sliced ripe fresh peaches	1 1/2 teaspoons baking powder
1 tablespoon lemon juice	1/2 cup milk

1. Preheat oven to 400°F. Combine 1/2 cup sugar, 2 tablespoons flour and dash of salt; mix well. In a medium bowl, sprinkle peaches with lemon juice; add flour mixture and stir to coat peaches. Place in a buttered 9-inch baking pan, dot with butter and sprinkle with cinnamon.

2. Combine remaining flour, 1 tablespoon sugar, baking powder and 1/4 teaspoon salt. Cut 3 tablespoons butter into flour mixture until it resembles coarse cornmeal. Add milk and mix until dry ingredients are moistened.

3. Spoon 9 rounded mounds of dough over peaches. Sprinkle remaining sugar over top. Bake at 400°F for 30 minutes, or until topping is golden brown. Makes 9 servings.

Kingsburg Apple Asian Pear or Pluot Crisp ▼

Asian pears are crisp and juicy like apples but have a distinctive texture and flavor more reminiscent of pears. Pluots are a complex hybrid fruit that blends the delicious flavors of plums and apricots. Both Asian pears and pluots lend themselves well to this fruit crisp recipe.

4 large Kingsburg Apple Asian pears, peeled, cored and sliced, or 8 large pluots, pitted and sliced	1/2 cup water
	1/2 cup cold butter, cut in pieces
2 1/2 teaspoons cinnamon, divided	3/4 cup flour
	3/4 cup sugar
4 tablespoons brown sugar, divided	

1. Preheat oven to 375°F. Arrange fruit in a buttered 10-by-10-inch baking dish. Sprinkle 1 1/2 teaspoons cinnamon, 2 tablespoons brown sugar and water over fruit.

2. Combine butter, flour and sugar until crumbly. Cover fruit with butter mixture. Sprinkle remaining brown sugar and cinnamon over topping. Bake for about 50 minutes, or until topping is browned and bubbly. Makes 8 servings.

Carter Thomas Roasted Mendocino Gold Pears with Cinnamon and Wine ▶

This easy-to-make recipe can be served at any time of year. You can find fresh Mendocino Gold Bartlett pears at Costco from February through December.

6 fresh Mendocino Gold*
  Bartlett pears, cut in
  quarters and cored

1/4 cup honey

1/4 cup light brown sugar

1/4 cup dry red wine

1 teaspoon cinnamon

1. Preheat oven to 400°F. Place pears in a 9-by-13-inch glass baking dish.

2. Mix honey, brown sugar, wine and cinnamon in a small bowl. Spoon over pears and toss gently to coat. Bake for 20-30 minutes, or until tender.

3. Spoon into individual dessert bowls. Makes 6 servings.

Tip: Toss with nuts and serve with your favorite wine and cheese.

Brands may vary by region; substitute a similar product.

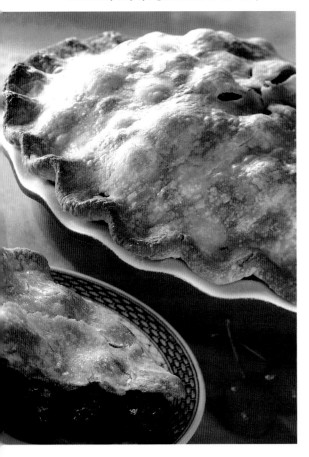

Grower Direct Cherry Pie ◀

3/4-1 1/4 cups sugar

1/3 cup flour

1/2 teaspoon salt

1/2 teaspoon nutmeg

1/2 teaspoon cinnamon

8 cups pitted Grower Direct
  California Bing cherries,
  about 3 1/2 pounds

Purchased 9-inch
  double piecrust

2 tablespoons butter,
  cut in pieces

Sugar

1. Preheat oven to 425°F. Combine sugar, flour, salt, nutmeg and cinnamon in a large bowl. Toss cherries with the sugar mixture. Pour into bottom piecrust. Dot cherry filling with butter pieces.

2. Moisten edges of bottom crust with cold water. Cover pie with top crust. Crimp edges and slit center. Sprinkle sugar lightly over top.

3. Bake for 10 minutes; reduce the heat to 350°F and bake for 1 hour, or until the crust is golden brown. Makes 6-8 servings.

Bee Sweet Citrus Orange Blossom Pie ▼

When you crave the fresh natural sweetness of oranges, try this easy recipe from Bee Sweet Citrus growers in the heart of California's Central Valley.

2 cups fresh squeezed
  Bee Sweet Citrus*
  orange juice

1/2 cup sugar

1/4 cup cornstarch

2 egg yolks, well beaten

Pinch of salt

1 tablespoon butter

1 tablespoon lemon juice

Purchased 9-inch pie
  shell, baked

2 cups whipped cream

1 tablespoon grated Bee Sweet
  Citrus orange peel, optional

1. Combine orange juice, sugar and cornstarch in a saucepan. Cook over low heat until thick, about 10 minutes.

2. Stir in egg yolks and salt; cook, stirring, 2 more minutes.

3. Remove from heat and stir in butter and lemon juice.

4. Pour into pie shell; chill. Before serving, top with whipped cream and orange peel. Makes 6-8 servings.

Brands may vary by region; substitute a similar product.

Jeremiah Tower

Considered a "dish for all seasons" by chef Jeremiah Tower, this timeless classic can be prepared in 10 minutes. This stew is just as perfect served over ice cream as it is on pound cake. Remember that fragile fruits such as raspberries should be added in the last minute of cooking.

Warm Fruit Stew ▶

1 cup strawberries, halved

1 cup blueberries

1 cup blackberries

¼ cup light syrup

1 tablespoon sweet butter, cut in cubes

Salt

2 teaspoons fresh lemon juice

1 pint vanilla ice cream

1. PREPARE LIGHT SYRUP: Combine water and sugar in a 2:1 ratio in a sauce pan. Bring to a boil, stirring constantly until all the sugar is dissolved. Simmer 5 minutes; cool.

2. Combine berries in a large frying pan with the syrup. Cook over medium heat for 2 minutes, shaking the pan gently to coat the berries with syrup.

3. Add butter, a pinch of salt and lemon juice and continue to cook, swirling the berries and butter around in the pan for 1 minute or until the butter is melted. Spoon the fruit onto 4 plates and place scoops of ice cream in the center of each serving. Makes 4 servings.

Ghirardelli Almond
Latte Brownies ▼

1 20-ounce package Ghirardelli Brownie Mix	1 cup (8 ounces) cream cheese, softened
1/3 cup water	1/4 cup (1/2 stick) butter, softened
1/3 cup vegetable oil	1 cup confectioners' sugar
1 egg	1 cup chocolate chips
1/2 cup sliced almonds, divided	1 teaspoon vegetable oil
2 teaspoons instant coffee crystals	

1. Preheat oven to 325°F. Blend brownie mix, water, oil, egg and 1/4 cup almonds until moistened. Spoon into a lightly greased 8-by-8-inch pan. Bake for 40-45 minutes. Cool thoroughly.

2. Dissolve coffee crystals in 1 1/2 teaspoons hot water. Set aside. Using an electric mixer, beat cream cheese and butter until fluffy. Add coffee mixture and sugar; beat until smooth. Spread over cooled brownies. Chill.

3. Melt chocolate chips with oil in the microwave for 2-3 minutes at 50% power, stirring occasionally. Spread over latte icing. Sprinkle with remaining 1/4 cup almonds. Makes 16 brownies.

Carol Burns, Culver City, California

Carol's Oh Wow Brownies ▲

Here's another variation on Ghirardelli Brownie Mix that member Carol Burns says always gets the "Oh, wow!" response.

2 20-ounce packages Ghirardelli Double Chocolate Brownie Mix	12 ounces semisweet chocolate chips
2/3 cup water	1/4 cup butter
2/3 cup vegetable oil	2 cups creamy peanut butter
2 eggs	2 cups crispy rice cereal
1 10.5-ounce package miniature white marshmallows	

1. Preheat oven to 325°F. Prepare brownies according to package directions with water, oil and eggs, baking in a large greased pan for 40-45 minutes.

2. Sprinkle marshmallows on top and return to the oven for 5 minutes, or until mostly melted. Cool pan on a rack.

3. Melt chocolate chips and butter in a large saucepan over low heat, stirring constantly until melted; add peanut butter, stirring gently until mixture is melted; add rice cereal 1 cup at a time, stirring gently. Spread the chocolate mixture over the marshmallows with a wet spatula. Cool. Cut into 1-inch squares. Makes 15 servings.

Caffe D'Vita Cappuccino Mousse ▸

9 teaspoons Caffe D'Vita* Cappuccino mix	3/4 cup chilled whipping cream
4 ounces black coffee	2 tablespoons sugar
4 ounces boiling water	1 teaspoon vanilla
2 ounces favorite liqueur, optional	Caffe D'Vita Cappuccino mix for dusting
	Coffee beans

1. Heat Caffe D'Vita mix, black coffee, boiling water and liqueur in a saucepan until dissolved.

2. With an electric mixer, beat cream on medium speed to soft peaks. Sprinkle with sugar, then increase speed to high and beat to stiff, firm peaks.

3. Pour cappuccino-coffee mixture into a large bowl; stir in vanilla. Fold in whipped cream.

4. Spoon into 6 goblets and chill for 2 hours. Dust lightly with cappuccino mix and garnish with coffee beans. Makes 6 servings.

Brands may vary by region; substitute a similar product.

Nestlé Candy Bar Ice Cream Pie ◂

Nestlé makes a variety of delicious foods that make any occasion even better. Nestlé Candy Bar Ice Cream Pie features Nestlé candy bars nestled between layers of Häagen Dazs ice cream. All your favorites in one dish.

1 pint chocolate ice cream, softened	4 (1.55-2.1 ounces each) Nestlé Crunch, Butterfinger or Baby Ruth candy bars, chopped, divided
1 9-inch (6-8 ounces) cookie-crumb crust	1 pint vanilla ice cream
	Chocolate-flavor syrup, such as Nestlé Nesquik

1. Spread chocolate ice cream over crust. Sprinkle with half of the chopped candy bars; cover with plastic wrap. Freeze for 1 hour.

2. Remove vanilla ice cream from the freezer to soften for 10 minutes. Spoon vanilla ice cream over chopped candy bars, forming a mound. Sprinkle with the remaining chopped candy bars; cover with plastic wrap. Freeze for 1 hour.

3. Drizzle with chocolate syrup. Makes 6 servings.

FROM THE COSTCO *Wine* EXPERT

Wine with (or as) Dessert

For some people, dessert wine is dessert rather than something to serve with dessert. Whatever your preference, the wine should be served nice and cold, with the exception of red port. Here are some sweet musings from David Andrew, Costco's global wine director:

Fruit: *Either on its own or in tarts, fruit flatters sweet wines wonderfully. The acid in the fruit is a nice foil to the sweetness of the wine: peaches (Sauternes, Coteaux du Layon, Late Harvest Riesling); oranges (Muscat); apples and pears (Sauternes, Orange Muscat).*

Chocolate: *It's hugely popular in desserts but tough to match with wine. Sweet reds like Banyuls are often suggested, but I like Tawny Port (or espresso). The creamy richness of the port marries extremely well with chocolate, blending into a heady hazelnut swirl.*

Cream: *Desserts such as crème brûlée or cheesecake are especially good with Sauternes-style wines (see below).*

Moscato d'Asti: *When the dessert is already sweet and heavy, the last thing you want is a sweet, heavy wine. Enter Moscato d'Asti. Gently sparkling, light and grapey, it works well with a variety of desserts but has a special affinity with strawberries.*

Sauternes and Barsac: *The great sweet wines of Bordeaux can be dessert in themselves, but they also work well with fruit tarts and cream desserts.*

Late Harvest Riesling *and* ***Eiswein*** *(ice wine): These truly can be dessert all by themselves. The great thing about the best German and Austrian examples is that although they have very high sugar levels, the sweetness is balanced by good acidity, so the wines are still refreshing. If you must have dessert with them, try peaches, apricots, raspberries and tropical fruits.*

Champagne: *The finesse of Champagne can be just what a fluffy sponge cake or soufflé needs.*

Jon Donaire Desserts
Strawberry Short-Cheesecake ▶

Jon Donaire Desserts dreams up more comfort food by serving cheesecake with a fresh strawberry topping.

4 strawberries, hulled and sliced	5 ounces Jon Donaire Baked New York Cheesecake* (1 precut slice)
1 tablespoon sugar	
1 teaspoon water	Whipped cream

1. Combine strawberries with sugar and water in a small mixing bowl. Refrigerate at least 1 hour for flavors to meld.

2. Place cheesecake on a large dessert plate.

3. Spoon berry mixture over the cheesecake slice. Garnish with a generous amount of whipped cream. Makes 1 serving.

Brands may vary by region; substitute a similar product.

Jelly Belly Movie Night
Snack Mix ◀

Only Jelly Belly dares to make more than 50 flavors of taste-defining jelly beans. Jelly Belly beans are in a class by themselves—a sweet treat for every taste and every occasion.

1 tablespoon sugar	1/2 cup dried cranberries
1 teaspoon cinnamon	Nonstick cooking spray
2 cups prepared air-popped popcorn	2 cups fat-free mini pretzels
1 cup bite-size crispy wheat squares cereal	2 1/2 cups Kirkland Signature Jelly Belly jelly beans, assorted flavors

1. In a small bowl, combine sugar and cinnamon. In a large bowl, combine popcorn, cereal and cranberries.

2. Spray the popcorn mixture lightly for 4-5 seconds with cooking spray; quickly toss with the sugar mixture. Stir in pretzels and jelly beans. Store in a covered container. Stir well before serving. Makes 8 cups.

Tip: For a fun hostess gift, spoon this mix into a clear container and finish with a pretty ribbon.

Dessert Ideas for Kirkland Signature Macadamia Nut Cereal

With a hearty, wholesome, crunchy, sweet mixture such as this specially crafted cereal, why enjoy it only at breakfast? Here are a few ideas for adding nutrition and protein to dishes beyond breakfast. They may save time as well.

✔ Make a fruit crisp topping quickly using Macadamia Nut Cereal instead of flour, sugar and nuts.

✔ Pulverize in a food processor and press into a pie pan for a rich, nutty pie crust.

✔ Make macadamia nut cookies by substituting Macadamia Nut Cereal for rolled oats in your favorite oatmeal cookie recipe.

✔ Turn this wholesome, crunchy cereal into a cookie snack that's easy to carry to school or play. Combine 3 cups of cereal with 1 cup of toasted coconut flakes in a large bowl. Gently mix into the cereal 3 egg whites beaten to soft peaks and sweetened with 1/2 cup of sugar and 1 teaspoon of vanilla. Bake at 350°F on a cookie sheet lined with parchment paper for 15 minutes or until lightly golden brown. Cool before removing from the sheet. Makes about 36 cookies.

Vicki's Baklava ▼

Vicki Kemmerer puts a California spin on baklava. Her version is lighter, featuring cashews in addition to pistachios and the floral flavor of Meyer lemon, a lemon-orange hybrid favored in California cuisine.

3 cups salted shelled pistachios	1 pound unsalted butter, melted
1 1/2 cups unsalted cashews	1-pound package phyllo dough, thawed
2 tablespoons sugar	
1 teaspoon cinnamon	1 1/2 cups water
1/2 teaspoon ground nutmeg	1 1/2 cups sugar
Pinch of ground cloves	1 Meyer lemon, halved
	1/4 cup honey

1. Preheat oven to 350°F. Grind pistachios, cashews and sugar in a food processor until crumbly. Add cinnamon, nutmeg and cloves.

2. With a pastry brush, coat the sides and bottom of a 9-by-13-inch baking dish with melted butter. Cover bottom and sides with 2 sheets of phyllo dough. Brush phyllo with melted butter. Add 2 more sheets and brush with butter. Add 2 more sheets, brush with butter and sprinkle with 1/3 cup of nut mixture.

3. Repeat the layers until all of the nut mixture is used, ending with phyllo dough on the top.

4. Create the traditional diamond shapes by slicing parallel diagonal lines in one direction through all but the bottom layer of the phyllo dough. Turn the pan 90 degrees and slice parallel diagonal lines through all but the bottom layer.

5. Bake about 45 minutes, or until the top is flaky and golden brown.

6. Combine water, sugar and lemon halves in a heavy saucepan. Bring to a boil, then simmer for 15 minutes. Remove lemon. Stir in honey.

7. When baklava and sugar syrup are slightly cooled, pour the syrup over the baklava. Let it sit at room temperature overnight and then cut through the bottom of the phyllo. Cover and refrigerate. Makes about 24 servings.

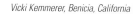

Vicki Kemmerer, Benicia, California

Lipton Sparkling Sangria Tea ▲

3 cups boiling water	1 medium orange, sliced, plus more for garnish
5 Lipton Brisk Cup-Size Tea Bags	1 medium lemon, sliced, plus more for garnish
1/3 cup sugar	
2 cups purple grape juice, chilled	1 medium lime, sliced, plus more for garnish
	Club soda, chilled

1. Pour boiling water over tea bags in a teapot; cover and brew for 5 minutes. Remove tea bags; stir in sugar and cool.

2. Combine tea with grape juice and fruit slices in a large pitcher; chill for at least 2 hours.

3. Just before serving, add a splash of soda. Pour into ice-filled glasses and garnish with additional orange, lemon and lime slices. Makes 8 servings.

Traffic-Light Smoothie from Zespri Kiwifruit and the California Strawberry Commission ▾

2 green kiwifruit

6 tablespoons orange juice, divided

2 Zespri gold kiwifruit

3/4 cup fresh California strawberries, hulled

1 tablespoon honey, or to taste

1. Cut green kiwi in half and scoop pulp by spoonfuls into a blender with 2 tablespoons orange juice; puree. Pour into 2 glasses. Rinse blender.

2. Cut gold kiwi in half and scoop into the blender with 3 tablespoons orange juice; puree. Pour slowly over the back of a spoon on top of the green puree to form two layers. Rinse blender.

3. Puree strawberries with the remaining tablespoon of orange juice and the honey. Pour over the gold puree to form a third layer. Makes 2 servings.

Tip: For a gravity-defying fruit garnish, thread a slice of kiwi or a strawberry on a bamboo skewer.

Kirkland Signature/Silk Razzleberry Smoothie ◀

Healthy body, happy taste buds—it all starts with Silk, America's favorite soymilk. Silk is lactose and cholesterol free and is easily found near the dairy case at Costco warehouses across the country.

1 cup Kirkland Signature/ Silk Vanilla Soymilk

1/2 cup frozen raspberries

1/2 cup frozen strawberries

1/2 sliced frozen banana

1 teaspoon honey, optional

1. Combine all ingredients in a blender; puree until smooth and creamy.

2. Pour into glasses and enjoy. Makes 2 servings.

Make Soymilk Part of Your Day

The health benefits of soymilk—high in protein, calcium and iron; low in fat; and cholesterol-free—are compelling. But actually consuming it every day is the challenge. It's white, sweet and cold. What's the problem? Drinking a glass with meals puts some people off because soymilk is sweeter than plain milk but not as sweet as chocolate milk. It has a bit more body than dairy milk. If you love milk and cookies you can probably make the switch. If you're lactose intolerant, you may learn to love it. But if you're not a milk drinker, it might seem impossible to get on the soy bandwagon.

Here are several ideas for including soymilk where you'll never notice the difference:

- ✓ Latte: heat 1 cup of vanilla soymilk; stir in 1 teaspoon of instant coffee
- ✓ Hot cocoa: heat 1 cup of chocolate soymilk in the microwave for 1-2 minutes and top with mini-marshmallows
- ✓ French toast batter or pancake and waffle mixes
- ✓ Fruit smoothies and milkshakes
- ✓ Blue cheese, cole slaw and ranch-style salad dressings
- ✓ Sour cream–based dip for chips

San Francisco Bay Coffee
Authentic Irish Coffee ▼

1-2 teaspoons sugar	3-5 ounces brewed
1 ounce Irish whiskey or	San Francisco Bay*
Irish liqueur	French Roast coffee
	1 ounce heavy cream

1. Fill a 6- to 8-ounce coffee mug with hot water to warm.

2. Pour out water and add sugar and liquor to mug. Add coffee and stir.

3. Hold a spoon upside down over the mug. Slowly pour cream over the inverted spoon, creating a layer on top of the coffee. Makes 1 serving.

Brands may vary by region; substitute a similar product.

Pacific Fruit Famous Bonita
Banana "Daiquiri" ▲

For more than 40 years, Pacific Fruit Inc. has been growing premium-quality bananas in Ecuador, the largest banana-exporting country in the world. Guests will line up for this refreshing twist on an old favorite.

2 Bonita* bananas	2 cups crushed or
1/2 can frozen lime	small cubed ice
daiquiri mix	2 1/2 cups water
	Whipped cream

1. Place bananas, daiquiri mix, ice and water in a 40-ounce blender. Blend at high speed until smooth and frothy.

2. Garnish with whipped cream or low-calorie whipped topping and banana slices. Makes 4 servings.

Brands may vary by region; substitute a similar product.

Tree Top Apple Strawberry
Banana Smoothie ▼

Perfect for an on-the-go breakfast, post-workout snack or afternoon pick-me-up, this smoothie tastes almost too good to be healthy.

1 cup Tree Top* Apple Juice	1 apple, peeled,
1 pint strawberries, hulled	cored and sliced
1 banana	6 ounces vanilla yogurt
	1 teaspoon vanilla extract

Put all ingredients in a blender and process until smooth. Makes 2 servings.

Tip: For a thicker smoothie, use frozen fruit or freeze the apple juice in an ice cube tray.

Brands may vary by region; substitute a similar product.

Islands of plenty

The land of the luau shares its exotic delights

H AWAII IS A TROPICAL OASIS *with a cuisine that reverberates with the cultures of its people, most notably Polynesians, Portuguese, Chinese, Japanese, Koreans, Filipinos and Caucasians of European descent.*

One of the easiest (and most fun) ways to be introduced to the foods of this region is to visit any of the six Costco warehouses located on the islands of Oahu, Hawaii and Maui. (See www.costco.com's warehouse locator for information and locations.)

Common tropical food sightings at the warehouses include poi, Manoa lettuce, Maui Gold pineapples, purple sweet potatoes, cluster tomatoes, local green- and red-leaf lettuce, sweet onions, Japanese cucumbers and eggplant, string beans, local bananas, papayas, avocados and corn, apple bananas and ginger root. Also look for Hawaiian-made sweet breads, fish such as opah (moonfish) and ono (wahoo), plus ahi sashimi trays (yellowfin tuna cut in bite-sized pieces with vegetables and seasonings) and numerous pokes (raw fish delicacies).

At the forefront of the local cooking scene is Hawaii's Culinary Ambassador, Sam Choy. A four-time nominee for the prestigious Best Regional Chef Award from the James Beard Foundation, he is the

Sam Choy

Native Hawaiian "Uncle" Sam Choy's greatest childhood food memory is of having dinner with his mom at a restaurant where he was served a Cornish game hen; he couldn't believe that a whole chicken was just for him. He now dreams of the day when poke, a Hawaiian delicacy made of raw fish and seasonings, will be as well known around the world as sushi, sashimi—and game hens.

author of 11 top-selling cookbooks, including Sam Choy's Island Flavors, Sam Choy's Polynesian Kitchen *and the recently released* Hawaiian Luau, *manager of a chain of restaurants and a television personality extraordinaire. This charismatic Hawaiian is passionate about his family and friends and the regional cuisine of his beloved islands.*

Q: *What are the common threads that bind all of Hawaii's diverse food cultures together?*

A: The bond is fresh—fresh ingredients, fresh fish and a variety of fresh herbs that are used by all the different cultures.

Q: *You've described your recipes as "somma" because usually all you need is "somma this" and "somma that." What are somma the ingredients always found in your kitchen?*

A: "Somma" the ingredients I use most are Aloha Shoyu (Hawaiian soy sauce), hot peppers, cilantro, garlic, ginger and Hawaiian sea salt.

Q: *In* Sam Choy's Island Flavors *you compare building a dish to building a house. If someone just wants to build a hut, what's the simplest Hawaiian dish to prepare?*

A: Poke and the no-imu kalua pig, which is prepared in the oven.

Q: *And your signature dish is?*

A: One of my signature dishes is my oriental lamb chops on creamy rotelli pasta—so simple and always a hit!

Q: *How would you describe a Hawaiian Costco warehouse?*

A: Costco in Hawaii is like no other. There are a variety of local foods offered here that you can't find anywhere else. It's the perfect example of where you can get a true taste of Hawaii.

Q: *If you were given a bag of Costco baking potatoes, what would you prepare?*

A: With a bag of Costco potatoes, I'd make a garlic mashed potato, scalloped potato casserole and fresh fries. 🍽

Sam Choy

For Chef Sam Choy, the biggest culinary accomplishment is creating a dish and watching people enjoy it. His creations are known for being fresh, simple and tasty, with great presentations. "Most important," he notes, "they should be memorable." Stateside, this festive pork roast goes well with cold fish dishes, sweet potato salad, fruit salad and coconut pudding.

No-Imu Kalua Pig ▷

Kalua pig, a Polynesian favorite, is traditionally cooked in an *imu*, an earth oven or large hole in the ground filled with heated rocks and wood. No-imu means you can cook it in an oven, not the traditional way. Ti leaves are popular with Hawaiian cooks because they are sturdy enough to steam food in and give a subtle flavor. Substitute banana leaf, oiled parchment paper or aluminum foil if you cannot get ti leaves where you live. In the United States, special-order ti leaves through any florist, or look for banana leaves in Asian or Latin food shops, fresh, dried or frozen in one-pound packages.

4 pounds pork butt	2 garlic cloves, minced
Hawaiian salt or other coarse salt	6 large ti leaves, ribs removed
3 tablespoons liquid smoke, plus a few more drops	2 cups boiling water

1. Preheat oven to 350°F. Score pork on all sides with 1/4-inch-deep slits about 1 inch apart; rub with salt, then 3 tablespoons liquid smoke and garlic. Wrap pork completely in ti leaves, tie with string and wrap in foil.

2. Place meat in a shallow roasting pan with 2 cups of water and roast for 4 hours.

3. Dissolve 1 tablespoon Hawaiian salt in 2 cups boiling water and add a few drops of liquid smoke. Shred the cooked pork and let stand in this solution for a few minutes before serving. Makes 12 servings.

Up-Country Sweet Potato Salad

4 cups diced cooked sweet potatoes	1/2 cup minced celery
3 hard-boiled eggs, chopped	1/4 cup minced carrot
	1 cup mayonnaise
1/4 cup minced onion	Salt and pepper

In a large bowl, combine sweet potatoes, eggs, onion, celery, carrot and mayonnaise; toss lightly. Adjust seasoning with salt and pepper. Makes 8-12 servings.

Oriental Lamb Chops with Rotelli Pasta

1/2 cup soy sauce	1 1/2 tablespoons minced garlic
3/4 cup minced fresh garlic	1 medium carrot, julienned
1 tablespoon minced fresh ginger	2 medium zucchini, julienned
2 cups brown sugar	12 ounces rotelli pasta, cooked according to package directions, drained
1/2 teaspoon crushed red pepper	
1/2 cup minced fresh basil	
1/2 cup minced fresh cilantro	6 cups heavy cream
Salt	Salt and pepper
8-18 lamb chops (2-3 per serving)	3/4 cup grated Parmesan cheese
	1/2 cup coarsely chopped Chinese parsley
2 tablespoons butter	
4 tablespoons olive oil	Basil sprigs

1. Combine soy sauce, garlic, ginger, brown sugar, red pepper, basil, cilantro and salt to taste. Massage into meat for 5-10 minutes; marinate for 4-6 hours in the refrigerator. Broil chops 2-3 minutes per side, or to an internal temperature of 130°F for medium-rare.

2. In a large saucepan, heat butter and olive oil over medium-high heat. Cook garlic for about 1 minute, without browning, then add carrots and zucchini; stir-fry for 2-3 minutes. Add pasta and stir-fry for 1 minute. Add cream, bring to a boil and immediately reduce to a simmer. Adjust seasoning with salt and pepper. Just before serving, fold in Parmesan and Chinese parsley and cook for 1 minute.

3. Serve in large pasta bowls with 2 or 3 lamb chops on top, garnished with sprigs of fresh basil. Makes 4-6 servings.

Orca Bay Grilled Mahi Mahi with Corn and Tomato Relish ▼

Mahi mahi is found throughout the world's tropical and subtropical oceans. It has a mild flavor and is excellent grilled. Chef Tony Casad of Food Concepts NW in Oak Harbor, Washington, created this tasty recipe especially for Costco.

4 6-ounce Orca Bay* Mahi Mahi fillets	Salt and pepper
3 tablespoons extra-virgin olive oil, plus more for brushing	2 cups fresh corn kernels
	2 large ripe tomatoes, cored and roughly chopped
	1/2 cup chopped fresh basil

1. Brush mahi mahi fillets with olive oil and season to taste with salt and pepper.

2. In a large skillet over medium-high heat, cook corn in olive oil, stirring, until slightly brown. Add tomatoes and basil; stir and cook approximately 1 minute. Season to taste with salt and pepper.

3. Grill mahi mahi over medium heat for approximately 4 minutes on each side, or to an internal temperature of 150°F. Top each fillet with the corn and tomato relish. Makes 4 servings.

Brands may vary by region; substitute a similar product.

FROM THE COSTCO *Meat* EXPERT

Short Ribs Secret

Thin-cut kobe-style beef short ribs are great on the grill. Always considered an excellent cut for braising, short ribs can also be quickly grilled, notes Doug Holbrook, Costco meat buyer.

- ✓ Short ribs come from the flavorful chuck section.
- ✓ A high marble content gives maximum flavor.
- ✓ Marinate, sear on both sides and serve.
- ✓ Costco removes the bones for you.

Sherry's Kobe-Style Short Ribs Marinade ▲

Sherry Holbrook, wife of Costco meat buyer Doug Holbrook, shares one of her recipes for preparing short ribs at home.

1 cup soy sauce	2 large green onions, chopped
1/4 cup each: mirin (Japanese rice wine) or sweet sherry, packed dark brown sugar, rice vinegar, oriental sesame oil, minced garlic (about 15 cloves)	5 pounds short ribs

Combine all ingredients and marinate in a large resealable bag overnight. Discard marinade. Grill ribs about 3 minutes per side. Makes 4 servings.

J&J Snack Foods Hawaiian Mocha Ice Cream Sandwiches ▲

Aloha, taste buds! Mocha Ice Cream Sandwiches are made with rich and creamy mocha ice cream nestled between two freshly baked Hawaiian Macadamia White Chunk Cookies rolled in toasted coconut for additional tropical flavor. Indulgence has never tasted so good!

6 scoops (1/2 cup each) mocha ice cream	1 dozen Kirkland Signature Double Nut White Chunk Cookies
1 cup sweetened coconut flakes, toasted	

1. Let the ice cream soften at room temperature until a spreadable consistency, about 5 minutes.

2. Spread coconut in a shallow dish.

3. Place 6 cookies on a baking sheet. Place a scoop of ice cream in the center of a cookie. Press down on the ice cream with the scoop, pushing it out to the edges. Top with another cookie, pressing together to form a sandwich. With a butter knife, smooth the ice cream around the edges.

4. Roll the ice-cream edge of the sandwich in the toasted coconut and place on the baking sheet. Repeat with remaining cookies. Freeze until just set, about 10 minutes, before serving. Or, wrap tightly in plastic and keep frozen until ready to serve. Makes 6 servings.

FROM THE MEMBER'S KITCHEN

Debra's Lilikoi Shortbread Cookies ▽

The winning recipe in a local contest is a distinctive shortbread cookie infused with lilikoi (passion fruit) flavoring. The winning baker, Debra Godwin, adapted a basic shortbread recipe, adding oat flour for a healthy touch— "to counter the butter and sugar"—and to give the cookie a nutty texture and appearance.

1 cup butter, softened	2 cups flour
1 cup confectioners' sugar	1/2 cup oat flour (3/4 cup rolled oats ground in a food processor)
2 1/2 tablespoons lilikoi (passion fruit) juice or orange juice concentrate	
	1/4 teaspoon salt

1. Preheat oven to 325°F. Beat butter and sugar 2-3 minutes, until creamy. Beat in lilikoi juice. Add flours and salt slowly while mixer is running. Cover and refrigerate 1 hour, or until firm.

2. Working with half the dough at a time (keep the other half chilled), roll out on a lightly floured surface to 1/4-inch thickness. Cut with 2-inch cookie cutter. Place on ungreased cookie sheets and bake 12-14 minutes, or until edges are lightly browned. Makes 2 dozen.

Tip: Make cookies sparkle by giving the edges a gold trim courtesy of a product called Luster Dust, available at gourmet kitchen stores.

Debra Godwin, Honolulu, Hawaii

Hearth *and* home

Pioneer farmers create a prairie garden cuisine

Judith Fertig

Author Judith Fertig, a caretaker of Midwestern recipes, keeps her larder full of unsalted butter, garlic, fresh lemons because lemon juice makes anything taste better, blue cheese because she loves it, and always a frozen raw pie ready to bake, as well as various kinds of frozen fruit that can be whipped up into a dessert at the last minute.

THE LAND OF MILK AND GRAIN *is filled with lush pasturelands, rolling prairies, wheat and cattle ranches, craft festivals, state fairs crammed with award-winning pickles, preserves and giant pumpkins, and plenty of hearty eaters.*

The region is our country's main source for most food crops, producing 75 percent of all tart red pie cherries, nearly half of all butter and cheeses, and a majority of beef and wheat. Here, culinary treasures aren't as much new or trendy as they are tried-and-true, reflecting contributions of pioneers from Sweden, Scotland, Germany, Ireland, Poland and Switzerland, and also Native American tribes, all of whom have brought basic dishes to the cuisine.

Midwesterners proudly claim that their corn is the tenderest, beef the most flavorful, sausages the most succulent, honey the sweetest and red pie cherries sublimely balanced with just the right amount of tartness and sugar.

Midwest Costco warehouses report that there's a great appetite among members for traditional Chicago deep-dish pizza, quality sausage and confectionery cuisine. (See www.costco.com's

warehouse locator for information and location of all Midwest Costco warehouses.) A loyal following has been established for Kirkland Signature extra-virgin olive oil and balsamic vinegar, Parmigiano-Reggiano and fresh mozzarella as well as antibiotic- and hormone-free chicken sausage. Not to be missed are Kirkland Signature's Atlantic salmon, pork loin boneless chops, beef brisket and veal chops, plus Michigan apples and blueberries, Canadian hothouse peppers and tomatoes, Wisconsin potatoes, asparagus and golden kiwis.

Judith Fertig, a recipe historian and classically trained cook, is renowned for celebrating the rich culinary traditions of Midwestern America. She has written a trilogy of prairie cookbooks, starting with Pure Prairie. Next came Prairie Home Cooking, which was nominated in 2000 for a James Beard award, followed by Prairie Home Breads in 2001. Her latest book, All-American Desserts, is destined to be classified as a national treasure, with such treats as sweet cherry cobbler with snickerdoodle topping and Mamie Eisenhower's million-dollar fudge.

Q: What is Midwest, or as you phrase it, prairie cuisine?
A: It's a cuisine that is rooted in farm living. Midwest cooking is all about abundance and bounty and eating from the garden. It's the real taste of homemade.

Q: And your idea of a great Midwest meal?
A: The centerpiece of the meal has to be a really, really good pot roast, a slow-smoked prime rib roast or wonderful fried chicken that you've fried in lard. (You're only going to do this once a year, so it's an extravagance.) And then you'd add seasonal side dishes.

Q: In this region of old pioneer recipes, what recipe do you consider the granddaddy of them all?
A: The recipes you're able to trace the best are desserts. They were written down because measurements had to be precise. There's an intriguing dessert called Bess Truman's Ozark pudding. It's basically butter and sugar mixed together with black walnuts and baked. The recipe actually goes back to French Huguenots

of the late 1600s who found their way to Charleston, South Carolina, and somehow over the years this recipe made its way to Missouri.

Q: *What items in a food basket speak instantly to you of this region?*
A: Anything barbecue, such as barbecue sauces, grill tools, spices, rubs and hardwood charcoal. This would say Midwest to me because people really like to grill and smoke foods here.

Q: *For someone visiting the region for the first time, what dishes would you tell them not to miss?*
A: You need to get to Cincinnati for chili and homemade coffee cake, Indiana for Hoosier cream pie, around the Great Lakes I'd suggest fresh fish like lake perch or walleyed pike (just sautéed) or smoked whitefish, Wisconsin for artisan cheeses, Kansas and Nebraska for steak. Not to be missed are the bake sales throughout small Kansas towns.

> *"Midwest cooking is all about abundance and bounty and eating from the garden. It's the real taste of homemade."*

Q: *Off the top of your head, what is the best food taste for each Midwest season?*
A: In the fall, it's apples, for the winter I'd say pot roast, spring would be asparagus and wild morel mushrooms, and finally, summer fresh fruits made into homemade ice cream, such as peaches-and-cream or strawberry ice cream.

Q: *You note that "food tells a story." What's a particularly juicy Midwestern food story?*
A: We didn't really get good steaks until the late 1800s and that's thanks to Midwesterners. The Texans had their longhorns, but their meat was stringy. The English brought over Herefords, but they only had meaty front quarters. One day a Texas longhorn had a clandestine affair with a

Hereford bull. Their offspring, named Texas Jane, was exhibited in a livestock show in Kansas City in 1883. This was the beginning of great steaks.

Q: *In this land of the past, are there any new culinary revolutions?*
A: It used to be that restaurateurs were the stars, then chefs, but now it's food producers. It's back to the land and a salute to the people who grow the foods. Also, using regionally grown products is very important.

Q: *Would you care to share your first Costco warehouse experience?*
A: Oh my—what grabbed me was very, very fresh seafood that looked great and a wonderful meat counter. The clincher was the lemons in the bags. They still had stems and leaves on them. I was a goner; that clinched the deal.

Q: *What would you make with one bag of Costco baking potatoes?*
A: People think of the Midwest and comfort foods, so mashed potatoes—but I'd add a more contemporary twist. I'd peel, boil and mash them with crème fraiche or a combination of half whipping cream and half sour cream, plus salt, freshly grated nutmeg or white pepper.

Q: *When shopping at a Costco warehouse, what items do you just find irresistible?*
A: That's hard, as there are a lot of things that are irresistible. Hmmm … lemons, salmon, boutique Italian items such as stuffed pastas and sausages, cheese, pound cake (it's a steal), roasts, briskets for smoking at home, organic salad mixes, and I just love the tri-color peppers.

Q: *Any last thoughts about Costco?*
A: Costco offers more of the things that good cooks want. It's getting the finer things of life but not having to pay through the nose. Just look at the olive oil, lemons and wines—you can really buy everything for a wonderful dinner and save money at the same time. 🍽

Pocket Meals Pepperoni Pizza Dipping Sauce

This great-tasting marinara sauce can be prepared ahead of time and refrigerated for up to 24 hours.

2 tablespoons olive oil	Pinch of dried basil
1/4 cup chopped onions	Pinch of dried oregano
1 garlic clove, minced	Salt and pepper
12 ounces plum tomatoes, chopped	12 Pocket Meals Pepperoni Pizza sandwiches
8 ounces tomato puree	

1. Heat oil in a medium saucepan over low heat and cook onions for about 10 minutes. Add garlic and cook until transparent.

2. Add tomatoes and puree; simmer for about 20 minutes. Add herbs and simmer for 1 minute.

3. Season to taste with salt and pepper. Serve as a dipping sauce for Pocket Meals sandwiches, or serve on pizza, bread, over pasta or however you choose. Makes 12 servings.

Hormel Foods Crumbled BLT Dip

2 cups mayonnaise, regular or light	1 1/4 cups Hormel Premium Real Crumbled Bacon
2 cups sour cream, regular or light	Melba toast, crackers or bread
3 medium tomatoes, seeded and diced	

1. Combine mayonnaise and sour cream in a mixing bowl.

2. Gently fold in tomatoes until evenly distributed. Stir in crumbled bacon to taste.

3. Serve as a dip with melba toast, crackers or bread. Makes 1 quart or 12-15 servings.

Jennie-O Turkey Store Thai-Style Turkey Spring Rolls

Jennie-O Turkey Store, based in Minnesota, is the largest producer of turkey in the United States. Here is a great new way to use turkey in a Thai-style roll. Try their precooked turkey in any recipe that calls for cooked poultry.

12 ounces Jennie-O Turkey Store Golden Roast Turkey Breast, minced	3/4 cup peanuts, toasted, salted and coarsely chopped
1 cup shredded carrots	1/2 cup loosely packed cilantro, minced
6 green onions, minced	16 rice paper spring roll wrappers
2 tablespoons minced fresh mint	Purchased peanut sauce for dipping, optional

1. Combine turkey, carrots, onions, mint, peanuts and cilantro in a large bowl.

2. Lay out rice paper wrapper in a "diamond" position. Place mound of turkey mixture in center. Fold nearest corner over filling. Fold in left corner over filling, then right corner. Roll up tightly.

3. Dab water on wrapper's inside tip to seal. Place seam side down on plate. Repeat with remaining ingredients.

4. Serve with peanut dipping sauce. Makes 16 servings.

Variation: To make egg rolls, use wonton wrappers. Fry rolls in peanut oil 3-4 minutes, or until golden brown.

Kellogg's

Since 1906, people have come to know Kellogg's as a company they can rely on for great-tasting, high-quality foods. Kellogg's is the world's leading producer of cereal and a leading producer of convenience foods, including cookies, crackers, toaster pastries, cereal bars, frozen waffles, meat alternatives, piecrusts and cones. Their products are manufactured in 19 countries and marketed in more than 160 countries around the world.

Kellogg's TV Time Cheez-It Snack Mix

2 tablespoons margarine, melted	2 cups prepared popcorn
4 cups Sunshine Cheez-It Original Crackers	1 cup candy-coated chocolate pieces
3 cups pretzel sticks	1 cup cashews
	1 cup raisins

1. Toss all ingredients in a large mixing bowl.
2. Store in an airtight container.
Makes about 12 cups.

Shultz Seasoned Pretzels

1 cup canola oil	2 teaspoons dried dill
3 tablespoons dry ranch salad dressing mix	1 teaspoon garlic powder
	16 cups Shultz* pretzels

1. In a small bowl, whisk together oil, dressing mix, dill and garlic powder.
2. Place pretzels in a large plastic bowl with a lid. Pour oil mixture over pretzels and toss to coat well. Toss every 15 minutes for 2 hours, then let rest overnight, tightly covered.
Makes 16-20 servings.

Brands may vary by region; substitute a similar product.

Joe Basse, Woodinville, Washington

Mountain View Fruit
Peachy Pasta Salad

1 8-ounce package
   dried bowtie or
   wagon wheel pasta

2 tablespoons vegetable oil

3 Summertime Label*
   California peaches, sliced

1 red bell pepper, cut in slivers

1/2 cup pecan or walnut halves

1/4 cup nonfat plain yogurt

DRESSING:

3/4 cup vegetable oil

1/3 cup white wine vinegar

1/4 cup chopped fresh basil

2 teaspoons minced garlic

1/2 teaspoon salt

1. In a large saucepan, cook pasta in boiling salted water with 2 tablespoons oil until tender, about 8 minutes. Drain and rinse under cool water.

2. In a large bowl, combine pasta, peaches, bell pepper, nuts and yogurt.

3. In a jar, combine dressing ingredients; shake.

4. Pour dressing over pasta and toss gently.

5. Refrigerate until chilled, if desired. Makes 6 servings.

Tip: If fresh basil is not available, substitute 2 tablespoons chopped fresh parsley and 1 tablespoon dried basil.

Brands may vary by region; substitute a similar product.

Spicy Granny Smith Potato Slaw

This garden-fresh recipe makes a great salad to serve with grilled meats. It showcases the talents of three independent companies working together: Brewster Heights Packing, Mack Farms and South Florida Potato Growers.

4 cups shredded
   napa cabbage

2 cups Granny Smith
   apples, cut in cubes

2 cups cooked potatoes
   cut in cubes

1-2 fresh jalapeño
   peppers, minced

1/2 cup diced sweet onion

1 tablespoon sugar

1/4 cup lemon juice

1 cup mayonnaise

Salt and pepper

1. Toss cabbage, apples, potatoes, jalapeños and onions in a large bowl.

2. Stir sugar into lemon juice in a medium bowl to dissolve. Stir in mayonnaise.

3. Toss with cabbage mixture. Season to taste with salt and pepper. Makes 8-10 servings.

Kirkland Signature/Maple Leaf
Bacon and Spinach Salad

1/2 cup sugar

1 cup safflower oil

1 teaspoon mustard

1 teaspoon salt

1/2 cup vinegar

1 teaspoon celery seeds

2 bunches spinach,
   washed and drained,
   stems removed

1 red onion, sliced thin

6 slices Kirkland Signature/
   Maple Leaf bacon, cut in
   2-inch pieces and fried

1/4 cup walnut halves

2 tomatoes, sliced

1/4 cup grated
   Romano cheese

1. Prepare dressing by blending together sugar, oil, mustard and salt. Add vinegar and celery seeds; shake or beat well. Chill.

2. In a large bowl, mix together spinach, onion, bacon and walnuts. Add chilled dressing and toss until well coated. Arrange tomatoes on top. Chill well.

3. Sprinkle with cheese before serving. Makes 8 servings.

Ritz-y Broccoli Casserole

3 10-ounce packages
 frozen chopped broccoli,
 thawed and drained

1/2 pound Velveeta
 Pasteurized Prepared
 Cheese product, cut up

36 Ritz Crackers, coarsely
 crushed, divided

1/4 cup (1/2 stick) butter or
 margarine, melted

1. Preheat oven to 350°F. Mix broccoli, Velveeta and half of the crushed crackers in a 3-quart baking dish until well blended.

2. Mix remaining crushed crackers with butter; sprinkle over broccoli mixture.

3. Bake for 45 minutes, or until heated through. Makes 8 servings.

Tip: To quick-thaw frozen broccoli, microwave for about half the amount of cooking time indicated on the package.

FROM THE MEMBER'S KITCHEN

Linda's Sweet and Sour Red Cabbage

This old family recipe is sweet, tart and hearty eating from the gardens of the German immigrants who settled in the Cleveland area.

1 medium head red cabbage,
 cored and shredded

1 teaspoon salt

1 tablespoon butter

1/2 cup cider vinegar

1/2 cup sugar

2 red cooking apples,
 unpeeled, diced

1. Combine cabbage, salt, butter, vinegar, sugar and 1/2 cup cold water in a large pot. Cook, covered, over medium heat, stirring occasionally, for 15 minutes.

2. Add apples to cabbage and cook 20 minutes more, or until cabbage is tender but still crisp. Adjust vinegar and sugar to taste. Sweeter apples may require less sugar or more vinegar. Makes 6 servings.

Linda G. Kelly, West Haven, Connecticut

King Pak Potato Salad

3 pounds King Pak white potatoes	3 tablespoons sweet pickle relish
6 eggs, hard-boiled	1 tablespoon vinegar
1 onion, chopped	Garlic salt
2 teaspoons celery seed	Salt and pepper
2/3 cup mayonnaise	Paprika
2 teaspoons yellow mustard	

1. Place potatoes in a pot. Add salted water to cover by 1 inch. Bring to a boil, reduce heat and simmer until tender. Drain and run cold water over potatoes until cool. Peel and cut into chunks.

2. Place potatoes in a bowl; chop 4 eggs and stir into potatoes with onion and celery seed.

3. Combine mayonnaise, mustard, relish and vinegar; stir into salad. Season to taste with garlic salt, salt and pepper.

4. Slice remaining 2 eggs. Arrange on top of salad and sprinkle with paprika. Refrigerate. Makes 8-12 servings.

Russet Potato Exchange
Twice-Baked Potatoes

Russet Potato Exchange of Bancroft, Wisconsin, uses soil from rich glacial deposits and water from deep underground aquifers to grow large, tasty russet potatoes.

4 large Biggins* russet potatoes	3 tablespoons crumbled cooked bacon
2/3 cup grated Monterey Jack cheese	2 tablespoons butter
1/2 cup crumbled blue cheese	2 tablespoons sliced green onions
3/4 cup sour cream	1/2 teaspoon ground nutmeg
1/3 cup heavy cream	Salt and pepper

1. Preheat oven to 350°F. Pierce potatoes with a fork (do not wrap in foil); bake on oven rack for 70-85 minutes, or until tender; remove and let cool for 10-15 minutes.

2. In a large bowl, mix cheese, sour cream, cream, bacon, butter, onions and nutmeg.

3. Preheat broiler. Cut a thin slice off the top of each potato. Scoop out centers, leaving a shell. Combine potato centers with cream mixture and blend. Season to taste with salt and pepper. Spoon mixture into shells.

4. Place on a baking sheet 5 inches from broiler. Broil for 4-6 minutes, or until golden brown. Turn off heat; close door and leave for 7-10 minutes, or until heated through. Makes 4 servings.

*Brands may vary by region; substitute a similar product.

Kirschenman Hot German Potato Salad

For three generations the Kirschenman family has been involved in growing potatoes. This recipe from Ginny Kirschenman is a favorite made with California red or white potatoes.

10 medium white potatoes	2 tablespoons sugar
1/2 pound butter	1 1/2 teaspoons salt
1 onion, minced	1/4 teaspoon pepper
2 1/2 cups water	3 tablespoons flour
2 tablespoons vinegar	

1. Preheat oven to 275°F. Boil, peel and slice potatoes. Place in a large covered baking dish.

2. Melt butter in a large frying pan over medium heat and cook onion until translucent. Stir in water, vinegar, sugar, salt, pepper and flour to make a sauce.

3. Pour sauce over the cooked potatoes, cover and bake for about 1 1/2 hours. Makes 12 servings.

Hot Potatoes! Cold Potatoes!

Here's the lowdown on potato varieties from Frank Padilla, Costco's produce buyer:

Russet, Idaho and russet Burbank are all names for the same long, rounded potato with rough brown skin. These big potatoes are excellent for baking and frying. Buy them firm and store in a cool, dark place for several weeks, but not in the refrigerator. Remove them from the plastic bag so they can breathe. Keep them out of the light so they won't turn green.

Long white potatoes have a thin skin and are good for baking, boiling and frying. When harvested early and small, they are called fingerling potatoes.

Round white or **red potatoes** are medium sized, thin skinned and excellent for roasting, boiling and mashing or in potato salad.

Yukon Gold potatoes, with their yellow skin and flesh, are best for boiling and mashing or in potato salad.

New potatoes can be any variety, harvested young and small. They don't keep well, so enjoy them immediately, roasted, boiled or in potato salad.

Jif and Crisco Muffins

Generations of choosy moms have chosen Jif and Crisco. Here's a recipe that uses both in a muffin that's perfect for meals and snacks.

3 tablespoons sugar	2 tablespoons sugar
3 tablespoons all-purpose flour	1 tablespoon baking powder
3 tablespoons Jif Creamy or Crunchy Peanut Butter	1 teaspoon salt
1/8 teaspoon salt	1 egg
2 cups sifted all-purpose flour	1 cup milk
	1/3 cup Crisco Oil

1. Preheat oven to 400°F. In a small bowl, combine the 3 tablespoons each of sugar, flour and peanut butter and 1/8 teaspoon salt with a fork until crumbly. Set aside.

2. In a large bowl, stir together the 2 cups flour, 2 tablespoons sugar, baking powder and 1 teaspoon salt.

3. Combine egg, milk and oil. Add to dry ingredients and stir just until moistened. Fill 12 greased muffin cups 2/3 full.

4. Spoon a small amount of peanut butter mixture over each muffin and lightly stir into the batter.

5. Bake for 20 minutes, or until golden brown on top. Makes 12 muffins.

Quaker Apricot-Banana-Almond Bread

2 1/2 cups all-purpose flour	1 cup mashed ripe bananas
1 cup Old Fashioned Quaker Oats, uncooked	1/2 cup low-fat buttermilk
2 teaspoons baking powder	1/2 cup vegetable oil
1 teaspoon baking soda	1/2 cup packed light brown sugar
1/2 teaspoon salt	2 eggs
2/3 cup finely chopped dried apricots	1/4 teaspoon almond extract
1/4 cup plus 2 tablespoons unblanched sliced almonds, divided	

1. Heat oven to 350°F. In a large bowl, combine flour, oats, baking powder, baking soda and salt; Stir in apricots and 1/4 cup almonds.

2. In a medium bowl, whisk together bananas, buttermilk, oil, brown sugar, eggs and almond extract. Add to dry ingredients. Stir just until dry ingredients are evenly moistened. Pour into a greased and floured 5-by-9-inch loaf pan. Sprinkle with remaining almonds.

3. Bake for 55-65 minutes, or until golden brown and a toothpick inserted in the center comes out clean. Cool for 10 minutes on a wire rack. Remove bread from pan and cool completely on rack. Makes 16 servings.

Kirkland Signature Canned Salmon—Quick and Healthful

Fast as a can opener and just as nutritious as a fillet hot off the grill is Kirkland Signature Canned Salmon for dinner or a snack. Everyone knows a few tricks with tuna, the most famous fish out of a can, and they all apply here. It makes a great salad, sandwich or topping for a cracker.

With its large, sweet, boneless, skinless chunks, Kirkland Signature Canned Salmon exceeds the quality of conventional canned salmon, according to Doug Luke, Costco buyer. He helped develop this new product, which meets the usual high standards of all Kirkland Signature fresh or frozen fish.

Everything from quality control at the source to the definition of chunk is part of the process. This is definitely not ordinary canned salmon.

Here are a few more ideas for quick meals and snacks with Kirkland Signature canned salmon:

- ✔ *Toss with hot pasta, oil and lemon.*
- ✔ *Stir into a fresh tomato sauce and serve over rice.*
- ✔ *Add it to a spicy salsa for a special dip with chips.*
- ✔ *Make a fish taco with chopped lettuce and onion.*
- ✔ *Blend with cream cheese to make a spread for canapés.*

Clear Springs Foods
Roasted Rainbow Trout with Lime Ginger Sauce

1 teaspoon grated lime zest	1 tablespoon soy sauce
1 tablespoon vegetable oil	Pinch of crushed red pepper
3 tablespoons lime juice	1 Clear Springs Dressed Rainbow Trout
1 teaspoon grated fresh ginger	1 green onion, thinly sliced

1. Preheat oven to 450°F. Mix lime zest, vegetable oil, lime juice, ginger, soy and pepper in a blender.

2. Rinse trout and pat dry. Score 3 slashes across the fish on both sides at the thickest part.

3. Place in a greased baking pan and roast until the fish is firm, about 12 minutes.

4. Skin and fillet fish. Pour lime sauce over the fish, sprinkle with green onions and serve. Makes 2 servings.

Kirkland Signature Meatballs
in Fresh Green Cream Sauce

A generous quantity of spinach adds flavor and color to this easy and healthful one-dish pasta meal. Substitute 2 cups of frozen spinach if fresh is not available.

1 2-pound package spinach, blanched and drained, reserving 1/2 cup or more cooking water	1 teaspoon crushed red pepper
	12-16 Kirkland Signature Meatballs, thawed
2 10.5-ounce cans cream of mushroom soup	4 4-ounce cans mushroom pieces
1 cup ricotta cheese	Salt and pepper
1 tablespoon red wine vinegar	1 pound pasta, cooked according to package directions
	Grated Parmesan cheese

1. Pulse spinach in a food processor to coarsely chop. Add soup, ricotta, vinegar and red pepper; pulse 2-3 times to combine.

2. Pour into a large skillet and bring to a simmer over medium heat. Thin sauce with hot blanching water if desired.

3. Add meatballs and mushrooms; simmer for 20 minutes, stirring occasionally. Season to taste with salt and pepper.

4. Serve over pasta. Pass grated Parmesan at the table. Makes 6-8 servings.

Tip: A large pot of boiling water prepared for pasta is a perfect excuse to blanch vegetables for that meal or another use before cooking the pasta. It also adds an extra layer of flavor and nutrients to the pasta.

FROM THE
COSTCO
Meat
EXPERT

Best Value Cuts of Beef

In the heartland of the country, where having a whole or half side of beef in the freezer is a tradition, every cut of meat is utilized and appreciated for its distinctive value.

You can maximize your food budget with these slow-cooker ideas from Doug Holbrook, Costco meat buyer:

✓ Pot roast pleases every time, and a beef shoulder roast is the perfect cut.

✓ Beef stew is most economical if you cut your own cubes from eye of round or sirloin tip roast.

✓ If you prefer the convenience of pre-cut fresh stew meat, Costco offers choice 1-inch cubes, with no gristle, fat or connective tissue, in 4-pound packages that make 8 to 12 servings.

Judith Fertig

For a lazy Sunday lunch, a picnic supper or a summer night's light dining, this is the perfect entrée. Vary the vegetables according to what is fresh and colorful in the garden. Serve with Cloverleaf Rolls.

Vegetable Garden Pot Roast

3 tablespoons vegetable oil	2 cups cherry tomatoes
5 pounds top or bottom round roast (or rump)	1 cup pitted black olives
	1 bunch scallions
1 1/2 cups dry red wine	2 cloves garlic
1 green bell pepper	2 tablespoons wine vinegar
1 small yellow zucchini or crookneck squash	1/4 cup olive oil

1. Preheat oven to 350°F. In a large skillet or roasting pan, heat the oil and brown the meat on all sides. Add the wine to the pan, cover and bake in the oven (or simmer over low heat on stove top) for 2 1/2 to 3 hours, or until the roast is tender.

2. Seed and chop the green bell pepper, chop the yellow zucchini, stem and quarter the cherry tomatoes, quarter the black olives, and slice the scallions (include some of the green). Mince the garlic.

3. Combine the bell pepper, zucchini, tomatoes, olives, scallions and garlic in a large bowl. Whisk wine vinegar and olive oil together and toss with the vegetables. Cover and let marinate at room temperature until the roast is done.

4. Cut a large piece of aluminum foil big enough to completely enclose the roast. Set the cooked roast in the center of the foil. Using a serrated knife, cut the beef into 1/2-inch slices, three-quarters of the way through the roast but not all the way. Spoon the marinated vegetable mixture between each slice and pack down firmly. Wrap with aluminum foil and let marinate for 30 minutes at room temperature, then cut the meat through and serve each slice with a spoonful of the marinated vegetables. Makes 6-8 servings.

Recipes adapted from Prairie Home Cooking, *by Judith M. Fertig.*

Home-Churned Butter

2 cups heavy cream

1. Place the cream in the bowl of a food processor and process for 1-3 minutes, or until the cream whips into a solid mass and separates from the liquid whey.

2. Line a sieve with a single thickness of cheesecloth. Place the sieve over a bowl. Transfer the cream mixture in the food processor to the lined sieve and press the butter solids to remove the liquid whey. Draw up the cheesecloth and gently squeeze out the remaining liquid.

3. Transfer the butter to a large ramekin, cover, and keep in the refrigerator. Makes 1 cup.

Great-Grandmother's Cloverleaf Rolls with Home-Churned Butter

Golden fields of wheat rustle in the hot June sun, ready to be harvested and then milled into all-purpose flour to make bread and yeast rolls. This vintage Midwestern recipe from my great-grandmother is easy enough that you should invite your children to help make it. And these tender rolls are oh, so delicious when served with Home-Churned Butter.

3 tablespoons unsalted butter, cubed

1/4 cup sugar

1 teaspoon salt

3/4 cup milk

1 (1/4-ounce) package or 2 1/4 teaspoons active dry yeast

1/2 cup warm (about 100 to 110 degrees) water

1 large egg, beaten

3 1/2 cups all-purpose flour

6 tablespoons unsalted butter, melted

1. Put the butter, sugar and salt in a bowl. Heat the milk and pour it over the butter mixture; let it cool to lukewarm (about 90 degrees). Sprinkle the yeast over the warm water in a small bowl and set aside to proof until foamy, about 5 minutes.

2. When the yeast has dissolved, stir it into the butter mixture. Mix in the egg. Then mix in the flour until you have a soft dough. Cover and refrigerate until ready to bake (up to 2 days).

3. Two hours before baking, divide the dough in half. Divide each half into 6 equal portions. Divide each portion into 3 pieces. Roll each piece into a ball, dip into the melted butter, and place in a muffin tin, 3 balls to a muffin cup. Cover and let rise in a warm place until double in bulk, about 1 1/2 hours.

4. Preheat oven to 350°F. Bake the rolls for 15 minutes, or until risen and browned. Makes 1 dozen rolls.

FROM THE EMPLOYEE'S KITCHEN

Alan's Smoked Duck with Pepper Berry Sauce and Fresh Herbs

2 1/4 cups Calvados, divided	2 cups marionberry preserves
1 cup balsamic vinegar	1 cup honey
1/4 cup chopped garlic	1 cup Dijon-style mustard
3 sprigs crushed fresh thyme	2 teaspoons crushed red pepper
Freshly ground black pepper	Fresh thyme, rosemary and sage or other fresh herbs
3 pounds boneless duck breasts	

1. Combine 2 cups Calvados, vinegar, garlic, thyme and black pepper in a large nonreactive bowl. Marinate duck breasts for at least 6 hours. Remove and pat dry.

2. Cook duck in a stove top smoker following the manufacturer's instructions.

3. In a medium saucepan, combine preserves, honey, mustard, red pepper and 1/4 cup Calvados; cook over medium heat, stirring occasionally, until boiling. Reduce heat and simmer for 15 minutes.

4. Pour sauce over duck. Garnish with fresh herbs. Makes 6 servings.

Alan Webster, Auburn, Washington

FROM THE EMPLOYEE'S KITCHEN

Kristin's Barbecue Ribs

This delicious rib recipe is from my mother in the Midwest. For a potluck, cut the boneless ribs into bite-size pieces before browning.

Oil	1 teaspoon salt
5 pounds Kirkland Signature Pork Shoulder Country Style Boneless Ribs	1 teaspoon paprika
	1/2 teaspoon black pepper
	1 teaspoon chili powder
2 onions, diced	3/4 cup ketchup
2 tablespoons vinegar	2 tablespoons brown sugar
2 tablespoons Worcestershire sauce	3/4 cup water

1. Preheat oven to 350°F. Brown the ribs in batches in a Dutch oven or large skillet in a small amount of oil, adding more if necessary. Pour off surplus fat. Place ribs in a large baking pan.

2. Mix onions, vinegar, Worcestershire sauce, salt, paprika, pepper, chili powder, ketchup, brown sugar and water in a bowl. Pour over the ribs.

3. Cover and bake 1 1/2 hours, or until fork tender. Makes 10-12 servings.

Kristin Granquist, Graham, Washington

Tyson Foods

Tyson Foods, Inc., founded in 1935 with headquarters in Springdale, Arkansas, is the world's largest processor and marketer of chicken, beef and pork and the second-largest food company in the Fortune 500. Tyson Foods produces a wide variety of brand-name protein-based and prepared food products marketed in the United States and more than 80 countries around the world.

Tyson Midwestern Messy BBQ Chicken Sandwich

1 pound Tyson Fully Cooked Grilled Chicken Strips	1 tablespoon dark chili powder
3/4 cup purchased barbecue sauce	1/2 teaspoon ground cumin
3/4 cup chili sauce	8 Texas toast slices, toasted
1/2 cup fresh lime juice	8 bacon slices, cooked crisp
1/2 cup chopped canned mild green chiles	1/4 cup chopped onion
	4 slices American cheese, each cut into 2 triangles
1/2 cup canned black beans, rinsed and drained	8 canned pepperoncini

1. Combine chicken, barbecue sauce, chili sauce, lime juice, chiles, beans, chili powder and cumin in a saucepan and mix thoroughly. Cover and bring to a boil over medium heat. Reduce heat and simmer for 2-4 minutes. Remove from heat; keep warm.

2. Arrange 2 slices of toast, slightly overlapping, on each plate. Top with 2 slices bacon and 1 cup chicken mixture. Sprinkle with 1 tablespoon onion and top with 2 cheese triangles and 2 pepperoncini. Makes 4 servings.

Tyson Caramel Apple Pork Chops

4 boneless pork chops, 3/4 inch thick	1/8 teaspoon ground mace
	1/8 teaspoon ground nutmeg
Vegetable oil	2 tablespoons butter
2 tablespoons brown sugar	2 tart red apples, cored and sliced into 1/2-inch wedges
1/4 teaspoon salt	
1/4 teaspoon pepper	3 tablespoons chopped pecans

1. Brush chops lightly with oil and cook in a large skillet over medium-high heat for 5-6 minutes, turning occasionally, until evenly browned on both sides. Remove chops to a serving platter; keep warm.

2. In a small bowl, combine brown sugar, salt, pepper, mace and nutmeg. Melt butter in the skillet over low heat; stir in brown sugar mixture and apples. Cover and cook for 3-4 minutes, or until tender. Remove apples and arrange on top of pork chops.

3. Continue cooking the sauce remaining in the skillet, uncovered, until it thickens slightly. Spoon over the apples and chops. Sprinkle with pecans. Makes 4 servings.

Tyson Crescent-Topped Beef Pot Pie

1 pound boneless top sirloin steak, 3/4 inch thick	1/2 teaspoon dried thyme
	12 ounces canned mushroom gravy
Vegetable oil cooking spray	
1/4 teaspoon pepper	8 ounces refrigerated crescent rolls
16 ounces frozen potato, green bean, onion and red pepper mixture	

1. Preheat oven to 375°F. Cut steak lengthwise into 2 or 3 strips, then crosswise into 1/2-inch-thick slices. Coat a large ovenproof skillet with cooking spray and heat over medium-high heat. Stir-fry steak in batches for 1 minute. Remove from the skillet and season with pepper.

2. Add vegetable mixture, 2 tablespoons water and thyme to skillet and cook, stirring, for 3 minutes, or until vegetables are defrosted. Stir in gravy and bring to a boil. Remove from heat; return beef to pan.

3. Separate rolls into 8 triangles. Starting at the wide end, roll up halfway. Arrange rolls on the beef mixture with pointed ends toward the center. Bake for 17-19 minutes, or until golden brown. Makes 4 servings.

Stove Top
One-Dish Chicken Bake

1 6-ounce package Stove Top Stuffing Mix for Chicken*	1 cup frozen mixed vegetables
1 2/3 cups water	1 10 3/4-ounce can condensed cream of mushroom soup
4 boneless, skinless chicken breast halves (about 1 1/4 pounds)	1/3 cup sour cream or milk

1. Preheat oven to 375°F. Mix contents of vegetable/seasoning packet, stuffing crumbs and water; set aside.

2. Place chicken in a 9-by-13-inch baking dish or 2-quart casserole. Pour mixed vegetables over chicken. Mix soup and sour cream; pour over chicken. Top with stuffing.

3. Bake for 35 minutes, or until chicken is cooked through. Makes 4 servings.

Tip: This dish can be made ahead by assembling as directed and then refrigerating, covered, for several hours or overnight. When ready to serve, bake, uncovered, at 375°F for 45 minutes, or until chicken is cooked through.

Brands may vary by season; substitute a similar product.

Eat Smart Sesame Chicken and Garden Vegetables

Located on California's central coast, Apio, Inc., takes pride in producing its convenient and nutritious Eat Smart brand products. Broccoli, the main ingredient, is high in vitamin C and folate and is a good source of vitamin A, fiber and potassium.

1 tablespoon sesame seeds, toasted	1 green onion, sliced
2 tablespoons soy sauce	3/4 pound boneless chicken breast, cubed
2 tablespoons water	3 cups Eat Smart Garden Vegetables*
1 1/2 teaspoons brown sugar	Steamed rice
1 garlic clove, chopped	
1/8 teaspoon grated ginger	

1. Combine sesame seeds, soy sauce, water, brown sugar, garlic, ginger and green onion in a bowl. Add chicken, coat thoroughly and marinate for 30 minutes.

2. Blanch vegetables in 4 cups of boiling water for 1 minute. Drain thoroughly.

3. Place chicken and marinade in a single layer in a large baking pan; broil for about 5 minutes, or until golden brown.

4. Stir in vegetables; broil for 3 minutes more, or until vegetables are hot but still crisp.

5. Serve over steamed rice. Makes 4 servings.

Brands may vary by region; substitute a similar product.

Kirkland Signature
Rotisserie Chicken

Rotisserie chicken is so good because the rotation delivers a beautifully browned, evenly cooked, tender, juicy bird. Costco's bird is bigger than those you get elsewhere, which may be why many members buy several at one time. It's the most popular item in the Service Deli.

What do you do with it when you get home besides take the night off from cooking? Here are a few more ideas for rotisserie chicken:

School lunches: Cut the chicken into 8 pieces and store in resealable sandwich bags for quick lunch-box packing in the morning with fruit and chips.

Wilted dinner salad: Toss cold salad greens with warmed vinaigrette and top with hot slices of chicken.

Quick stir-fry: Stir-fry a 10-ounce package of cole slaw until crisp-tender; season to taste with chili-garlic sauce and sweetened rice vinegar; stir in chunks of rotisserie chicken until hot.

DESSERTS

L&M Cheesy Granny Smith Apple Pie

L&M Northwest represents the largest supply of Granny Smith apples year-round from the "Apple Capital of the World." This luscious recipe is from Janet White, an apple grower in Grandview, Washington.

3/4 cup sugar	CRUMB TOPPING:
1 tablespoon brown sugar	1/3 cup sugar
2 tablespoons flour	1/2 cup flour
1/2 teaspoon cinnamon	3/4 cup grated Cheddar cheese
1/8 teaspoon salt	3 tablespoons butter
4 large L&M Northwest* Granny Smith apples, cored, peeled and thinly sliced	Vanilla ice cream, caramel sauce
1 9-inch piecrust, unbaked	

1. Preheat oven to 400°F. Combine sugars, flour, cinnamon and salt. Toss with apples.

2. Spread apples in piecrust. Bake for 15 minutes. Reduce heat to 350°F.

3. Prepare the crumb topping: Mix sugar, flour, cheese and butter until crumbly. Sprinkle evenly on the pie and bake for 30 minutes more, or until the apples are tender and the topping is golden. Cover lightly with foil if the topping starts to darken before the apples are tender.

4. Serve with vanilla ice cream, caramel sauce or both. Makes 8 servings.

*Brands may vary by region; substitute a similar product.

Domex Baked Cherry Delight

3 cups fresh cherries, pitted	1 teaspoon almond extract
1/3 cup sugar	1 package white cake mix
2 teaspoons cornstarch	1 cup chopped walnuts or pecans
1/2 cup water	1 cup melted butter
2 tablespoons lemon juice	Whipped cream

1. Preheat oven to 325°F. In a saucepan combine cherries, sugar, cornstarch, water, lemon juice and almond extract; cook over low heat, stirring occasionally, until the sauce thickens.

2. Spread in a 9-by-13-inch pan. Sprinkle dry cake mix evenly over cherries.

3. Sprinkle nuts over cake mixture; pour melted butter evenly over nuts. Bake for 1 hour 15 minutes, or until golden brown. Chill. Garnish with whipped cream. Makes 12 servings.

FROM THE
COSTCO
Produce
EXPERT

Storing Fresh Cherries

From blossom to fruit, the cherry tree has been celebrated since 300 BC. The Bing cherry is perhaps the most regal variety, with its large, plump fruit and sweet, juicy flesh. Not only do cherries taste great, but they are also a rich source of fiber and potassium.

Frank Padilla, Costco's produce buyer, suggests storing cherries in the refrigerator, loosely covered. They will stay fresh for up to 3 days. They can also be bagged (stemmed and pitted) and frozen for up to 3 months.

Multifoods

Costco has enjoyed a long relationship with Multifoods, which produces and markets customized baking mixes and ingredients for quality-minded bakery and food-service customers. Other leading consumer brands owned by Multifoods include Pillsbury desserts and baking mixes, Hungry Jack, Martha White, Robin Hood and Pet evaporated milk.

Multifoods
Muffins Grilled with Fruit

4 tablespoons butter or margarine, softened	6 ounces flavored yogurt
2 Kirkland Signature muffins, cut in 4 equal slices	1 cup canned mandarin oranges or apple pie filling or 2 kiwis, sliced

1. Lightly butter each side of the muffin slices. Heat a nonstick skillet over medium-high heat; cook muffin slices until golden brown on both sides. Cool on a rack.

2. Arrange 2 slices on each plate; top each slice with yogurt and fruit. Makes 4 servings.

Muffin and fruit suggestions: Lemon poppy seed muffin—peach yogurt, sliced kiwi and mandarin oranges. Apple walnut muffin— vanilla yogurt and apple pie filling.

Puratos Cocktail Dessert

Indulge yourself and your guests with a new dessert idea. Create this innovative treat by combining a classic dessert with your favorite liqueur to give the perfect finishing touch to your meal.

1 Kirkland Signature iced chocolate or white sheet cake filled with chocolate mousse	Chocolate or caramel sauce
	Chocolate chunks, chips or shavings for garnish
Flavored liqueur: Irish cream, almond, coffee, hazelnut, chocolate or peppermint	Whipped cream, optional

1. Cut cake into 2-inch squares. For each serving, place one square in a large cocktail or fancy drink glass. Pour 1 shot (2 ounces) liqueur over cake.

2. Drizzle with chocolate or caramel sauce.

3. Decorate with chocolate chunks, chips or shavings, and garnish with a whipped cream, if desired. Serve. Makes 48 servings.

Dessert idea developed by Heinz Wiechmann of Puratos Corporation U.S.

Multifoods Blueberry Muffin French Toast

2 eggs, beaten	4 large fresh strawberries, hulled and sliced
1/3 cup milk	
3 fresh Kirkland Signature blueberry muffins, cut in 4 equal slices	1 11-ounce can mandarin oranges
	1 1/2 cups fresh or frozen blueberries
1 cup confectioners' sugar	1 cup blueberry-flavored syrup

1. Combine eggs and milk. Dip each muffin slice in egg mixture. Heat a skillet coated with nonstick cooking spray over medium-high heat; cook muffin slices until golden brown on each side.

2. Arrange 3 slices on each plate and sprinkle with confectioners' sugar. Serve with fruit and syrup. Makes 4 servings.

Multifoods Muffin Splits

4 Kirkland Signature apple walnut muffins, sliced in half	2 medium bananas, sliced in 1/2-inch pieces
1 14-ounce can vanilla pudding	1 14-ounce tub chocolate fudge frosting, warmed

1. Arrange the bottom half of a muffin on a serving plate. Spread with vanilla pudding and sliced bananas.

2. Place the top of the muffin on the bananas; spread with another layer of vanilla pudding and sliced bananas.

3. Drizzle with warmed frosting. Makes 4 servings.

Equal Apple Pie

Equal Spoonful, the zero-calorie sweetener that measures cup-for-cup like sugar, is perfect to try in this delicious apple pie recipe for an all-American dessert without all the sugar.

Pastry dough for 2-crust 9-inch pie	3/4 teaspoon ground cinnamon
3 tablespoons cornstarch	1/4 teaspoon ground nutmeg
1 cup Equal Spoonful or 24 packets Equal sweetener	1/4 teaspoon salt
	8 cups peeled, sliced Granny Smith apples

1. Preheat oven to 400°F. Line a 9-inch pie pan with pastry dough.

2. Combine cornstarch, Equal, spices and salt in a large bowl; add apples and toss. Arrange apples in pie shell.

3. Place top crust on the pie. Seal edges and flute; cut a few slits in top. Bake 40-50 minutes, or until crust is brown and juices are bubbly. Cool on a wire rack. Makes 8 servings.

Act II Classic Popcorn Balls

1/3 cup light corn syrup

2 tablespoons butter

1 teaspoon cold water

1 1/4 cups
  confectioners' sugar

1/2 cup marshmallows

10 cups (approximately
  1 1/2 bags) popped
  Act II* Microwave
  Butter Popcorn

Vegetable shortening

1. In a saucepan over medium heat, combine corn syrup, butter, water, confectioners' sugar and marshmallows.

2. Heat, stirring, until the mixture comes to a boil. Carefully combine the hot mixture with the popcorn, coating each kernel.

3. Grease hands with shortening and quickly shape the coated popcorn into balls. Makes 15-20 servings.

Brands may vary by region; substitute a similar product.

Kellogg's Tony the Tiger Cookies

1 3/4 cups all-purpose flour

1/2 teaspoon baking soda

1/2 teaspoon salt

1 cup margarine, softened

1 cup sugar

2 eggs

1 teaspoon vanilla extract

3 cups Kellogg's Frosted
  Flakes cereal, crushed
  to 1 1/2 cups

1 6-ounce package (1 cup)
  semisweet chocolate
  chips, melted

1. Preheat oven to 350°F. Stir together flour, baking soda and salt.

2. Beat margarine and sugar in a large mixing bowl until light and fluffy. Beat in eggs and vanilla. Add flour mixture slowly, beating thoroughly. Mix in cereal.

3. Drizzle melted chocolate on the dough. With a knife, swirl melted chocolate gently through the dough to achieve a marbled appearance. Drop by rounded tablespoonfuls onto ungreased baking sheets.

4. Bake for about 12 minutes, or until lightly browned. Remove immediately from baking sheets and cool on racks. Makes about 48 cookies.

Dannon Peach Smoothie

1 pound or 4 medium peaches, peeled and sliced

1 cup Dannon Light 'n Fit* peach nonfat yogurt

1/2 cup unsweetened orange juice

1 tablespoon chopped fresh mint

2 teaspoons sugar, optional

5 ice cubes

Mint leaves

1. Place peaches, yogurt, orange juice, mint, sugar (if desired) and ice cubes in a blender. Pulse until well combined and ice is crushed.

2. Serve in tall glasses, garnished with mint leaves. Makes 2 servings.

*Brands may vary by region; substitute a similar product.

Splenda Raspberry Tea Punch

This refreshing recipe has 42 percent fewer calories, is 50 percent lower in carbohydrates and has 60 percent less sugar than a full-sugar version!

1 quart water

6 bags raspberry-flavored tea

2 bags English tea

2/3 cup Splenda Granular or 16 Splenda packets

1/4 cup fresh lemon juice

1 quart club soda

2 cups raspberries, fresh or individually quick frozen

1. Bring water to a boil; pour into a large heat-resistant pitcher or bowl. Steep tea bags in hot water to make a strong tea; remove tea bags. Stir in Splenda No Calorie Sweetener; chill 2 hours or until ready to serve.

2. Just before serving add lemon juice, club soda and raspberries. Serve immediately after adding soda. Makes about 2 quarts, or 8 8-ounce servings.

Spices of life

Finding flavor with the fires of Tex-Mex

I
T'S A REGION OF LIMITLESS SPACE *and tremendous vistas where horses run free, wheat bends to the wind, flat-topped mesas majestically rise from the desert floor and the mighty Colorado River and Rio Grande thread through narrow gorges and grand canyons.*

Without a doubt, the cuisine reflects the deep cultural roots of Native American tribes, Mexicans and Spaniards. It is a land of beef, cumin, chili powder, red chiles, green chiles, highly seasoned chorizo (pork) sausage, arroz (rice), pinto beans, corn, squash, jicama, pumpkins, potatoes, onions, tomatillos, red grapefruit, oranges, lemons, limes, gulf shrimp, prickly pear cactus and masa harina *(finely ground dried corn).*

This cuisine of strong and tart flavors yet subtle character requires a balance of herbs and earthy, smoky ingredients. The desire is to shock and please the palate. Pivotal to most southwestern masterpieces is the trinity of corn, beans and squash. Dishes include fajitas, which originally were created using marinated skirt steak, chiles rellenos (stuffed peppers), flautas (white or yellow corn tortillas stuffed with beef, chicken or pork and fried),

Grady Spears
Cowboy chef Grady Spears is said to fill his saddlebags with "*piloncillo,* a traditional cone-shaped Mexican brown sugar, kosher salt, a good cut of beef… and Lone Star Beer." His rip-roaring cooking attitude has made him a star of Southwest cuisine and one of the Most Wanted chefs across the land.

tamales (cornmeal and cheese, meats or vegetables steamed in corn husks), chili con carne (with meat), burritos (corn or wheat tortillas enclosing a savory filling), refried beans, vegetable stews, guacamole (mashed avocado used for dip, sauce, side dish or topping), tortilla soup and carne adovada (braised pork and pureed red chiles).

Nationally popular Tex-Mex cuisine is a child of the Southwest. It focuses on fresh, seasonal products highlighted with intricate seasonings such as cumin and chili powder, rich flavorings and generous proportions.

Beef is still king, livened up with fiery spices, slow cooked over an open fire with a ketchup-based sauce, pounded into chicken-fried steak (served with gravy) or converted into one-pot "out on the range" dishes such as chili.

The Costco warehouses of the Southwest offer members national favorites such as Kirkland Signature private-label boneless, skinless chicken breasts, extra-fancy mixed nuts, canned chicken and salmon fillets. (See www.costco.com's warehouse locator for information and location of all Southwest Costco warehouses.) However, regional flavor preferences are given high priority. So these warehouses are a must if you have a hankerin' for smokehouse brisket, jalapeño sausage, chicken fajita kits, chicken or cheese enchiladas, pecans, brittle (breakable candy), pralines (confections made of almonds and caramelized sugar), divinity (fluffy candy made with egg whites), barbecue sauce or chili. In fact, the raspberry chipotle (dried, smoked jalapeño) sauce has become so sought after that other Costco regions now have it in stock.

On the fresh side, expect to find a very upscale food selection—cluster tomatoes, continental salad, avocados, strawberries, Fuji apples, limes, hot chiles (Anaheim, habanero, Serrano, jalapeño, wax and dried), Spanish onions, Rio Red grapefruit, Rocky Ford cantaloupes, Kirkland Signature beef such as extra-lean ground, ribeye, flap, brisket and filet mignon, plus Atlantic salmon and fryer breasts.

Grady Spears, a real-life cowboy turned chef, has been putting his own special signature brand on the flavors of the Southwest for well over a decade (Restaurants and Institutions *magazine named him one of the rising stars of 1998). He's the author of four cookbooks,* A Cowboy in the Kitchen, Cowboy Cocktails, The Great Steak Book *and most recently* Texas Cowboy Kitchen: Recipes from the Chisholm Club. *Passionate about Texas and his restaurants— The Chisholm Club in Fort Worth, Nutt House Restaurant on the square in Granbury, Texas, the soon-to-be-opened Burning Pear in Sugarland, Texas, and the Roadrunner in Las Vegas—Spears has established himself as a true Southwest icon, cowboy boots and all.*

Q: *What are the common threads running through most Southwest cuisine?*
A: Chiles are number one. Southwestern cuisine is always made up of bold, spicy, fresh foods that have a lot of flavor and don't need to be touched a lot.

Q: *Fundamental to the cuisine is the combination of corn, beans and squash. What's your favorite way to present these foods?*
A: For corn, it's barely cooking it. I like to roast squash. As for the beans, drunken beans would be my favorite. These are beans with beer, bacon, ham, cilantro, onions and other flavors. The rule is one beer for the beans and one beer for the cook.

Q: *What's the most misunderstood aspect of Southwest cuisine?*
A: Southwest food is not necessarily hot or spicy; it just means that it's full of flavor, using a lot of fresh ingredients that are indigenous to this area.

Q: *Your ideal West Texas cowboy meal would include?*
A: A great piece of beef, roasted whole with kosher salt and black pepper. Then Dutch oven potatoes with dried fruit, spoon bread with chorizo, roasted asparagus with blue cheese butter or green chili and cheese grits. All of this would be served family-style

with Grandma Spears' Coca-Cola cake for dessert, topped off with buttermilk ice cream. Oh, and of course a big ol' bucket of Lone Star Beer.

Q: *Do you have a food pet peeve?*
A: Only use fresh. We don't own a freezer except for ice cream, nor do we own a microwave.

Q: *The most versatile ingredient in your kitchen would be?*
A: Beef. I'm big on beef. I have a real weakness for it.

Southwestern cuisine is always made up of bold, spicy, fresh foods that have a lot of flavor and don't need to be touched a lot.

Q: *Speaking of beef, Costco warehouses are always well stocked with USDA Choice beef.*
A: We truly push Costco beef. Most people have not had the opportunity to buy whole [large cuts of] beef. What a luxury and a price savings. Everyone in my cooking classes thinks I work for Costco, but it's just such a perfect place to buy beef.

Q: *Are there irresistible Costco items besides beef that you just never pass up?*
A: The produce is great and always fresh, with so many varieties. Awesome onions and cantaloupes. Actually, they have great cheese, too.

Q: *If you were given a bag of Costco baking potatoes, what would you prepare?*
A: I'd mix up Dutch Oven Potatoes with Dried Cranberries. I'm telling you, this is the recipe. (Grady shares this recipe on page 113.)

Q: *Finally, any sage advice for Costco members?*
A: There are no food rules. Experiment. And don't be afraid to ask the Costco butchers for help. Knock on the glass window; these guys are so helpful. 🍽

Nate's Salsa del Mundo

This recipe makes a giant portion of wonderful salsa that has the right amount of spice to please a large crowd, including kids. And it's so easy to make, even a kid can do it, says 10-year-old Nate Fifield, whose dad, Will, is a Costco employee. Serve with tortilla strips, burritos, tacos or tostadas. There's always enough left over to send some home with guests.

1 128-ounce can diced tomatoes, drained, juice reserved	1-3 garlic cloves
	1 bunch cilantro, chopped, divided
1 jalapeño pepper, stemmed	1 white onion, chopped, divided
1 Anaheim chile or 2 yellow chiles, stemmed	Salt and pepper

1. Combine tomato juice, 2 cups of tomatoes, jalapeño, chile, garlic, half of cilantro and half of onion in a blender; puree.

2. In a large mixing bowl, combine pureed mixture with remaining tomatoes, cilantro and onion. Mix well; season to taste with salt and pepper. Makes 1 gallon.

Nate Fifield, Snohomish, Washington

Kirkland Signature
Three-Cheese Taco Dip

Kirkland Signature's rich, nutty Cheddar and smooth, creamy Monterey Jack cheeses complement the south-of-the-border flavors of this delicious, easy-to-make dip for nacho chips.

12 ounces Raskas* cream cheese	1 cup (4 ounces) shredded Kirkland Signature Cheddar cheese
1/2 cup sour cream	
2 teaspoons chili powder	1 cup (4 ounces) shredded Kirkland Signature Monterey Jack cheese
1 1/2 teaspoons ground cumin	
1/8 teaspoon ground red pepper	1/2 cup diced plum tomatoes
	1/2 cup sliced black olives
1/2 cup salsa	1/3 cup sliced green onions
2 cups shredded lettuce	Tortilla chips

1. Combine cream cheese, sour cream and seasonings, mixing until well blended. Stir in salsa.

2. Spread the cream cheese mixture out on a 10-inch serving platter. Sprinkle evenly with lettuce, cheeses, tomatoes, olives and green onions.

3. Serve with tortilla chips. Makes 10 servings.

Brands may vary by region; substitute a similar product.

Donna's Costco Double Blue Cheese Pizza

Originally from back east, the Moffas live near Phoenix now and enjoy this at least once a month, usually on a Friday night.

2 teaspoons yeast	Blue cheese dressing
4 cups flour	6-10 Tyson Buffalo Style Tenders, sliced
1 1/2 teaspoons salt	
3/4 teaspoon sugar	Blue cheese, crumbled
2 1/2 tablespoons olive oil	Mozzarella, cut in small pieces
1 12-ounce can beer	

1. Combine yeast, flour, salt, sugar, olive oil and beer in a 2-pound bread machine on the dough cycle. Roll or stretch dough on a floured surface into a 12-by-17-inch shape. Place on a 12-by-17-inch baking sheet coated with cooking spray. Let rise in a warm place for about 1/2 hour.

2. Preheat oven to 450°F. Pour blue cheese dressing evenly over the dough. Arrange tenders on top. Sprinkle with blue cheese. Top with mozzarella. Bake for 20 minutes, or until crust is golden brown. Makes 4-6 servings.

Tip: To raise dough in your oven, preheat the oven to 200°F. Turn off the heat and place the dough the oven.

Donna Moffa, Peoria, Arizona

Heinz Superb Snack Platter

Heinz Poppers, Delimex Taquitos and Bagel Bites only get better when you serve them together in a deluxe snack platter with your favorite dipping sauce.

Poppers Cream Cheese Jalapeños

Delimex Beef and Cheese Taquitos*

Ore-Ida Bagel Bites Deluxe Cheese

1. Preheat oven to 450°F. Place 7 poppers on an unlined, ungreased cookie sheet, spaced well apart.

2. Bake 7 minutes on the middle rack.

3. Remove from oven and add 7 Taquitos and 7 Bagel Bites. Bake 7 minutes longer.

4. Remove from oven and let sit 1 minute before serving. Makes 4 servings.

*Brands may vary by region; substitute a similar product.

Grady Spears

Chef Grady Spears is passionate about one-pot meals as well as cookin' without a lot of frills. He suggests serving this baked bean dish with coleslaw and corn pone, also known as johnnycake or cornbread, with more beans in the batter for a real cowboy-style lunch. The secret ingredient in his Mac and Texas Cheeses recipe is the roasted green chiles. Roast, as you would red peppers, remembering to remove and discard the charred skins along with the seeds.

Shiner Bock and Molasses Baked Beans ▼

2 tablespoons oil	1 bottle
2 garlic cloves, minced	Shiner Bock* beer
2 red onions, diced	1 cup barbecue sauce
2 pounds bacon, diced	1 cup brown sugar
6 jalapeño peppers,	¹/₂ cup molasses
seeded and diced	4 cups cooked and
2 red bell	drained pinto beans
peppers, diced	Kosher salt

1. Preheat oven to 375°F. Heat oil in a large skillet. Cook garlic and onions over medium heat until they start to soften; add bacon, jalapeños and bell peppers and cook, stirring occasionally, until bacon is browned.

2. Combine beer, barbecue sauce, brown sugar and molasses in a large bowl, stirring until sugar is dissolved. Stir in beans and the bacon mixture; season to taste with salt. Transfer into a large casserole and bake for 45-60 minutes, until very hot. Makes 6-8 servings.

*Shiner Bock is a bock-style German beer made in Texas and considered by many fans to be the best American bock beer. If you must substitute, look for a slightly sweet dark lager.

Mac and Texas Cheeses with Roasted Chiles ▶

2 cups heavy cream	Kosher salt
1 cup milk	1 ¹/₂ pounds macaroni,
8 tablespoons	cooked
unsalted butter	4 poblano chiles, roasted,
¹/₂ cup flour	cleaned and cut in
3 cups grated cacciota	thin strips
or jack cheese	1 cup seasoned bread crumbs
1 cup crumbled	2 cups grated Asiago or
goat cheese	Parmesan cheese

1. Preheat oven to 375°F. Heat cream and milk in a saucepan over medium-high heat.

2. In a separate saucepan, melt butter over medium heat. Whisk in flour and cook, stirring, over medium heat for 1 minute. Slowly pour in the heated cream, whisking until the mixture thickens. Remove the saucepan from the heat and stir in both cheeses. Season to taste with salt.

3. In a large mixing bowl, combine the cream mixture, macaroni and chiles, mixing gently until well combined.

4. Pour into a buttered medium-size casserole. Sprinkle with bread crumbs and Asiago. Bake for 50 minutes, or until the top is browned. Makes 6-8 servings.

Dutch Oven Potatoes with Dried Cranberries

2 pounds russet potatoes, scrubbed	Kosher salt
1/2 cup grated Parmesan cheese, divided	Freshly ground black pepper
	2 1/2 cups heavy cream
2 cups dried cranberries	3 tablespoons unsalted butter, cut in small pieces

1. Preheat oven to 300°F. Slice potatoes 1/16 inch thick with a mandolin, or paper thin by hand. Layer one-fifth of the sliced potatoes in a buttered 8-by-8-inch baking dish, making 2 thin overlapping layers.

2. Sprinkle 2 teaspoons Parmesan over potatoes. Top with 1/2 cup cranberries, salt and pepper to taste, and 1/2 cup cream. Repeat this step 3 more times, ending with potatoes. Top potatoes with remaining cream and dot with butter. Sprinkle with remaining cheese.

3. Cover the pan with foil and bake for 2 hours. Uncover and bake for 15 minutes more to lightly brown the top. For a darker brown, place the potatoes under the broiler for a few minutes.

4. Remove from the oven and let potatoes sit for 15 minutes before serving. Cut into squares with a sharp knife. Makes 6-8 servings.

Grandma Spears' Coca-Cola Cake and Buttermilk Ice Cream, on page 125, complete the ideal West Texas cowboy meal.

Land O'Lakes Easy Fiesta Sausage and Eggs

6 (6-inch) corn tortillas, cut in 1/2-inch strips	1/2 cup milk
1 pound chorizo or hot Italian sausage, cooked, sliced and drained	8 eggs
	1/2 teaspoon chili powder
	1/2 teaspoon garlic salt
12 slices (3/4 ounce each) Land O'Lakes* American Cheese Singles	2 large tomatoes, each cut in 6 thin slices
	Paprika
1 4-ounce can chopped green chiles, drained	3/4 cup Land O'Lakes* sour cream
	Cilantro leaves

1. Arrange half each of the tortilla strips, sausage and cheese in a greased 9-by-13-inch baking pan. Layer with remaining tortilla strips and sausage; sprinkle with green chiles. Top with remaining cheese slices.

2. Combine milk, eggs, chili powder and garlic salt in a large bowl; mix well. Pour over cheese. Arrange tomato slices over cheese; sprinkle with paprika. Cover and refrigerate for at least 2 hours or overnight.

3. Preheat oven to 350°F. Bake, uncovered, for 40-55 minutes, or until center is set and edges are lightly browned. Let stand 5 minutes.

4. Cut into squares; top with a dollop of sour cream and cilantro. Makes 12 servings.

Brands may vary by region; substitute a similar product.

Swanson Broth

Cooking with Swanson Broth gives you so many opportunities to enhance the natural flavor of food. Substitute broth for water to simmer vegetables, cook rice, braise meats or splash on leftovers before reheating. Use broth instead of cream to enrich mashed potatoes, sauces, dressings and gravies without fat. Create soups that get dinner on the table in a hurry.

Swanson Southwestern Chicken and White Bean Soup ▶

With Swanson Broth and a small supply of canned beans, frozen vegetables and salsa on hand, it's easy to make soup. Add chicken, pork or beef to make it hearty. This spicy Southwestern soup is a perfect example of a quick dinner that tastes like you spent hours cooking it.

1 pound boneless chicken breasts, cubed	1 cup Pace Chunky Salsa
3/4 cup chopped onion	1 15-ounce can small white beans, rinsed and drained
3 garlic cloves, minced	
1 teaspoon ground cumin	1 cup frozen whole-kernel corn
1 14-ounce can Swanson Chicken Broth	

1. Spray a large saucepan with cooking spray and heat over medium heat for 1 minute. Add chicken and cook until browned, stirring often. Add onion, garlic and cumin and cook until onion is tender.

2. Add broth, salsa, beans and corn. Bring to a boil. Cover and cook over low heat for 20 minutes. Makes 6 servings.

General Mills Chunk Breast of Chicken Salad ◄

Pillsbury of Minneapolis has been making all-butter croissants for more than 20 years. This fun and easy recipe uses their regular-size all-butter croissants and is a summertime Texas favorite. It tastes so good that you'll want to serve it year-round.

1 1/2 cups cooked chicken chunks	1/2 cup diced Granny Smith apple
1/2 cup mayonnaise	1/8 teaspoon black pepper
1/4 cup diced onion	Celery salt
1/4 cup diced celery	Kirkland Signature croissants
1/2 cup chopped walnuts	Lettuce
	Alfalfa sprouts

1. In a medium bowl, combine chicken, mayonnaise, onion, celery, walnuts, apple, pepper and celery salt to taste; mix well.

2. Spread salad on sliced croissants; garnish with lettuce or alfalfa sprouts. Or serve the salad on a bed of lettuce. Makes 4 servings.

Seasoning and ingredient variations:

Tarragon or dill	Shredded Swiss cheese
Dijon-style mustard	Diced boiled eggs
Slivered almonds	Cucumber dressing
Sweet or dill pickle relish	instead of mayonnaise

FROM THE MEMBER'S KITCHEN

Mitzi's Jalapeño Cornbread ►

1 16-ounce container sour cream	1 8 1/2-ounce can cream-style corn
3 large eggs, lightly beaten	1 4-ounce can chopped jalapeño peppers or green chiles
1/3 cup vegetable oil	
2 cups self-rising cornmeal mix	2 cups shredded sharp Cheddar cheese
1 medium onion, chopped	

1. Preheat oven to 350°F. Combine sour cream with eggs and oil in a large bowl. Beat in cornmeal mix. Stir in onion, corn, jalapeños and cheese.

2. Pour batter into a lightly greased 9-by-13-inch pan. Bake for 1 hour, or until the top is golden. Makes 12-24 servings.

Mitzi Siracusa, San Gabriel, California

What to Drink with Spicy Food

There are two ways to look at pairing wine with spicy food: You either want a clean, refreshing wine to counteract the spiciness and put out the fire, or you want a spicy wine that can take the heat. While it's hard to generalize when spices and preparations vary so widely, here are a few helpful hints from David Andrew, Costco's global wine director:

Whites should be cold; reds often benefit from being on the cooler side of room temperature. Keep the wine fairly simple, as fine, delicate wines may be overpowered. Keep in mind that some dishes—certain curries, for example— are extremely difficult to match with wine, so if all else fails, have a nice cold beer!

***Gewürztraminer** is a classic accompaniment for Asian foods—it has a little spiciness of its own. The best comes from the Alsace region of France.*

***Grenache** wines, mostly from the south of France, are spicy themselves without being heavy. Try a Côtes-du-Rhône or Gigondas, among others.*

***Pinot Grigio** is pretty neutral, which makes it a refreshing choice that doesn't interfere with the spices.*

***Dry Riesling,** especially those from Alsace and Australia, can be an excellent foil for spicy food. Australian Riesling has delicious, mouthwatering lime-juice acidity to refresh the palate between spicy mouthfuls.*

***Sauvignon Blanc,** especially Sancerre and Pouilly-Fumé, as well as those from New Zealand and Australia, has bright, zesty gooseberry and lemongrass flavors that make it a lively, refreshing partner to many spicy dishes.*

***Zinfandel,** big, juicy and spicy, can go several rounds with the most intense foods. Zin tends to be higher in alcohol than most, so go easy. It's a specialty of sunny California.*

Carolyn's Southwestern Chicken-Stuffed Peppers ▽

Carolyn suggests serving these with your favorite crusty bread and a good bottle of wine.

---

2 tablespoons olive oil, divided	2 teaspoons Worcestershire sauce
1 small onion, diced	1 1/2 cups long-grain rice
2 garlic cloves, finely chopped	2 14.5-ounce cans chicken broth or more
1 small jalapeño pepper or more, finely chopped	3/4 cup chopped golden raisins
1 pound boneless chicken or turkey breasts, cut in 1/2-inch pieces	3/4 cup pine nuts, toasted
	Salt and pepper
1 1/2 teaspoons each dried thyme, oregano, marjoram and tarragon*	6-8 green bell peppers or Mexican poblano chiles or 12-16 Anaheim chiles
1 tablespoon chopped fresh cilantro	8 thin slices Monterey Jack or low-fat mozzarella cheese
4 medium mushrooms, finely chopped	3-4 bunches fresh spinach, steamed

1. Preheat oven to 350°F. Heat 1 tablespoon oil in a large skillet over medium heat; cook onions, garlic and jalapeño until onions are soft. Remove from pan.

2. Cook chicken or turkey in remaining oil over medium heat until opaque but not browned. Stir in onion mixture. Add herbs, mushrooms, Worcestershire sauce and rice. Mix thoroughly and cook for 5-7 minutes, or until the rice is browned.

3. Stir in chicken broth. Cook over low heat for 10 minutes, or until rice begins to soften. Stir in raisins and pine nuts. Season to taste with salt and pepper. Cook until rice is almost done but the mixture is still moist.

4. Blanch bell peppers or chiles for 1 minute. If using peppers, cut off tops, clean out seeds and membranes, and stuff with meat mixture. If using chiles, leave the stems on, slit down one side, clean out seeds and membranes, and carefully stuff with meat mixture.

5. Arrange stuffed peppers or chiles and any remaining rice mixture in a large baking dish and cover. Bake for 1 hour, or until peppers are soft Add more chicken broth if rice becomes dry. Top each pepper with a slice of cheese and put the cover back on until the cheese melts.

6. Arrange a bed of steamed spinach on each plate. Add a pepper or two and a scoop of the rice mixture if any remains. Makes 6-8 servings.

*If fresh herbs are available, use twice the amount specified for dried herbs.

Carolyn Foster, Pleasant Hill, California

Sunkist

For more than a century, the Sunkist name has evoked images of the plumpest, juiciest fresh citrus, bursting with sun-ripened flavor. One of the oldest grower-owned citrus cooperatives in the world, Sunkist originated in the fertile valleys of the desert Southwest. Today, more than 6,000 Sunkist growers continue to set the standard for the citrus industry. In addition to producing premier-quality citrus, Sunkist has become a worldwide leader in fruit marketing, helping millions enjoy the healthful benefits of delicious fresh citrus with recipes like Orange Barbecued Chicken and Real Old-Fashioned Lemonade.

Sunkist Orange Barbecued Chicken ▲

Don't limit this citrus-flavored barbecue sauce to chicken—it's excellent on pork ribs as well.

1/3 cup diced onion	Grated peel of 1/2 Sunkist orange
3 tablespoons butter or margarine	1 1/2 tablespoons cornstarch
1/3 cup honey	Juice of 3 Sunkist oranges, about 3/4 cup
Juice of 1 fresh Sunkist lemon	2 broiler-fryers (about 2 1/2 pounds each), quartered
3 tablespoons soy sauce	Vegetable oil

1. In a small saucepan, cook onion in butter until tender. Add honey, lemon juice, soy sauce and orange peel.

2. Stir cornstarch into orange juice; add to the onion mixture. Cook over medium heat, stirring, until thickened.

3. Lightly brush chicken quarters with oil.

4. Grill chicken over medium-low coals for about 20 minutes on each side.

5. Brush chicken with sauce. Continue cooking, turning and brushing occasionally with sauce, until chicken is tender, with an internal temperature of 160°F. Makes 6-8 servings.

Sunkist Real Old-Fashioned Lemonade ▲

A Sunkist classic—zesty, thirst quenching and not too sweet.

Juice of 6 fresh Sunkist lemons, approximately 1 cup	4 cups cold water
	Ice cubes
1 cup sugar, or to taste	1 Sunkist lemon, cut into cartwheel slices

1. In a large pitcher combine lemon juice and sugar; stir until sugar is dissolved.

2. Stir in cold water.

3. Serve over ice. Garnish each glass with a lemon slice. Makes 6 servings.

Reprinted with permission from Sunkist Growers, Inc. All rights reserved.

ENTRÉES

Janet's Fresh Fish Tacos

*3/4-1 pound fresh
white fish (mahi mahi,
grouper or tuna)*

2 teaspoons ground cumin

*1/2 cup reduced-fat
sour cream*

*1/4 cup finely chopped
red onion*

1 tablespoon fat-free milk

*2 teaspoons fresh
lemon juice*

*2 teaspoons
prepared horseradish*

*6 6-inch flour, corn or
whole wheat tortillas*

Fresh spinach leaves

*1 11-ounce can mandarin
oranges, drained*

1 tomato, chopped

Seasonal fruit

1. Sprinkle both sides of fish with cumin. Pan-fry, grill or broil fish until it reaches an internal temperature of 145°F. Flake the fish.

2. Combine sour cream, onion, milk, lemon juice and horseradish in a small bowl.

3. Place tortillas in a resealable plastic bag and heat in the microwave on high for 1 minute.

4. Arrange spinach evenly over tortillas. Add pieces of fish. Top each serving with 2 tablespoons of oranges. Spoon sour cream sauce over oranges. Sprinkle with chopped tomato.

5. Garnish plate with fruit of the season. Makes 6 servings.

Janet Kurtz, Lakewood, Colorado

WilsonBatiz Red Snapper with Red Grape Vinaigrette

*2 tablespoons rice
wine vinegar*

2 ounces cold water

Juice of half a lemon

*1 tablespoon
Dijon-style mustard*

*1 tablespoon
chopped shallots*

*1 tablespoon each chopped
fresh basil and tarragon*

1 tablespoon sugar

1/3 cup extra-virgin olive oil

*10-14 WilsonBatiz
Divine Flavor* red
grapes, quartered*

Salt and pepper

*4 (4-6 ounces each) fresh
Gulf red snapper fillets*

Flour

1/4 cup olive oil

Fish stock or clam juice

1. PREPARE THE VINAIGRETTE: Combine vinegar, water, lemon juice, mustard, shallots, basil, tarragon and sugar. Whisk in olive oil in a slow, steady stream. Stir grapes into vinaigrette. Season to taste with salt and pepper.

2. PREPARE THE FISH: Preheat oven to 400°F. Lightly dust fish with flour. In an ovenproof pan, cook in olive oil over medium-high heat until lightly browned on both sides.

3. Remove fillets. Pour off oil. Add enough fish stock or clam juice to the pan to come halfway up fish. Bring to a simmer and return fillets to the pan.

4. Bake 15 minutes, or until fish reaches an internal temperature of 150°F. Season to taste with salt and pepper. Spoon vinaigrette over fish and serve. Makes 4 servings.

*Brands may vary by region; substitute a similar product.

SeaPak Santa Fe Shrimp Scampi Salad with Roasted Corn and Black Beans

4 cups baby greens

*1/2 cup purchased
vinaigrette, divided*

1 cup roasted corn

1 cup black beans

*48 SeaPak Shrimp Scampi,
cooked according to
package directions*

*4 corn tortillas cut in 1-by-3-
inch batons, fried crisp*

*2 corn tortillas cut in 1/8-by-
4-inch strips, fried crisp*

1/2 cup diced tomatoes

2 tablespoons chopped chives

4 green onions, sliced

1 tablespoon pine nuts

1 tablespoon lime juice

1. Toss greens with half of the vinaigrette in a large bowl. Mound greens in soup bowls; scatter corn and black beans over greens; arrange shrimp on top.

2. Plant tortilla batons vertically around the edge of the greens; top shrimp with tortilla strips. Sprinkle with tomatoes, chives, green onions and pine nuts. Drizzle with remaining vinaigrette and a splash of lime juice. Makes 4 servings.

Hebrew National
Sizzling Franks with Grilled Corn and Black Beans ▼

2 ears corn, shucked

2 tablespoons vegetable or olive oil, divided

1 12-ounce package Hebrew National Beef Frankfurters

1/2 cup chopped red or yellow onion

1/2 cup chopped red bell pepper

1 16-ounce can black beans, drained

1/2 cup prepared chunky salsa

Chopped cilantro for garnish

1. Brush corn with 1 tablespoon oil. Grill corn and franks over medium heat 10-12 minutes, or until corn is tender and franks are heated through.

2. Heat remaining oil in a medium saucepan over medium heat. Add onion; cook 3 minutes. Add bell pepper; cook 2 minutes. Add beans and salsa; cover and simmer 5 minutes.

3. Cut corn from cobs; stir into bean mixture. Cut franks into 1-inch pieces. Serve the beans topped with franks and cilantro. Makes 6 servings.

Nalley's Enchilada Chili Bake ▲

1 6 1/4-ounce package tortilla chips, divided

1 8-ounce package shredded sharp Cheddar cheese, divided

1 19-ounce can Nalley's Original Chili with beans

1 15-ounce can enchilada sauce

1 8-ounce can tomato sauce with chopped onion

1 4 1/2-ounce can chopped olives, drained

2 cups sour cream

1. Preheat oven to 375°F. Reserve 1 cup tortilla chips and 1/2 cup shredded cheese.

2. Combine remaining tortilla chips and shredded cheese with the canned ingredients in an 11-by-7-inch baking dish.

3. Bake, uncovered, for 30 minutes, or until bubbling hot. Spread sour cream on top; sprinkle with reserved tortilla chips and cheese. Bake 5 minutes more, or until cheese is melted. Makes 6 servings.

Grace Baking Chipotle Poblano Strata ▼

Since 1987, Grace Baking, San Francisco's award-winning bread maker, has been committed to providing their loyal customers with time-honored recipes using only the finest ingredients. Their recipes are specially formulated to meet their high standards of authentic, old world, artisan bread—with all-natural starters and no preservatives or artificial ingredients.

1/2 pound chorizo, removed from casing

1 onion, diced

18 slices Grace Baking* Pugliese bread, divided

4 roasted poblano peppers, cut into strips, divided

1 1/2 cups shredded Cheddar cheese, divided

1 14.5-ounce can diced tomatoes, drained

1 chipotle pepper in adobo sauce

2 tablespoons adobo sauce

4 eggs

2 cups milk

1. Cook chorizo and onions on medium heat for about 6 minutes.

2. Place 6 bread slices in a buttered 3-quart casserole. Sprinkle with half of chorizo mixture, 1/3 of poblano strips and 1/3 of cheese. Repeat layering.

3. Arrange remaining slices of bread on top and sprinkle with tomatoes and remaining poblano strips and cheese.

4. Puree chipotle pepper, adobo sauce, eggs and milk. Pour over casserole. Refrigerate 1 hour.

5. Preheat oven to 350°F. Bake for 50 minutes, or until bubbling hot. Makes 6-8 servings.

Brands may vary by region; substitute a similar product.

Leah Hermsen, Corvallis, Oregon

PrairieFresh Peppered Pork Roast with Cherry Salsa ▾

Natural PrairieFresh Premium Pork comes fresh from their farms located throughout the rolling prairies of the Southwest. Because every step of production is controlled, you'll be serving the safest, best-tasting pork available.

1/3 cup chopped onion	*1 1/2 tablespoons vinegar*
1/3 cup chopped green bell pepper	*1 1/2 tablespoons chopped cilantro*
1/3 cup chopped jalapeño peppers	*2 tablespoons black pepper*
	2 teaspoons garlic salt
1/3 cup dried cherries	*3-pound PrairieFresh* boneless pork loin*
1/3 cup red cherry preserves	

1. PREPARE CHERRY SALSA: Combine onion, peppers, dried cherries, preserves, vinegar and cilantro; mix well. Cover and chill overnight.

2. Preheat oven to 350°F. Rub black pepper and garlic salt onto pork loin. Place pork in a shallow pan and roast for about 1 1/2 hours, or until the internal temperature is 150°F.

3. Remove from oven and let pork rest for 10 minutes. Slice and serve with Cherry Salsa. Makes 6-8 servings.

*Brands may vary by region; substitute a similar product.

FROM THE MEMBER'S KITCHEN

Leah's Popeye Burritos ▴

2 cups cooked and drained hamburger, or any combination of chopped beef, chicken or pork	*1 8-ounce can tomato sauce*
	1/3 cup water
	2 tablespoons oil
1 10-ounce package frozen chopped spinach, thawed and squeezed dry	*8 8-inch flour tortillas*
	2 cups shredded Cheddar or Cheddar/jack mix, divided
1 1.25-ounce package taco seasoning mix	*Sour cream*
	Refried beans

1. Preheat oven to 325°F. Combine meat, spinach, seasoning mix, tomato sauce and water in a large saucepan. Bring to a boil over medium heat and simmer for 5 minutes, stirring occasionally.

2. Heat oil in a skillet over high heat. Warm both sides of tortillas to soften, about 1 minute on each side. Drain on paper towels.

3. Spoon 2 heaping tablespoonfuls of the meat mixture onto each tortilla. Sprinkle with cheese. Roll up tortillas and place seam side down in a large baking dish coated with cooking spray. Sprinkle with remaining cheese. Bake for 20 minutes, or until cheese is melted. Top each tortilla with sour cream and serve with refried beans. Makes 4 servings.

Charlie's Mexican Spiced Pork Chops with Pineapple Lime Salsa ▲

4 Kirkland Signature pork chops	1/4 teaspoon ground cinnamon
4 garlic cloves, crushed	2 tablespoons red wine vinegar
1 teaspoon dried oregano	3 tablespoons orange juice
1 teaspoon ground cumin	1 tablespoon honey
1/2 teaspoon ground coriander	1 tablespoon olive oil
1 teaspoon crushed red pepper	Salt and black pepper
1/2 teaspoon black pepper	

1. With scissors, cut snips through the fat on the pork chop edges at 1 1/2-inch intervals.

2. Combine garlic, oregano, cumin, coriander, red pepper, black pepper, cinnamon, vinegar, orange juice, honey and oil. Pour over the chops, turning several times to coat thoroughly. Cover and refrigerate for 4 hours.

3. Grill chops over medium/hot coals until there is no trace of pink near the bone but pork is still juicy, with an internal temperature of 150°F. Season to taste with salt and pepper. Serve with Pineapple Lime Salsa. Makes 4 servings.

Pineapple Lime Salsa ▲

1/2 fresh pineapple, cored and finely chopped	Chopped fresh cilantro or mint
	Grated peel of 1 lime
1 fresh red chili, seeded and finely chopped	3 tablespoons fresh lime juice
	Salt
1 red onion, finely chopped	Hot pepper sauce

1. Combine pineapple, chili, onion, cilantro, lime peel and lime juice. Add salt and hot pepper sauce to taste.

2. Cover and let stand for 30 minutes at room temperature to allow flavors to blend.

3. Serve chilled or at room temperature. Makes 1 1/2 cups.

FROM THE
COSTCO
Meat
EXPERT

Best-Value Pork Cuts

When you want to cook once and serve twice, or freeze half a recipe to enjoy another day, vice president Charlie Winters suggests pork. Conveniently sold in six-pound packages, either of these economical meat selections makes 12 or more servings:

Whole pork shoulder butt roast
- ✔ Delicious choice for pot roast
- ✔ Perfect for shredding to use in carnitas

Country-style ribs
- ✔ Excellent roasted or grilled
- ✔ Succulent simmered in a slow-cooker

Charlie's country-style rib tip: Boil ribs for 15 minutes; drain and chill. Marinate in barbecue sauce for 1 hour. Finish on the grill for color or in the oven at 350°F for 20 minutes.

Charlie's spare-rib tip: Cut in 2- or 3-rib sections to fit your slow-cooker; cook for 1 1/2 hours on medium in barbecue sauce.

Bourbon-Basted **Swift** BBQ Beef

Swift & Company is a leading supplier of fresh beef and pork under the Swift Premium and Swift brands. Tri-tip used to be the butcher's secret, but now the word is out about what a tender cut this is. Tri-tip is perfect for grilling and matching with a zesty sauce.

2 pounds Swift beef tri-tip	*BOURBON BBQ SAUCE:*
STEAK RUB:	2 cups ketchup
1 teaspoon ground cumin	1/3 cup dark molasses
1 tablespoon garlic powder	1/2 cup bourbon
2 tablespoons sweet paprika	1/4 cup Dijon-style mustard
2 tablespoons ground black pepper	3 tablespoons hot pepper sauce
3 tablespoons salt	2 tablespoons Worcestershire sauce
3 tablespoons brown sugar	2 tablespoons sweet paprika
1/4 cup bourbon	2 garlic cloves, minced
	1/2 medium onion, minced

1. Combine all steak rub ingredients except the bourbon. Sprinkle a generous amount of rub on each side of the tri-tip and place in a plastic bag or bowl. Add bourbon and work into the mixture to coat the meat. Marinate in the refrigerator for at least 1 hour, or overnight (preferred).

2. Combine BBQ sauce ingredients in a large, heavy saucepan. Bring to a simmer over medium heat, stirring occasionally. Cover, reduce heat to low and cook another 20 minutes, until thickened. This can be made several days in advance and stored in the refrigerator.

3. Apply a light coating of BBQ sauce to each side of the meat. Grill over medium heat about 10 minutes per side, or to an internal temperature of 130°F for medium-rare. Serve with BBQ sauce for dipping. Makes 4 servings.

Excel Corporation
Perini's Ranch Steak Rub

Tom Perini, one of the most popular cooks of authentic Texas cuisine in the country, says, "I'm a believer in letting the flavors of the meat speak for themselves." This is the standard rub used in his restaurant, the Perini Ranch Steakhouse, located in Buffalo Gap, Texas; *www.periniranch.com.*

1 tablespoon cornstarch or flour	1 teaspoon dried oregano
2 tablespoons salt	4 teaspoons garlic powder
4 teaspoons coarsely ground black pepper	1 teaspoon paprika
	1 teaspoon granulated beef stock

Mix all ingredients together. Sprinkle or rub into steaks before grilling or broiling. Makes 1/2 cup. Will cover 4-10 steaks, depending on size and flavor preference.

Grady Spears

Chef Spears notes in A Cowboy in the Kitchen that cowboys have always been weak for sweets and that dessert usually gets a wild reception in cowboy country. This cake, created by Grandma Spears herself, is one of the most requested dishes at the chef's Nutt House Restaurant in Granbury, Texas.

Grandma Spears' Coca-Cola Cake ▸

1 cup butter	2 cups sugar
1 cup Coca-Cola	2 cups flour
3 tablespoons cocoa	FROSTING:
1/2 cup buttermilk	1 cup butter
1 teaspoon baking soda	3 tablespoons cocoa
1 teaspoon vanilla extract	6 tablespoons Coca-Cola
2 eggs, beaten	1 1/2 cups confectioners' sugar

1. Preheat oven to 350°F. Combine butter, Coca-Cola and cocoa in a medium saucepan and cook over low heat until boiling; cool.

2. Beat buttermilk, baking soda and vanilla in a small bowl. In a separate bowl, beat together eggs, sugar and flour.

3. Stir all three mixtures together, mixing well. Pour the batter into a greased 9-by-13-inch baking dish and bake for approximately 1 hour, or until a toothpick inserted in the center comes out clean.

4. To make the frosting, combine butter, cocoa and Coca-Cola in a medium saucepan and bring to a simmer over low heat; whisk in sugar and remove from heat.

5. Pierce holes throughout the hot cake with a fork. Spread the frosting on the cake and let cool. Makes 16 servings.

Buttermilk Ice Cream

1 cup water	1 tablespoon corn syrup
1 cup sugar	
2 cups buttermilk	Kosher salt
Juice and grated peel of 1 lime	

1. Place water and sugar in a small saucepan and bring to a boil over high heat. Cool and refrigerate until chilled.

2. Combine buttermilk, lime juice, lime peel, corn syrup and chilled sugar syrup. Season to taste with salt. Freeze in an ice-cream maker according to the manufacturer's instructions. Makes 6 servings.

Cuisine
of the
colonies

Seafood harvests seasoned with Yankee pride

T HE MARITIME HERITAGE *of the Atlantic seaboard anchors this region to its cuisine. Oysters, scallops, clams, cod, salmon, lobster and blue and soft-shell crabs reign supreme—in a myriad of preparations.*

The area is known for its craggy coastlines, colonial heritage, fall foliage, clambakes, rolling hills, maple syrup and intense seasons. It is here that the oldest fruit orchards, dairies, vegetable farms and grain mills in the United States reside. Small boutique farms producing prize-winning cheeses, ciders, jams and preserves dot the landscape. New England and mid-Atlantic cooking has evolved today into a sophisticated, contemporary cuisine, yet dishes from its early colonial history continue to thrive.

Urban centers filled with ethnic groups from Ireland, Greece, Portugal, Italy and other nations offer a melting pot of food experiences. Jewish delicatessens, with their bagels and Reuben sandwiches, can be found next to Greek restaurants and Irish pubs.

Jasper White
Jasper White, the New England chef who recently wrote an entire cookbook on North American chowder (*50 Chowders*) and who dreams of writing another cookbook on clams, notes that many American foods can be traced back to immigrants. As a result, great American culinary fare is not about how fancy the tables are but about the food and people gathering together.

Costco's Atlantic states warehouses report that regional specialties are always in great demand. The mid-Atlantic area shows a preference for seafood, including crabmeat, oysters, salmon and cod, while the New York/New Jersey corridor favors Italian and seafood items, and the Northeast shows a strong liking for salty snacks such as pretzels, granola bars and cereal bars. (See www.costco.com's warehouse locator for information and location of all Atlantic Costco warehouses.)

Depending on the location, expect to find regional specialties such as stuffed tilapia, preserves, pure maple syrup, frozen crab cakes, marinated mozzarella cheese balls, Italian cheeses, crabmeat and bruschetta topping.

As for fresh fruits and vegetables, look for red seedless grapes, continental and spring mix salad blends and other basics. Seasonal offerings include New York apples (Empire and Red Delicious), cranberries, Italian chestnuts, Spanish and Moroccan clementines (mandarin oranges), Holland peppers, Asian pears, persimmons, dates and Spanish lemons.

Jasper White was named the Best Chef in the Northeast by the James Beard Foundation in 1991 and is considered a leading teacher of contemporary American cooking. He embraces food and cooking with great gusto. His three Summer Shack restaurants, located in Boston and Cambridge, Massachusetts, and at the Mohegan Sun in Uncasville, Connecticut, with their lobster tanks and indoor clambakes, as well as his tradition-filled cookbooks Jasper White's Cooking from New England, Lobster at Home and 50 Chowders, reflect the best of Atlantic cuisine.

Q: What distinguishes Atlantic fare from other American regional cuisines?
A: It was the first American cuisine. It is also seasonal because our seasons are so dramatic up here. For example, in the winter you'll find a lot more hearty fare such as slow-cooked dishes, rich chowders and more use of dairy products.

Q: *Could you share a New England culinary trait that has been passed down through the centuries?*
A: Originally the only way that New Englanders cooked was in the hearth, and the only control over the food was the distance from the heat of the fire. So the dishes that have really passed the test of time are the ones that were and still are slow cooked. Look at baked beans. That dish was prepared by Native Americans way before the British ever came over here.

> *"There is nothing more Yankee than a lobster roll. When it's perfectly made it, has got to be one of the most exquisite things you will ever eat."*

Q: *Does one dish come to mind that epitomizes the notion of "no-nonsense Yankee practicality"?*
A: There is nothing more Yankee than a lobster roll. When it's perfectly made, it has got to be one of the most exquisite things you will ever eat. It's normally served in roadside stands in a paper hot-dog holder with a pickle and a bag of potato chips. It is quintessential New England—truly humble and yet rich and beautiful. [Jasper shares his recipe on page 144.]

Q: *What provisions do you consider indispensable in your kitchen today?*
A: Other than seafood, because seafood is the main provision, I'd say local cornmeal, farm-fresh eggs (people forget how good local eggs can be), fresh herbs, dry spices, maple syrup, good New England naturally bleached flour, dried beans (A-1 yellow eyes from Maine for making baked beans and limas for succotash) and fresh shell beans, which we only get in July and August. I've seen them at Costco.

Q: *Are there any recipes found in this region that you consider authentically American?*
A: Chowder is at the top of the list. Potpies are way up on the list, too. Pies originated in England

but were perfected in New England and were a way to preserve food. People would make pies at harvest time and put them in pie sheds, where they would freeze naturally.

Q: *Describe a classic Atlantic regional meal.*
A: It totally depends on the season. So let's pick summer. In New England it is the clam/lobster bake, and farther down the coast in the Jersey shore, Chesapeake and Baltimore area it's what I call smashing crabs. This is where the crabs are dumped out on the table. It's just the most wonderful feast. You sit and you drink beer and pick crabs. These two feasts define the Atlantic region.

Q: *And the most misunderstood aspect of Atlantic cuisine would be?*
A: In terms of food, the Northeast probably has more real ethnic people than anyplace else in America and more great ethnic foods. This cuisine is not boring.

Q: *Your three new restaurants are all called Jasper White's Summer Shack. What's the story behind this name?*
A: The word summer evokes so many pleasant things—freshness, simplicity, family, fun, relaxation— and the word shack brings it down a notch so that it doesn't get too far away from this planet.

Q: *If you were given a bag of Costco baking potatoes, what would you prepare?*
A: Clean the potatoes, rub them with olive or vegetable oil, sprinkle with a little salt and poke through to allow the steam to escape. Roast at 400 degrees for about an hour and serve with sour cream and caviar. Sorry, it's not very New England, but that's the ultimate baked potato.

Q: *What are your hopes for contemporary American cooking?*
A: My hope is that while contemporary cooking keeps expanding, it does so without replacing the simple classics that define each region, like the chowders, steamers and brown bread. I would hate to see us throw out the good stuff, the old stuff. 🍽

Evelyn's New York Baked Clams

Evelyn tells us, "I grew up in New York City with Italian and Hungarian heritage. My family loves these clams as an appetizer or a main dish with spaghetti."

3/4 pound margarine	2 tablespoons chopped parsley
1 small onion, chopped	3 tablespoons grated Romano cheese
8 garlic cloves, chopped	
1 51-ounce can chopped clams, drained, reserving 1 cup broth	1 pound shredded mozzarella
	1/2 teaspoon salt
1 pound firm sliced white sandwich bread, crumbled	1/2 tablespoon pepper
	4-5 dozen tin clam shells
	Paprika

1. Preheat oven to 350°F. Melt margarine in a large skillet over medium heat; cook onion and garlic until soft.

2. Stir in clams, broth, bread, parsley, cheeses, salt and pepper. Mound mixture in shells. Sprinkle with paprika.

3. Bake for 15-20 minutes in the middle of the oven, or until hot. Makes 4-5 dozen.

Evelyn Lyshir, Holbrook, New York

Frank's RedHot
Buffalo Chicken Wings

Frank's Original RedHot Sauce, they proudly say, was the secret ingredient in the first Buffalo Wings in 1964.

2 1/2 pounds chicken wings	1/3 cup melted butter
1/2 cup Frank's RedHot Cayenne Pepper Sauce	Celery sticks
	Blue cheese dressing

1. Preheat oven to 425°F. Bake wings for 1 hour or deep-fry for 12 minutes at 400°F; drain thoroughly.

2. Combine Frank's RedHot Sauce and butter; toss wings in sauce to coat. Serve with celery sticks and blue cheese dressing. Makes 6-8 servings.

Variations: Add to RedHot Sauce; cook until hot:
SWEET AND SPICY
1/4 cup orange juice concentrate
3/4 teaspoon cinnamon
TEX-MEX
1 teaspoon chili powder
1/4 teaspoon garlic powder

Kirkland Signature

Pine nuts, harvested by hand from pine trees around the world, play an indelible role in the history of cuisines of China, Italy, Spain, North Africa, Mexico and the American Southwest. They are delicious ground raw in pesto sauce, toasted as a garnish in salads or baked in cookies and casseroles. Store pine nuts in the refrigerator for up to a month and in the freezer for up to a year.

Mussels with **Kirkland Signature** Pine Nuts and Pesto ◀

Costco's Seafood Roadshows, on the first and third Friday and Saturday of each month, present the six best-selling seafood items in the world. Top-quality regional mussels are offered debearded and ready for cooking.

1 pound mussels (15-20), scrubbed and debearded	1/2 cup Kirkland Signature pine nuts
1 cup pesto	

1. Steam mussels over simmering water for 2 minutes, or until the shells open. Discard any that do not open. Cool.

2. Break off half the shell and discard.

3. Scoop out the mussel with a spoon and break the membrane attaching the mussel. Return mussel to the shell. Arrange shells on a baking sheet.

4. Warm pesto in the microwave for 1 minute on high. Place a dollop of pesto on each mussel. Sprinkle pine nuts on top. Broil for 2 minutes, or until nuts are lightly browned. Makes 2 servings.

Tip: Debearding, or removing the beard from, mussels is easy with a pair of needle-nose pliers.

Ore-Ida Savory Fries ▼

Put fresh flavor and a new face on Ore-Ida savory fries with feta cheese and crumbled bacon.

2 tablespoons olive oil	2 strips bacon, cooked and crumbled
1 teaspoon chopped fresh oregano,	¼ cup crumbled feta cheese
½ pound Ore-Ida Golden Crinkles, prepared according to package directions	Salt and pepper

1. Mix together olive oil and oregano in a small bowl. Drizzle the olive oil mixture over the warm fries. Sprinkle with crumbled bacon and feta cheese.

2. Season to taste with salt and pepper. Makes 4 servings.

Hannah International Foods
Bruschetta Appetizer ▶

Hannah Bruschetta is made with only the finest-quality ingredients—fresh plum tomatoes, basil, oregano and garlic. It is a versatile sauce that complements many different foods. Traditionally, it is used on Italian bread and topped with cheese.

1 loaf of Italian or French bread	1 cup grated cheese (mozzarella, Romano, Parmesan or a mixture)
Olive oil	
1 39-ounce jar Hannah* Bruschetta	

1. Preheat broiler. Slice bread on the diagonal and brush slices with olive oil. Place under the broiler for 1 minute, or until golden brown.

2. Remove from broiler, spoon Hannah Bruschetta on bread and sprinkle with cheese. Place under the broiler for 1 minute to warm and melt cheese. Makes 10-15 servings.

Tip: Use bruschetta to spice up pizza, pasta, burgers, chicken or fish. For a great marinara sauce, heat and pour over pasta, vegetables or meat.

*Brands may vary by region; substitute a similar product.

Cabot's Golden Dollars ◀

An old-time favorite recipe from the New England farm families who own Cabot, this luxuriously rich blend of aged-to-perfection Cheddar and award-winning sweet cream butter is easy to prepare, elegant and utterly delicious.

1 ½ cups grated Cabot Vintage Choice or Private Stock* Cheddar cheese	1 teaspoon garlic powder
	1 cup all-purpose flour
6 tablespoons butter, softened	¼ cup poppy seeds or toasted sesame seeds
1 teaspoon hot pepper sauce	

1. Preheat oven to 400°F. Combine cheese, butter, hot sauce and garlic powder in a food processor. Add flour and process until the mixture forms a ball.

2. Divide in half. Shape into 2 long rolls, each about 1¼ inches in diameter. Roll in poppy seeds or toasted sesame seeds to coat. Refrigerate for at least 30 minutes.

3. Slice in ¼-inch rounds. Place on a baking sheet coated with cooking spray, poking each slice with a fork to mark. Bake for 10-12 minutes, or until golden. Cool on a rack. Makes 36 pieces.

*Brands may vary by region; substitute a similar product.

Say Cheese

Cheese provides so much flavor, pleasure and protein that you should serve it more often. Costco offers a variety of cheeses that can be used in many different ways. Store cheese in the refrigerator, but let it come to room temperature before serving.

Blue Cheeses: Three international styles of blue cheese are typically available: Gorgonzola, the Italian-style blue; Société Roquefort, the French-style blue; and Danish blue. All come in wedges that are easy to slice for an appetizer or dessert cheese tray with fresh fruit. Sharp, spicy, full-flavored blue cheese seems to have a natural affinity with wine. Blue cheeses crumble easily to sprinkle on salad, hamburgers or steak for a jolt of flavor and creamy texture. The creaminess also works well in dips and spreads for crackers or fruit.

Brie: Serve it with fresh fruits and nuts. The white rind is edible, but not everyone agrees that it's tasty. A wheel of Brie is often dressed up for parties by baking it with a wrapping of puff pastry or a topping of sweetened nuts.

Jarlsberg: Made in Norway in the Emmental style, with large holes, it is milder in taste than the Swiss or French versions and very versatile. Purchase it in wedges or slices.

Parmigiano-Reggiano: This well-known, hand-made Italian cheese with a piquant, salty flavor is potent enough to sprinkle sparingly and achieve great effects. The extraordinary flavor results from the milk of grass-grazed cattle, the traditional production methods and aging for two, three or even four years. It's popular in cooking or freshly grated on salad, soup or pasta. It also works on a cheese tray for an appetizer or dessert course with dried fruit and nuts.

Swiss Emmentaler: Memorable for the holes in every wedge, this cheese is truly all-purpose. The nutty, golden flavor is savored in Reuben sandwiches, in fondue and other hot dishes or on a cheese tray with fresh fruit. Purchase it in wedges or slices.

General Mills
Gorgonzola Squares ▲

Savory cheese squares make a quick hot snack.

1/2 cup crumbled Gorgonzola cheese	1/2 cup pistachio nuts
	3/4 cup Original Bisquick
1/2 cup chopped green onions	1/2 cup milk
	2 eggs, beaten

1. Preheat oven to 400°F. Sprinkle cheese, onions and nuts in a greased 9-by-9-inch baking pan.

2. Combine Bisquick with milk and eggs in a medium-size bowl. Pour over cheese mixture.

3. Bake for 25-30 minutes, or until a knife inserted in the center comes out clean. Cool for 5 minutes before cutting in 1-inch squares. Makes 9 servings.

SOUP

Sea Watch New England Clam Chowder ◄

1 small (4-6-ounce) package salt pork, diced	3 medium potatoes, peeled and diced
1 onion, diced	2 cups milk
1/2 cup diced celery	1 cup half-and-half
2 tablespoons flour	Salt and pepper
1 51-ounce can Sea Watch chopped clams, drained, with juice reserved	3 tablespoons butter

1. Cook pork in a large soup pot over low heat until brown and the fat is rendered.

2. Cook onions and celery in pork fat for 3 minutes. Sprinkle flour over onions and cook, stirring constantly, for 3 minutes. Add clam juice, stirring until the sauce is smooth and simmering.

3. Add potatoes and simmer until tender, adding water if the mixture becomes too thick. Add clams, milk and half-and-half. Return to a simmer. Season to taste with salt and pepper. Stir in butter before serving. Makes 12 servings.

SALADS

Mott's Tuna Waldorf Salad ►

1 12-ounce can white tuna in water, drained	1/4 cup chopped scallions
1 tablespoon lemon juice	1/4 cup chopped walnuts
1/3 cup mayonnaise	1 tablespoon chopped fresh dill or 1 teaspoon dried dill
1/2 cup Mott's* Apple Sauce	Salt and pepper
1/2 cup seedless red grapes	Lettuce

1. In a medium bowl, combine tuna, lemon juice, mayonnaise and apple sauce. Stir in grapes, scallions, walnuts, dill, and salt and pepper to taste.

2. Serve chilled on a bed of lettuce. Makes 4 servings.

Brands may vary by region; substitute a similar product.

Big Valley Fruit Salad with Honey-Orange Dressing ▼

Big Valley is the premier brand of J.R. Wood, Inc., one of the largest manufacturers and processors of fresh frozen fruit. Try this exciting blend of fruit in a zesty salad recipe that complements any meal.

3/4 cup low-fat plain yogurt	4 1/2 tablespoons orange juice
1/3 cup nonfat mayonnaise	
1/3 cup honey	2 1/4 teaspoons vinegar
1 1/4 teaspoons grated orange peel	1 5-pound package Big Valley Deluxe Mixed Fruit,* semi-thawed
1/2 teaspoon dry mustard	

1. In a small bowl, whisk together yogurt, mayonnaise, honey, orange peel and mustard until blended. Gradually mix in orange juice and vinegar.

2. Place fruit in a large bowl, discarding juice; toss fruit gently with dressing. Cover and refrigerate until ready to serve. Makes 10-12 servings.

Brands may vary by region; substitute a similar product.

Mariann Raftery, Scarsdale, New York

FROM THE MEMBER'S KITCHEN

Mariann's Arugula Asparagus Salad ▲

1 bunch asparagus, steamed crisp-tender, cut in quarters	1/4 cup olive oil
	2 tablespoons red wine vinegar
1 bunch fresh arugula, stemmed	1/4 cup purchased Italian dressing
1 head endive, separated, sliced in 1-inch pieces	Salt and pepper
1/4 to 1/2 red onion, sliced thin	

1. Combine asparagus, arugula, endive and red onion in a bowl.

2. Whisk together oil, vinegar and Italian dressing. Season to taste with salt and pepper.

3. Toss dressing with salad mixture. Serve immediately. Makes 4 servings.

FROM THE COSTCO Produce EXPERT

Keeping Salad Mix Fresh

Have you ever avoided purchasing that big bag of salad mix because you thought it would probably spoil before you finished it? Costco produce buyer Frank Padilla says the best way to ensure that salad mix stays fresh is to remember six words: keep it cool; keep it sealed. He suggests making it the last item to go in your basket when you visit the warehouse, thus reducing the time the product is unrefrigerated.

Each bag of salad mix is maintained at a temperature below 40°F while it is at Costco. When the salad mix does not last as long as the printed use-by date on the bag, it is normally because of extreme temperature fluctuation between the time it left the warehouse and when it was placed in a refrigerator.

Once opened, the bag should always be reclosed in order to deter oxidation on the cut edges. A good plastic clip will help ensure a good seal. Keeping the bag refrigerated and sealed can prolong the usable life of salad mix.

Premio Foods

Premio, founded by a family from Naples, Italy, uses secret recipes passed down through the generations. Their summer salad is a lively addition to any summer day. The sweetness of the sausage plays against the apples and vinegar.

Premio Summer Salad ▶

1 package (8 links) Premio*
    Sweet Italian Sausage,
    cooked according to
    package directions,
    cut in 1/2-inch dice

3 medium potatoes,
    cooked, peeled and
    cut in 1/2-inch dice

3 Granny Smith apples,
    unpeeled, cut in
    1/2-inch dice

1 1/2 cups diced celery

1 1/2 cups sliced red onions

1/3 cup lemon juice

1/4 cup cider vinegar

1 1/2 teaspoons salt

1 teaspoon black pepper

1/4 cup sugar

3/4 cup olive oil

1/4 cup chopped fresh parsley

3/4 cup chopped walnuts

1. Combine sausage, potatoes, apples, celery and onions in a large bowl.

2. Whisk together lemon juice, vinegar, salt, pepper and sugar in a small bowl. Whisk in oil. Pour dressing over the salad; toss well. Refrigerate for several hours or overnight before serving.

3. Toss the salad again. Sprinkle parsley and walnuts on top. Makes 6-8 servings.

Brands may vary by region; substitute a similar product.

Andy Boy Romaine Hearts
Lettuce Wraps ▲

3 garlic cloves	3 chicken breasts, cooked and sliced
1 teaspoon salt	
1 bunch cilantro, stemmed	1 head Andy Boy* romaine hearts, separated
1/3 cup pine nuts	
1 tablespoon white wine vinegar	1 Hass avocado, peeled, pitted and sliced
1/2 cup oil	2 Roma tomatoes, cored, seeded and sliced thin
1/4 cup chicken stock	1 green onion, sliced
Salt and pepper	1/3 cup freshly grated cheese

1. Pulse garlic, salt, cilantro leaves, pine nuts and vinegar in a food processor until a paste forms. Add oil in a stream with the motor running. Add chicken stock; pulse to combine. Season to taste with salt and pepper.

2. Toss chicken with the cilantro pesto. Place a leaf of romaine on a plate and mound 1/4 of the chicken mixture on top; arrange avocado and tomato slices around chicken; sprinkle onions and cheese on top. Makes 4 servings.

Brands may vary by region; substitute a similar product.

Kirkland Signature Panzanella
Italian Bread Salad ▷

2 pounds Kirkland Signature ciabatta rolls, cut in 1/2-inch cubes	2 cups thinly sliced red onion
2 tablespoons capers	1/2 cup diced yellow bell peppers
4-6 garlic cloves	1/2 cup kalamata olives
4-6 anchovy fillets	1/2 cup fresh basil leaves, torn in pieces
1 cup Kirkland Signature extra-virgin olive oil	Kosher salt
2/3 cup Kirkland Signature balsamic vinegar	Freshly ground pepper
4 cups diced tomatoes	Grated Parmigiano-Reggiano cheese
2 cups diced cucumber	

1. Preheat oven to 375°F. Bake bread cubes on a baking sheet for 10 minutes, until dry and lightly browned.

2. Pulse capers, garlic and anchovies in a food processor until smooth. Add olive oil and vinegar, pulsing once or twice to combine.

3. Toss caper mixture with bread cubes in a large bowl. Add tomatoes, cucumber, onions, bell peppers, olives and basil. Toss again. Season to taste with salt and pepper. Sprinkle with grated cheese before serving. Makes 12 servings.

Mozzarella Fresca
Classic Caprese Insalata ◁

1 8-ounce ball Mozzarella Fresca* fresh mozzarella	2 tablespoons balsamic vinegar, optional
1 large (8-ounce) or 2 small (4-ounce) fresh tomatoes	2 ounces fresh basil, lightly chopped
1/4 cup extra-virgin olive oil	Salt and pepper

1. Cut mozzarella and tomato into 8 equal slices. Arrange tomato slices on a small platter. Place 1 mozzarella slice on each tomato slice.

2. Drizzle with olive oil. Add balsamic vinegar if desired. Garnish with basil and season to taste with salt and pepper. Makes 4 servings.

Brands may vary by region; substitute a similar product.

Sir Thomas Columbus Sandwich ◄

Here's a great sandwich to eat at any time of day. Crunchy English muffins and bacon topped with creamy eggs, cheese and tomatoes will satisfy cravings at breakfast, lunch or dinner.

4 Thomas' Original Flavor* English Muffins, split, toasted and buttered

8 slices bacon, cooked

4 eggs, scrambled

4 slices tomato

4 slices provolone cheese

1/2 cup chopped green bell pepper

1. Preheat broiler. Top each muffin bottom with bacon, egg, tomato, cheese and green pepper.

2. Broil for 2 minutes, or until cheese melts. Top with remaining muffin halves. Makes 4 servings.

Brands may vary by region; substitute a similar product.

ConAgra Brioche ▲

3 cups ConAgra Harvest Bread Flour

1 teaspoon salt

5 tablespoons honey

1/4 teaspoon vanilla extract

4 large eggs

1/2 cup milk

2 1/2 teaspoons instant yeast

6 tablespoons unsalted butter

1. Place all ingredients in the large bowl of a standing mixer. Mix 1 minute on low speed with the paddle attachment. Scrape down the bowl. Mix 5 minutes on medium speed with the dough hook attachment.

2. Roll dough on a floured work surface. Round into a smooth ball. Place dough in a large buttered bowl; cover and let rise for 4 hours in a warm spot, or until doubled.

3. Roll dough on a floured work surface. Shape to fit a greased loaf pan; cover and let rise in a warm area for 1 1/2 hours, or until dough reaches the top of the pan.

4. Bake in a preheated 375°F oven for 45 minutes, or until golden brown. Makes 1 loaf, about 16 servings.

Bagels, Bagels, Bagels

FROM THE
COSTCO
Bakery
EXPERT

Sue McConnaha, vice president and director of bakery operations, talks about bagels from Costco:

Sold in two sleeves of six, Costco bagels come in the following flavors: plain, cinnamon raisin, sesame and poppy seed, honey cracked wheat and either plain Parmesan cheese and olive oil or with onion. There also are "everything bagels," which contain onions, cornmeal, and poppy, sesame, caraway, fennel and sunflower seeds. Accommodate your taste by mixing sweet and savory or hearty and plain.

Bagels that will be eaten soon can be stored in their sleeves on the counter. For longer storage, bagels can be wrapped in plastic, frozen and then taken out one sleeve, or one bagel, at a time.

While bagels are considered primarily a breakfast food, they are also ideal for making sandwiches.

They are excellent toasted and served with spreads such as butter, cream cheese, jam or peanut butter. Add lox, honey or bananas for a flavor boost. For a sandwich, try sliced ham and honey mustard on the cinnamon raisin bagel. Or try pastrami and Swiss cheese on the everything bagel.

Pauline's Pesto and Peppers on French Bread ◀

Make two loaves at a time—one for now and one for later. This tastes good cold, too.

1 21-ounce jar Cibo Naturals basil pesto	1 24-ounce jar sweet red roasted peppers, drained, sliced
2 loaves French bread, 24 inches long, sliced lengthwise	8 ounces shredded mozzarella or shredded 3-cheese blend

1. Preheat oven to 350°F. Spread pesto on the cut sides of both loaves. Arrange red peppers on the two bottom halves; sprinkle cheese over peppers. Replace the top halves of bread. Wrap in aluminum foil.

2. Bake for 20 minutes, or until cheese melts. Cut into 2-inch pieces. Makes 24 pieces or 12 servings.

Pauline Dionne Mastronardi, Reading, Massachusetts

New World Restaurant
Bagel French Toast Platter with Seasonal Berry Relish ▷

BAGEL FRENCH TOAST	1/2 cup pecan pieces
4 Kirkland Signature by Noah's New York* plain bagels, each cut in 4 horizontal slices	1/4 cup corn syrup
	2 tablespoons water
French toast batter (use family recipe)	SEASONAL BERRY RELISH
	1 cup sliced strawberries
Butter	1/2 cup raspberries
	1/2 cup blackberries or blueberries
PECAN PRALINE GLAZE	1/4 cup sugar
1/2 cup butter	
3 tablespoons brown sugar	

1. Soak bagel slices in French toast batter for at least 1 minute. Cook in butter in a large skillet over medium heat until browned. Remove to a platter.

2. For the glaze, melt butter in the skillet over low heat; add brown sugar and stir until dissolved. Add pecans and cook for 1 minute. Stir in corn syrup and water; simmer for 3 minutes. Spoon onto French toast.

3. Toss berries with sugar in a bowl. Place on the platter. Makes 4-5 servings.

Look for Kirkland Signature by Einstein Brothers bagels in some regions.

Tarantino's

Forty years ago, Pete Tarantino Sr. traveled the world looking for just the right sausage recipes. Today, Tarantino Sausage Company still uses these now tightly guarded recipes from the world's master sausage-makers to prepare their succulent offerings. Made from only the finest meats, Tarantino's sausage is another way to spell dining success.

Tarantino's
Stuffed Bell Peppers Italiano ▶

1 1/2 quarts water

3 large green bell peppers, halved, stemmed and seeded

1 1/2 pounds Tarantino's* mild or hot Italian sausage

1/4 cup chopped onion

1 teaspoon minced garlic

1/2 cup partially cooked rice

1 cup tomato sauce, divided

2 teaspoons finely chopped parsley

2 teaspoons freshly grated Parmesan or Romano cheese

1. Preheat oven to 350°F. Heat water to boiling in a large saucepan. Blanch peppers for 2 minutes; drain and plunge into cold water to stop the cooking action and retain color. Drain.

2. Remove the sausage casing and discard. Cook sausage, onion and garlic in a large skillet over medium heat until sausage is light brown and crumbly. Add rice, half the tomato sauce, parsley and cheese. Stir well.

3. Stuff peppers with the sausage mixture. Bake in a shallow greased pan for about 50 minutes. Ten minutes before peppers are done, place a spoonful of the remaining tomato sauce on each pepper.

4. Serve immediately. Leftover peppers can be frozen. Makes 6 servings.

Brands may vary by region; substitute a similar product.

Tarantino's Italian Stuffed
Party Mushrooms ▶

36 fresh mushrooms, stemmed

Olive oil

1 pound fresh cooked Tarantino's* mild or hot Italian sausage, crumbled

1/2 pound grated mozzarella cheese

2 tablespoons grated Parmesan cheese

2 tablespoons fresh chopped parsley

1. Place mushrooms on cookie sheets. Rub olive oil on the outside of mushrooms.

2. Combine sausage with mozzarella, Parmesan and parsley. Stuff mushrooms with sausage mixture. Broil 6-8 minutes, or until sausage is crisp. Makes 36 servings.

Brands may vary by region; substitute a similar product.

Hidden Valley Original Ranch
Spinach Tortellini with Roasted Bell Peppers

2 9-ounce packages fresh spinach tortellini

2 tablespoons butter or olive oil

4 garlic cloves, minced

1 7-ounce jar roasted red peppers, rinsed, drained and sliced thin

1/4 cup chopped fresh basil or 2 teaspoons crushed dried basil

1/2 cup chopped walnuts or pine nuts, toasted

1 cup Hidden Valley Original Ranch Dressing

Fresh basil leaves, optional

1. Cook tortellini according to package directions.

2. Melt butter in a medium saucepan; add garlic and cook over medium heat for approximately 2 minutes. Stir in tortellini, red pepper and basil; add nuts. Stir in dressing so that mixture is creamy and tortellini are coated.

3. Garnish with basil. Makes 4-6 servings.

Tarantino's Italian Sausage Soup

1 tablespoon olive oil

1 medium onion, diced

1/2 pound Tarantino's* mild or hot Italian sausage, sliced

2 celery stalks, diced

2 garlic cloves, minced

1/2 teaspoon dried oregano

1/4 cup white or red wine, optional

4 cups water

2 small carrots, peeled and diced

1 cup diced tomatoes in juice

1-2 bay leaves

Salt and pepper

1 cup cooked ditalini, orzo or other small pasta

Grated Parmesan cheese

1. Heat olive oil in a deep saucepan over medium heat; add onion and cook for 1-2 minutes; add sausage and cook for 3-4 minutes. Add celery, garlic and oregano and cook for 1 minute.

2. Stir in wine and cook for 2 minutes. Add water, carrots, tomatoes and bay leaf and bring to a low boil. Simmer for 30 minutes. Season to taste with salt and pepper.

3. Remove bay leaf. Serve with small pasta and top with grated Parmesan. Makes 4 servings.

*Brands may vary by region; substitute a similar product.

Cardile Brothers
Famous Portobello Parmesan ▲

Cardile Brothers Mushroom Company has a long
history, spanning four generations, of growing
only the finest white and exotic mushrooms.

1 garlic clove, chopped	1 tablespoon milk
Olive oil	5 large eggs, well beaten
1 pound lump crabmeat	6-8 large Cardile Brothers portobello mushrooms, stemmed
1 1/2 cups seasoned bread crumbs	
3 tablespoons grated Parmesan cheese	1 cup or more tomato sauce, divided
1 teaspoon salt	Grated Parmesan cheese and/or mozzarella cheese
1/2 teaspoon pepper	

1. Preheat oven to 350°F. Cook garlic in oil in a
large skillet over low heat until lightly browned.
Add crabmeat and cook, stirring, just until mixed
thoroughly with garlic. Remove with slotted spoon
and set aside.

2. Combine bread crumbs, Parmesan, salt and
pepper in a large bowl.

3. Combine milk and eggs in a smaller bowl.

4. Dip portobellos in egg mixture, then in bread-
crumb mixture; repeat 2 times. Cook portobellos
in hot oil in a large skillet over medium heat until
golden brown and fork tender.

5. Spread a layer of tomato sauce in a large baking
pan. Arrange portobellos on top. Spoon some
crabmeat on each. Spoon additional tomato sauce
over portobellos and sprinkle with cheese.

6. Bake for 20 minutes, or until cheese is melted
and lightly browned. Makes 6-8 servings.

● ENTRÉES

Classico Tomato and Basil
Lasagna Roll-Ups **di Napoli** ▽

Lasagna noodles here are spread individually
with cheese, not layered, and then rolled up, covered with tomato sauce and baked until bubbly.
The colors enhance the presentation.

1 15-ounce container ricotta cheese	1 egg, slightly beaten
1 10-ounce package frozen chopped spinach, thawed and well drained	9 lasagna noodles, cooked according to package directions
1 cup (4 ounces) shredded mozzarella cheese	1 26-ounce jar Classico di Napoli Tomato and Basil Pasta Sauce
1/4 cup grated Parmesan cheese	

1. Preheat oven to 350°F. Combine ricotta,
spinach, mozzarella, Parmesan and egg in a
medium bowl. Spread about 1/3 cup cheese
mixture on each lasagna noodle; roll up.

2. Pour 1/3 cup pasta sauce into a 9-by-13-inch
baking dish. Arrange lasagna rolls seam side
down in dish. Top with remaining sauce.

3. Cover with aluminum foil. Bake 35 minutes,
or until hot. Makes 9 servings.

BelGioioso Cheese
Mild Provolone Pizza ◄

BelGioioso Cheese Incorporated, creators of Classic Italian Cheeses Made in the USA, shares one of its most famous recipes with you. BelGioioso Mild Provolone has a delicious full, rich flavor that will enhance any pizza, sandwich or cheese tray.

Pizza dough, freshly made or purchased

3 ounces BelGioioso Parmesan cheese, freshly grated, divided

1/2 pound pre-sliced BelGioioso Mild Provolone cheese

5 ripe Roma tomatoes, thinly sliced

Salt and pepper

Fresh basil, chopped

1. Preheat oven to 425°F. Roll dough out onto a lightly oiled 12-inch pizza pan or cookie sheet and sprinkle with some of the Parmesan.

2. Cover with slices of provolone. Top with tomatoes and salt and pepper to taste; sprinkle with the remaining Parmesan.

3. Bake for 15 minutes, or until crust is golden brown and cheese is melted. Top with fresh basil, cut and serve. Makes 4-6 servings.

NewStar Asparagus and Spinach
Frittata with Green Onion Cream ▲

1/2 pint sour cream

1 cup chopped NewStar* green onions, divided

1 teaspoon black pepper, or to taste

3 potatoes, cooked and sliced

1 tablespoon olive oil

1 pound NewStar Young and Tender* spinach, blanched and squeezed dry

1/2 pound NewStar* asparagus, cooked and sliced in 1/2-inch pieces

12 eggs

1/2 cup heavy cream

1/2 cup shredded Monterey Jack cheese

1. Preheat oven to 350°F. Prepare Green Onion Cream by combining sour cream, 1/2 cup green onions and pepper.

2. Brown potato slices in oil in a large nonstick, ovenproof skillet. Top with spinach and asparagus.

3. In separate bowl, combine eggs, cream, 1/2 cup green onions and cheese. Pour mixture over asparagus. Bake for 30 minutes, or until firm.

4. Gently slide from skillet onto a large serving platter. Cut into 4 wedges. Garnish with Green Onion Cream. Makes 6-8 servings.

Brands may vary by region; substitute a similar product.

Fresh Serving Ideas for
Sabatasso's Vegetable Lasagna

Choose one of these toppings for a garnish that adds color and flavor.

Before Baking:

1 cup pesto sauce
1 7-ounce can diced green chiles
Sliced green olives
Chopped mushrooms
Chopped jalapeño peppers
Minced sweet onions
Roasted poblano chile slices

Right Out of the Oven:

4 garlic cloves, minced and cooked in butter
Chopped fresh basil leaves
Minced rosemary and garlic
Minced sweet onions
Diced tomatoes, fresh or canned
Canned mushroom pieces
Bed of fresh spinach leaves
Cooked sausage, sliced or crumbled
Grated lemon peel

Jasper White

The lobster roll is "one of the most spectacular-tasting, wonderful dishes placed in such a humble presentation," notes Jasper White. *"It's a cool lobster salad in a warm buttery bun. When it's perfectly made, it has got to be one of the most exquisite things you will ever eat."* Scallions are used rather than raw onions, which tend to turn the salad bitter.

Traditional Lobster Salad ▶

1 pound fully cooked
    lobster meat or
    5 pounds live lobster

1 medium cucumber,
    peeled, seeded
    and finely diced

1/2 cup mayonnaise

3 small scallions,
    thinly sliced

Kosher or sea salt

Freshly ground black pepper

6 New England-style hot
    dog buns

Pickles and potato chips

1. If using live lobsters, steam or boil them. Let cool at room temperature. Use a cleaver to crack and remove the meat from the claws, knuckles and tails. Remove the cartilage from the claws and the intestine from the tails of the cooked meat. Cut the meat into 1/2-inch dice. Pick all the meat from the carcass and add it to the diced meat. Freeze the carcass for soup or broth.

2. Place the cucumber in a colander for at least 5 minutes to drain the excess liquid.

3. Combine the lobster meat, cucumber and mayonnaise. If the salad is to be served within the hour, add the scallions. If not, add them 30 minutes before serving. Season with salt if needed and pepper. Cover with plastic wrap and chill for at least 30 minutes before serving.

4. Preheat a large heavy skillet over medium-low heat; lightly butter both sides of each bun. Cook for about 2 minutes on each side, or until golden brown. Stuff the buns with the chilled lobster salad. Serve with pickles and potato chips. Makes 6 lobster rolls.

Recipe adapted from Lobster at Home, *by Jasper White (Scribner, 1998). Reprinted with permission.*

Gratin of Potato and Turnip ▲

2 tablespoons
   unsalted butter

2 garlic cloves,
   finely chopped

2 1/2-3 pounds Maine
   or other all-purpose
   potatoes, peeled and
   cut in medium-large
   (1/2-3/4-inch) dice,
   about 4 cups

2 pounds turnips or
   rutabagas, peeled and
   cut in medium-large
   (1/2-3/4-inch) dice,
   about 4 cups

4 cups heavy cream

Kosher salt and freshly
   ground black pepper

1. Preheat oven to 350°F. Grease the bottom of a 9-inch square baking dish with butter and sprinkle with the chopped garlic.

2. Mix the diced potatoes and turnips and spread in the dish.

3. Bring the cream slowly to a boil and season with salt and pepper.

4. Pour the cream over the vegetables and cover loosely with foil. Bake for 30 minutes; uncover and bake for 15-20 minutes more. The potatoes and turnips should be quite tender and the top brown and bubbling. Makes 6-8 servings.

Recipe adapted from Jasper White's Cooking from New England, *by Jasper White (Biscuit Books, 1998), available through Jessica's Biscuit/ecookbooks.com. Reprinted with permission.*

Phillips Crab-Stuffed Chicken Breasts ◄

1 6-ounce can corn, drained	3 tablespoons vegetable oil
1/2 cup diced onion	1 tablespoon chopped fresh parsley
2 ounces goat cheese, crumbled	2 teaspoons grated lemon peel
2 ounces cream cheese, cubed	1 tablespoon lemon juice
1/4 cup diced sun-dried tomatoes	1/2 teaspoon poultry seasoning
Salt and pepper	1/2 teaspoon black pepper
1 pound Phillips Crab Meat	
6 boneless, skinless chicken breasts	

1. Preheat oven to 375°F. Mix corn, onion, goat cheese, cream cheese and dried tomatoes in a bowl. Season to taste with salt and pepper. Fold in crab.

2. Cut a pocket in each chicken breast; stuff with crab mixture. Close opening with a toothpick. Place stuffed breasts in a baking pan.

3. In a small bowl, mix oil, parsley, lemon peel, lemon juice, poultry seasoning and pepper; brush onto chicken breasts.

4. Bake for 20-30 minutes, or until internal temperature is 160°F. Remove toothpicks before serving. Makes 6 servings.

High Liner Scallops Piccata ▶

1 tablespoon olive oil	2 tablespoons dry white wine
1/2 pound High Liner* sea scallops, thawed	2 tablespoons fresh lemon juice
1/2 tablespoon crushed fresh garlic	1/3 cup heavy cream
1 tablespoon capers	2 tablespoons salted butter

1. In a medium-sized saucepan, heat olive oil over medium-high heat. Add scallops and cook for 2 minutes. Remove scallops. Add garlic and capers and cook for 2 1/2 minutes.

2. Add wine and lemon juice. Simmer until the liquid is reduced by half.

3. Add heavy cream. Bring to a simmer again. Return scallops to the pan.

4. Slowly add butter and stir until it is blended into the sauce. Serve with your favorite pasta or rice. Makes 2 servings.

Brands may vary by region; substitute a similar product.

Kirkland Signature Lemon Dill Chicken Croissant Sandwiches

3 12.5-ounce cans Kirkland Signature Chunk Breast of Chicken

1 cup sliced celery

1/4 cup sliced green onion

1 1/4 cups mayonnaise

1/4 cup fresh lemon juice

1 1/2 teaspoons grated lemon peel

1/4 cup chopped parsley

1/2 teaspoon dill weed

1/2 teaspoon salt

12 croissants, halved lengthwise

Sliced tomato

Green-leaf lettuce

1. Combine chicken, celery and green onion in a large bowl.
2. Combine mayonnaise, lemon juice, lemon peel, parsley, dill and salt. Stir into chicken mixture.
3. Fill each croissant with 1/2 cup chicken filling.
4. Add tomato and lettuce. Makes 12 servings.

McCormick Old Bay Salmon

Once a seafood staple enjoyed by only a lucky few along the Chesapeake Bay, Old Bay Seasoning now brings spicy flavor to every part of the country and every meal occasion.

4 6-ounce salmon fillets

1 tablespoon McCormick Old Bay Seasoning

1 lime, sliced

1 tablespoon McCormick Pure Vanilla Extract

1. Preheat oven to 425°F or preheat grill. Arrange salmon on a large sheet of foil. Sprinkle both sides of salmon with Old Bay Seasoning. Place lime slices on top of salmon.
2. Pour vanilla on salmon; fold up the sides of the foil and pinch together at the ends.
3. Bake for 25 minutes or grill over medium-high heat, covered, for 14-16 minutes, or to an internal temperature of 145°F. Makes 4 servings.

Yoshida's Mandarin Chicken Salad

A touch of fruit flavor and Asian spice gives a refreshing twist to this chicken salad.

4 boneless, skinless chicken breasts

1/4 cup Yoshida's Gourmet Sauce

1 tablespoon orange juice concentrate

1/2 cup thinly sliced red bell pepper

1/2 cup thinly sliced cucumber

1/2 cup canned mandarin oranges, drained

6 cups bite-sized pieces of iceberg lettuce

1. Coat a medium skillet with cooking spray and heat over medium-high heat. Cook chicken approximately 2 minutes on each side, or until browned. Drain. Add Yoshida's Gourmet Sauce to pan. Turn chicken breasts to coat; cook over low heat, uncovered, for 10 minutes, or until chicken is no longer pink. Remove chicken from pan; cool and cut into slices.
2. Add orange juice concentrate to pan. Stir to blend and cook 1-2 minutes. Remove from heat.
3. Combine chicken, bell pepper, cucumber, oranges and orange juice mixture in a large bowl; toss to coat evenly.
4. Place lettuce on 4 salad plates. Top with chicken salad. Makes 4 servings.

Barilla Penne with Ricotta and Broccoli ▼

2 cups ricotta cheese	1 26-ounce jar Barilla* Marinara Sauce
1/2 cup grated Parmesan cheese	1 16-ounce box Barilla* Penne Pasta
1/2 teaspoon salt	3 cups broccoli florets
1/8 teaspoon black pepper	

1. Mix ricotta, Parmesan, salt and pepper in a large bowl.

2. Heat Barilla Marinara in a large skillet over low heat.

3. Cook penne according to package directions. During last 2 minutes of cooking time, add broccoli florets. Drain. Add penne and broccoli to ricotta mixture. Mix well.

4. Place on a serving platter, top with marinara sauce and serve. Makes 4-6 servings.

Brands may vary by region; substitute a similar product.

Bumble Bee Albacore Pasta Primavera ▲

1 16-ounce package pasta spirals	1 cup sliced yellow bell peppers
1 cup sliced carrots	1 cup sliced red bell peppers
1 cup sugar snap peas	2 6-ounce cans Bumble Bee* Solid White Albacore, drained and flaked
3/4 cup olive oil	
1/2 teaspoon crushed red pepper	1 cup sliced black olives
1 tablespoon finely chopped garlic	Salt and pepper
	Parsley

1. Prepare pasta according to package directions. During the last 5 minutes of cooking time, add carrots and snap peas. Drain well and return to the cooking pot.

2. In a large saucepan, heat oil over medium heat. Cook pepper flakes and garlic until garlic is golden; add bell peppers and cook for 2 minutes. Combine with the pasta and toss well. Add albacore and olives and toss lightly. Season to taste with salt and pepper. Garnish with parsley. Makes 6-8 servings.

Brands may vary by region; substitute a similar product.

Basil and Lemon Spaghetti with Cello Parmigiano Reggiano ▼

1-2 tablespoons coarse or regular salt	1/2 teaspoon salt
1 pound spaghetti	1/4 teaspoon black pepper
1/2 cup unsalted butter	1/3 cup packed fresh basil leaves, chopped
1 tablespoon grated lemon peel	3/4 cup freshly grated Cello Parmigiano Reggiano
2 tablespoons fresh lemon juice	6 sprigs fresh basil for garnish

1. Add 2 tablespoons coarse salt to 2 gallons of rapidly boiling water. Stir in spaghetti and cook until al dente. Drain. Return to the cooking pot.

2. Melt butter in a large sauté pan. Add lemon peel, lemon juice, salt and pepper. Heat gently for 1 minute. Toss with hot drained spaghetti. Add chopped basil and Cello Parmigiano Reggiano and toss until spaghetti is evenly coated.

3. Garnish with basil sprigs. Pass additional grated Cello Parmigiano Reggiano at the table. Makes 6 servings.

D'Orazio Foods Red Pepper Sauce

3 tablespoons olive oil

1/2 cup finely chopped onion

1 large garlic clove, minced

2 medium red
bell peppers, diced

1 cup canned crushed
tomatoes in tomato puree

1/4 teaspoon dried
basil, crushed

1/4 teaspoon salt

1/8 teaspoon
crushed red pepper

D'Orazio Stuffed Shells,*
prepared according to
package directions

1. Heat oil in a medium-sized skillet. Cook onions with garlic over medium heat until softened. Add peppers and cook, stirring occasionally, until softened, about 5 minutes.

2. Add tomatoes, basil, salt and red pepper. Cook, covered, over low heat for 10-15 minutes.

3. Puree in a blender or food processor until smooth.

4. Serve with Cheese Stuffed Shells. Makes 4 servings.

Brands may vary by region; substitute a similar product.

Giorgio Foods Spaghetti with Spicy Tomato and Mushroom Sauce

1 28-ounce can crushed
tomatoes in tomato puree

2 4-ounce cans
Giorgio/Penn Dutch or
Brandywine* pieces and
stems mushrooms

2 tablespoons olive oil

1 large garlic clove, chopped

1 teaspoon salt

1/2 teaspoon
granulated garlic

1/2 teaspoon onion powder

1/2 teaspoon dried basil

1/2 teaspoon dried oregano

1/4 teaspoon crushed
red pepper

1/8 teaspoon finely ground
black pepper

1 pound #11 spaghetti,
cooked according to
package directions

Grated Parmesan cheese

1. Combine tomatoes, mushrooms, olive oil, fresh garlic, salt, granulated garlic, onion powder, basil, oregano, red pepper and black pepper in a large saucepan. Bring to a boil over high heat; reduce heat and simmer, uncovered, for 15 minutes, stirring occasionally. Taste and adjust seasoning.

2. Serve over spaghetti. Pass Parmesan at the table. Makes 6 servings.

Brands may vary by region; substitute a similar product.

Monterey Pasta Fabulous Tricolor Tortelloni with Sausage

2 pounds Italian
sausage links

18 ounces Monterey Pasta
tricolor cheese tortelloni,
cooked according to
package directions

4 ounces roasted red
bell peppers

8 ounces canned quartered
artichoke hearts

4 ounces Monterey Pasta
pesto sauce

2 ounces pine nuts, toasted

5 ounces Monterey Pasta
shredded Parmesan cheese

1. In a large skillet, cook sausage over medium heat until lightly browned. Remove sausage from skillet, cool and cut into diagonal pieces.

2. After tortelloni is cooked, drain off the water and return the pasta to the pot.

3. Cook bell peppers and artichoke hearts in the skillet over medium heat for 3 minutes; add sausage pieces and pesto sauce and bring to a simmer, stirring. Pour over the tortelloni and cook for 2 minutes, or until hot.

4. Garnish with pine nuts and Parmesan. Makes 6 servings.

Australian Lamb

Easy as one, two, three. Fresh Australian Southern Cross lamb is naturally raised, is low in fat and cholesterol, and contains no artificial additives. Sweet and mild Australian lamb is so easy to prepare. Everything you need to season it is probably right in your kitchen cupboard. Here are three simple recipes:

Southern Cross Australian Rack of Lamb with Lemon Rosemary Baste ▶

3 tablespoons lemon juice

3 teaspoons dried rosemary

3 teaspoons dried oregano

Black pepper

1 tablespoon vegetable oil

1 medium 8-rib rack of Australian lamb

1. Preheat oven to 475°F. Combine lemon juice, rosemary, oregano and black pepper to taste in a small bowl. Add oil to a heavy skillet and sear lamb over high heat for 3 minutes per side.

2. Coat lamb with sauce. To roast, place the lamb rack, fat side up, in a roasting pan and roast in the middle of the oven for 14-16 minutes for medium-rare. To grill, place the lamb rack, fat side up, on the grill for 15-17 minutes for medium-rare (turn once after 10 minutes).

3. Transfer to a warm plate and let rest for 10 minutes before serving. Makes 2 servings.

Tip: You can test for doneness by touch. Just prod the lamb—when it has a springy but firm texture and is moderately juicy, the meat is done. The firmer the feel, the more well-done. Lamb is at its best when it's medium-rare or medium, with an internal temperature of 130°-140°F.

Australian Lamb Loin Chops with Barbecue Sauce ▼

3 tablespoons soy sauce

1 tablespoon brown sugar

3 tablespoons olive oil

1 clove garlic, minced

2-inch piece of
 fresh ginger, grated

8 Australian Lamb
 loin chops

Combine soy sauce, brown sugar, olive oil, garlic and ginger in a small bowl. If desired, reserve some of the sauce for dipping.

To grill: Preheat grill on high. Cook chops for about 2 minutes, until just starting to brown, before basting with sauce. Continue cooking for another 3-5 minutes on each side, basting occasionally.

To pan-broil: In a heavy frying pan, sear over high heat for 1-2 minutes on each side, until just starting to brown, before basting with sauce. Reduce heat to medium and cook chops for 2-4 more minutes, turning at least once. Makes 4 servings.

Southern Cross Australian Boneless Leg of Lamb with Cranberry Glaze ▲

HERB RUB

1/3 cup olive oil

1/2 teaspoon dried
 basil, crushed

1/2 teaspoon dried
 thyme, crushed

1 teaspoon ground
 black pepper

1 teaspoon garlic powder

1 teaspoon salt

1 teaspoon dried
 rosemary, chopped

1 Southern Cross Australian
 boneless leg of lamb

CRANBERRY GLAZE

1 cup white wine

1/2 cup cranberries,
 fresh or frozen

1/3 cup honey

1/2 cup orange juice

2 tablespoons butter

1. Preheat oven to 475°F. Combine ingredients for herb rub in a small bowl. Coat meat on all sides with the rub. Put meat on a rack in a baking pan.

2. Roast for 20 minutes, then reduce heat to 350°F. Roast for another 20 minutes per pound, or until internal temperature is 130°F. Remove lamb from oven and let rest for 15 minutes.

3. While the lamb is resting, combine white wine, cranberries, honey and orange juice in a skillet. Simmer for 12-15 minutes, until reduced by half. Add butter and blend well.

4. Cut lamb into 1/2-inch-thick slices. Serve with glaze. Makes 6-8 servings.

New York Style Sausage

In 1947, Frank D'Ambrosio Sr. left New Haven, Connecticut, to seek his fortune in Santa Clara, California. He immediately missed eating the sausage of his old neighborhood and seized the opportunity, distributing free samples from a family recipe to the local markets in his new home. The response was enthusiastic. Frank's sons still use the same recipe today. New York Style Sausage Company is proud of its tradition of high-quality lean sausage, made fresh daily with no preservatives or MSG. It's been family owned and operated for more than 50 years.

Baked New York Style Sausage Dinner ▼

8 links of any New York Style Sausage*	1 large onion, sliced
4 tablespoons olive oil	3 garlic cloves, chopped
4 medium potatoes, cut in quarters	1 tablespoon chopped parsley
6 carrots, cut in halves or quarters if large	1/4 cup water
	1/4 cup white wine

1. Preheat oven to 350°F. Brown sausage in olive oil in a frying pan on top of stove. Place sausage in a large casserole with a lid. Reserve drippings. Arrange potatoes and carrots between sausages.

2. Cook onions, garlic and parsley in reserved drippings over medium heat until onions are translucent; pour over sausage and vegetables evenly. Add water and wine.

3. Cover and bake for about 1 hour, or until the vegetables are tender. Remove lid for the last 15 minutes to allow potatoes to brown.
Makes 4-6 servings.

Brands may vary by region; substitute a similar product.

Morton's of Omaha
Pot Roast Strudel

Fully cooked, easy to prepare meat items are Emmpak's specialty. All their products are made with great care so you can cook to impress the most critical of guests or the closest of family. Morton's of Omaha Pot Roast is USDA Choice and available only at Costco.

2 pounds Morton's of Omaha* fully cooked choice beef pot roast, broken into bite-size pieces	7 ounces beef demi-glace
	1 teaspoon dried thyme
1/2 pound cooked baby carrots, sliced	Salt and pepper
	8 ounces phyllo dough, 14-16 sheets
1 medium onion, sliced thin, cooked in butter	Melted butter for brushing phyllo sheets

1. Preheat oven to 325°F. Combine pot roast, carrots, onion and beef demi-glace. Sprinkle with thyme and salt and pepper to taste.

2. On a jelly-roll pan lined with parchment paper, stack phyllo dough sheets, lightly brushing every other sheet with melted butter.

3. Place pot roast mixture down the center of stacked phyllo dough. Fold up the long sides and pull up the ends neatly. Lightly brush seams with butter to seal. Roll the strudel over so the seams are on the bottom. Lightly brush strudel with melted butter.

4. Bake for 25 minutes, or until golden brown.

5. Remove from oven and let stand for 10 minutes before slicing with a serrated knife.

Makes 4-6 servings.

Brands may vary by region; substitute a similar product.

Ella's Fabulous DC Brisket ▶

Member Bobby Rosenfeld writes, "This recipe is from my mother-in-law, Ella, who lived in Washington, D.C., for many years. Driving down from New Jersey on holidays and vacations, we always looked forward to eating brisket—and now I cook it whenever I feel nostalgic for the East Coast."

4-8 pounds first-cut brisket	6 carrots, whole or thinly sliced
2 or more garlic cloves, mashed	4 large sweet onions, thinly sliced, divided
Salt and pepper	3/4 cup ketchup
Paprika	1 cup chicken stock or more

1. Preheat oven to 400°F. Rub brisket with garlic and season to taste with salt, pepper and paprika. Scatter carrots and 2 onions in a large baking pan; arrange roast on top. Bake 20-30 minutes, or until browned.

2. Combine ketchup and stock; pour over the brisket. Arrange remaining onions on top of the brisket. Reduce the heat to 325°F. Cover and bake 3-4 hours, or until the meat is fork tender. If the pan becomes dry, add more stock. Cool and slice. Serve with pan gravy. Makes 8-16 servings.

Bobby Rosenfeld, Scottsdale, Arizona

Smithfield Ham with Cider Glaze ◀

This is the classic ham that makes the holiday or any day special. A touch of mustard, a hint of cloves and a splash of apple cider combine to make the traditional glaze.

1 Smithfield Ham* (15-16 pounds), semi-boneless, fully cooked	1 cup apple cider
	2 teaspoons spicy mustard
4 teaspoons cornstarch	1/8 teaspoon ground cloves

1. Preheat oven to 350°F. Place ham in a shallow roasting pan in the oven.

2. Stir cornstarch and 2 tablespoons of the apple cider together in a small saucepan. Stir in remaining apple cider, mustard and cloves; bring to a boil and cook, stirring, until thickened.

3. Pour glaze over ham and continue to bake, basting occasionally, until ham is heated through, about 45-60 minutes, or until internal temperature is 130-140°F. Makes 12-24 servings, with leftovers.

Brands may vary by region; substitute a similar product.

Marcho Farms
Veal Loin Chops Italiano

Marcho Farms, located in Pennsylvania Dutch country, is involved in all aspects of veal production and is the largest veal producer in the nation. Here is a tasty and easy veal loin chop recipe.

1 cup flour	1/2 green bell pepper, diced
1 teaspoon onion salt	1 medium onion, diced
1 teaspoon garlic salt	2 stalks celery, diced
1/4 teaspoon ground pepper	1/2 cup red wine
2 teaspoons olive oil	1 14 1/2-ounce can
2 teaspoons butter	tomato sauce
4 veal loin chops	Salt and pepper
2 garlic cloves, crushed	

1. Combine flour, onion salt, garlic salt and ground pepper. Heat oil and butter over medium heat in a large frying pan. Dredge chops in seasoned flour and brown on both sides. Remove chops and keep warm.

2. Add garlic, bell pepper, onion and celery to pan and cook on low heat, not browning.

3. Add wine, scraping pan with a wooden spoon; reduce liquid by half. Stir in tomato sauce. Return chops to the pan and cover with sauce.

4. Simmer, covered, for 30 minutes, or until tender. Season to taste with salt and pepper. Makes 4 servings.

Atlantic Veal and Lamb
Grilled Gremolata Veal Chops

Gremolata is a mixture of lemon zest, garlic and parsley that can be used as a rub or sprinkled as a garnish over meat, pasta or hearty salads to give a bright flavor. It is a traditional finishing touch with osso bucco, made with veal shanks.

3 tablespoons finely chopped fresh basil	4 8-ounce Atlantic Veal and Lamb* veal rib or loin chops, about 1 inch thick, well-trimmed
3 tablespoons finely chopped fresh parsley	
1 teaspoon freshly grated lemon peel	Salt and pepper
1 garlic clove, crushed	2 medium red bell peppers, halved lengthwise
	2 teaspoons olive oil

1. In a small bowl, combine basil, parsley, lemon peel and garlic. Reserve 1 tablespoon.

2. Season chops with salt and pepper to taste. Press herb mixture on both sides of veal chops. Brush bell peppers with oil. Grill chops and peppers uncovered over medium heat, turning occasionally, for 12-14 minutes, or until peppers are tender and veal reaches an internal temperature of 130-140°F, for medium-rare.

3. Cut each pepper half into three pieces to serve with a chop. Sprinkle reserved herb mixture over each plate. Makes 4 servings.

Brands may vary by region; substitute a similar product.

Van Diermen Cream Puffs with Raspberry Puree Sauce

2 8-ounce containers
   frozen raspberries, thawed

2 tablespoons sugar

1 teaspoon fresh lemon juice

Van Diermen* Cream Puffs

Blend raspberries, sugar and lemon juice in a food processor for 15-30 seconds. Press through a strainer to remove seeds. To serve, arrange cream puffs on serving plates and drizzle with raspberry sauce. Makes 2 cups, enough for about 20 cream puffs. This sauce keeps in the refrigerator for about 2 days.

Brands may vary by region; substitute a similar product.

Ocean Spray Cranberry Mousse ▲

1 cup Ocean Spray*
   Cranberry Juice Cocktail

1 3-ounce package
   raspberry-
   flavored gelatin

1 16-ounce can
   Ocean Spray* Jellied
   Cranberry Sauce

2 cups frozen non-dairy
   whipped topping, thawed

1. Heat cranberry juice cocktail to boiling in a saucepan. Remove from heat and stir in gelatin until dissolved. Transfer to a large mixing bowl.

2. Place cranberry sauce in a small bowl and beat with an electric mixer on high speed for 1 minute. Stir into gelatin mixture. Chill until mixture begins to thicken but is not set.

3. Gently mix in whipped topping with a rubber spatula. Spoon into serving dishes or a baked pie shell. Chill until firm. Makes 8 servings.

Brands may vary by region; substitute a similar product.

Naumes Butterscotch Braised Boscs ▶

4 Naumes* Bosc pears,
   peeled, halved and cored

Juice of 1/2 lemon in a
   large bowl of water

3/4 cup brown sugar

2 tablespoons unsalted butter

1/4 cup water

1. Preheat oven to 350°F. Place pears in the bowl of lemon water.

2. Combine brown sugar, butter and water in an 11-by-17-inch glass baking dish. Microwave on high 3 minutes, stirring after 90 seconds to dissolve sugar (or simmer in a saucepan on stove top for 3 minutes).

3. Arrange pear halves, cut sides up, in baking dish and spoon butterscotch mixture over pears. Cover with aluminum foil; bake 30 minutes.

4. Remove foil, turn pears over, spoon butterscotch over pears, and bake 10 minutes more, or until pears are tender. Makes 8 servings.

Brands may vary by region; substitute a similar product.

Countryside Baking Old World Rugala with Whipped Cream ▲

Rugala is a pastry made of paper-thin dough that was created by the royal chef for the king of Hungary in 1522. It is delicious on its own at room temperature or divine served warm with sweetened whipped cream.

1 cup heavy cream	1/2 teaspoon vanilla extract
2 tablespoons confectioners' sugar	8 pieces Countryside rugala

1. Preheat oven to 350°F. Whip cream in a medium bowl with an electric mixer until soft peaks form. Beat in sugar and vanilla.

2. Bake rugala for 5 minutes, or until heated through. Serve on a platter with the whipped cream in a bowl for dipping. Makes 8 servings.

Kirkland Signature Cookie Parfait ▶

1 ounce unsweetened chocolate, chopped	24 Kirkland Signature Danish Butter Cookies, 18 coarsely crumbled, 6 whole for garnish
3 cups whole milk	
1 1/2 cups sugar, divided	1 pint strawberries, hulled and sliced
1/2 cup flour	
3 eggs and 2 egg yolks, beaten	Whipped cream
	Mint leaves
2 teaspoons vanilla extract	

1. Melt chocolate in a bowl over simmering water or in the microwave.

2. In a saucepan, bring milk and 3/4 cup sugar to a boil.

3. Mix remaining sugar with flour in a bowl. Whisk in eggs until smooth.

4. Whisk boiling milk into egg mixture. Return to saucepan over medium-high heat and cook, whisking, until mixture thickens and comes to a boil. Strain. Stir in vanilla.

5. Remove 1 cup of the mixture and stir into the chocolate. Smooth plastic wrap on surface of the 2 custards. Chill until cool.

6. Layer six 8-ounce parfait glasses with chocolate custard, crushed cookies, vanilla custard, berries, crushed cookies, vanilla custard. Top with whipped cream. Garnish with strawberries, mint and whole cookies. Makes 6 servings.

Nonni's Biscotti Serving Ideas

Nonni's Biscotti are available in two flavors: Cioccolati, a light and crunchy almond cookie dipped in gourmet bittersweet chocolate, and Eggnog, a rich and spicy treat with a delicious white satin bottom. Nonni's Biscotti, traditionally served with coffee, can be eaten alone or enjoyed:

- ✔ Dunked in your favorite beverage
- ✔ Served with ice cream
- ✔ Crushed and used as a flavorful pie crust

Kirkland Signature Cranberry-Grape Mock Champagne ▽

Costco's Kirkland Signature private label Cranberry-Grape Juice lends a delightful tangy sweetness to this punch. Perfect for holiday festivities and children's parties, it's also a refreshing treat for warmer weather.

1/2 cup sugar	1 cup pineapple juice
1 1/2 cups water	2 2-liter bottles lemon-lime soda
1/2 cup orange juice	
2 cups Kirkland Signature Cranberry-Grape Juice	

1. In a saucepan, combine sugar and water and bring to a boil, stirring until sugar dissolves. Cool.

2. Combine orange, cranberry-grape and pineapple juices. Add sugar water. Add soda to taste just before serving. Makes 12-16 servings.

Amber and Jasen Libenson, Sammamish, Washington

Amber and Jasen's Italian Creme Cake ▲

Amber and Jasen write, "Our favorite cake recipe of all time is inspired by a small local restaurant called Sweet Addition in Issaquah, Washington."

1 teaspoon baking soda	1 cup chopped pecans
1 cup buttermilk	1 8-ounce package cream cheese, softened
2 cups sugar	
1/2 cup vegetable shortening	1 stick butter, softened
1 stick butter, softened	1 teaspoon vanilla extract
5 eggs, separated	1 16-ounce box confectioners' sugar (2 cups)
2 cups flour	
1 teaspoon vanilla extract	1/2 tablespoon evaporated milk or water
2 cups coconut	1/2 cup chopped pecans

1. Preheat oven to 350°F. Combine baking soda and buttermilk and let stand for a few minutes. Cream sugar, shortening and butter. Add egg yolks one at a time, beating well after each addition. Add buttermilk alternately with flour to creamed mixture. Add vanilla.

2. In a separate bowl, beat egg whites until stiff and fold into mixture. Gently stir in coconut and pecans. Pour into 2 greased 9-inch cake pans. Bake for 25-30 minutes, or until a toothpick inserted comes out clean. Cool on a rack before icing.

3. To make icing, cream together cream cheese and butter. Add vanilla. Beat in sugar a little at a time. Add evaporated milk. Mix in pecans. Makes 16 servings.

Tip: For a 3-layer cake, reduce the oven temperature to 325°F.

Sugar Foods Café au Lait ▲

1 cup skim milk

1 packet Sweet'N Low*

1/4 teaspoon ground cinnamon

1 teaspoon instant coffee granules, regular or decaffeinated

1. In a small saucepan over medium-low heat, heat the milk, Sweet'N Low and cinnamon until it simmers.

2. Place the coffee granules in a mug; add the hot milk and stir until blended. Makes 1 serving.

Brands may vary by region; substitute a similar product.

The facts about water

Perrier is the leading mineral water in the U.S. It is a top choice among beverages to accompany meals and a sophisticated no-calorie alternative to alcoholic beverages.

Perrier facts:

✔ Perrier is a natural, sparkling mineral water and therefore has no calories. The essences used in the lemon and lime flavored products are entirely natural and calorie-free.

✔ Perrier is sodium-free, according to U.S. government standards.

✔ Perrier's distinctive mineral content is at the heart of its exceptional composition. It includes traces of calcium, magnesium and bicarbonate. The mineral content of any water is measured scientifically as "total dissolved solids."

Perrier contains approximately 475 parts per million "TDS," which earns it the designation of mineral water.

Water facts:

✔ Water accounts for 60 percent of our total weight.

✔ Although we can go without food for a month or longer, we cannot do without water for more than two to five days.

✔ Dehydration begins when only 1 percent of body weight from water is lost and not replaced.

Grits to gumbo

The savory goodness of Southern hospitality

WHERE ELSE BUT THE SOUTH *could time-honored cooking techniques and traditional recipes from numerous generations of Native American, French, English, Spanish, African and West Indian families be so marvelously blended to create a rich and flavorful cuisine?*

The region, with its humid subtropical climate, frost-free growing season, mysterious swamps, heady flowering magnolia trees and swaying fields of cotton, sugarcane and tobacco, has a full plate of culinary history. For example, the French Huguenots are said to have added sauces, gratins and numerous meat dishes, the Spanish figs, pomegranates, peaches and red beans and the Africans rice, yams, sesame seeds, okra and black-eyed peas. And, of course, there was the always dominant culinary influence of the English.

Food icons of the Deep South include fried chicken with gravy, hoppin' John (black-eyed peas cooked with salt pork and rice), Carolina slow-cooked pulled pork, Frogmore stew, mint juleps, hush puppies (deep-fried cornmeal), fried green tomatoes, hominy (dried corn kernels), cracklings

Nathalie Dupree
Southern comfort guru Nathalie Dupree prefers such classics as soup with herbs, roasted chicken with root vegetables, biscuits, a pecan delectable, and grits in every shape and form—at any time of day.

(fried pork skins), fried catfish, country ham, grits, redeye gravy, greens, chitterlings (hog small intestine), gumbos made of okra, local oysters, crayfish and shrimp, jambalaya, coconut layer cake, key lime pie, gingerbread, divinity and pecan pie.

While fabulous, none of these foods would taste half as good if it weren't for the region's best ingredient: Southern hospitality. It is the glue that keeps traditions such as Sunday dinners and the public feasts of barbecues, oyster roasts, Low Country boils, Mardi Gras balls, hunt breakfasts, jazz, country and bluegrass festivals, and county fairs sacred for another generation.

Costco's private-label Kirkland Signature products such as boneless/skinless chicken breasts, extra-fancy mixed nuts, Atlantic salmon and solid white albacore canned tuna are mainstays in Southern warehouses (see www.costco.com's warehouse locator for information and locations). That's not to say, however, that regional products are slighted. Look for fresh farmed tilapia (originated in the South), beef brisket flap meat, top loin, veal, Vidalia onions, honey tangerines, Florida blueberries, strawberries, sweet corn, Indian River grapefruit, plantains, asparagus, raspberries, mangoes, sugar snap peas, papayas, melons and grape tomatoes (originated in Florida)—plus fresh made-on-site caramel flan and key lime pie.

Nathalie Dupree, the Southern belle of easy entertaining and a respected pioneer of the New Southern Cooking movement, is the author of eight books, including Comfortable Entertaining and Southern Memories, both of which received James Beard Awards, the food world's equivalent of the Oscars.

Q: What is classic Southern cuisine?
A: Many nationalities, from the British to African slaves, have left their culinary stamp, with influences such as curry, ginger, spices, okra, eggplant and peanuts. However, it's the down-home cooking caused by the Great Depression era mixed with the elegance of the meals from pre-slavery time that sets this cuisine apart.

Q: *It has been almost 20 years since you pioneered the New Southern Cooking movement. Can you share that vision?*

A: It's taking the foods of the region, cooking them in more updated ways and adding some of the new foods that are now easily grown here, such as zucchini.

Q: *What one dish is considered the belle of the South?*

A: Grits are historically a Southern specialty. I was having some people for dinner just recently, and one of the guests called to say he was going to be late. I thought, 'Oh God, I've got to have something to keep people from eating their fingers until he shows up,' so I pulled a cheese grit soufflé out of the freezer and microwaved it. It was perfect.

Q: *In* Southern Memories *you suggest adding a touch of grace when entertaining. What does this mean?*

A: You must remember that your guest is the important person, not you.

Q: *Many consider you to be the maven of entertaining tricks. Could you share a couple of fail-safe party ideas?*

A: My Thanksgiving trick is my favorite. In order to have an empty sink and dishwasher when the first guest walks in, fill a cooler that's been placed outside or a spare bathroom's bathtub with hot, soapy water and use it to soak all the last-minute pots and pans. Also, if you're afraid someone will put your good china, silver and crystal in the dishwasher when you aren't looking, then just hide the dishwasher soap.

Q: *Southerners take their barbecue very seriously, fiercely defending their secret sauces. What defines good Southern barbecue?*

A: Oh, this is such a controversial issue. North Carolina is famous for its vinegar barbecue sauce and South Carolina for those made with mustard. Just don't forget that Southerners barbecue only pork—unless you're with someone who thinks that Texas is part of the South.

Q: *What Southern ingredients best represent the region?*

A: Pork, Vidalia onions, corn, grits, peas, English butter beans [baby limas], pecans, peaches, seafood and, of course, bourbon!

Q: *What's the most misunderstood aspect of Southern cuisine?*
A: People confuse Southern food with what they get at a buffet line in a cheap restaurant. Southern food is not all fried.

Q: *Cajun versus Creole—these two cuisines can be so confusing to the neophyte. What culinary factors distinguish each?*
A: It's kind of like the city mouse and the country mouse. Creole is high style with much more finesse and richer flavors, whereas Cajun is more country.

> "North Carolina is famous for its vinegar barbecue sauce and South Carolina for those made with mustard."

Q: *Many Southern recipes are a marvelous blend of many cultures. Are there any new interesting food pairings?*
A: We are seeing grits with every form of seafood. In fact, we are seeing grits with all meals.

Q: *Costco's Southern warehouses are chock-full of regional specialties. As a newer member, have you discovered any great products while shopping Costco?*
A: Well, the first time I shopped at Costco, I spent 500 dollars just on meat. I had a great time . . . oh, the lamb, pork roast and veal. But I will say that everyone also seems to love Costco's fruit.

Q: *If you were given a bag of Costco baking potatoes, what would you prepare?*
A: I'd make mashed potatoes with turnips, or just a nice plain baked potato—there's nothing wrong with that. Or perhaps I'd peel the potatoes, drop them in boiling water and brown them off in the oven with butter. That's always tasty.

Q: *Do you have any final Southern comfort words of wisdom?*
A: People have become afraid to cook. Give yourself permission to experiment. 🍽

Caroline Kennedy, Lighthouse Point, Florida

Caroline's Shrimp Fritters and Tomato Marmalade

6 cups water	2 large eggs
1 pound unpeeled medium 31/40-count fresh shrimp	1/4 cup light or dark beer
	1 medium onion, minced
1 cup all-purpose flour	1 jalapeño pepper,
1 teaspoon baking powder	seeded and minced
1 teaspoon salt	4 garlic cloves, minced
1 teaspoon freshly ground black pepper	1/2 teaspoon dried thyme
	Vegetable oil

1. Bring water to a boil; add shrimp and cook for 3-5 minutes, or just until shrimp turn pink. Drain and rinse with cold water; chill.

2. Peel shrimp, deveining if desired, and coarsely chop.

3. Combine flour, baking powder, salt, pepper, eggs and beer in an electric-mixer bowl; beat at medium speed until smooth. Stir in shrimp, onion, jalapeño, garlic and thyme. Cover and chill for 2 hours.

4. Heat 5 inches of oil in a Dutch oven to 375°F.

5. Drop batter by rounded tablespoonfuls into hot oil and fry in batches for 5 minutes, or until golden brown. Drain fritters on paper towels. Serve with Tomato Marmalade. Makes 8 appetizer servings.

Tomato Marmalade

This is an excellent condiment to serve with shrimp fritters, grilled meat or crab cakes.

1 tablespoon olive oil	3 tablespoons minced fresh basil or
1 medium onion, finely chopped	2 teaspoons dried basil
4 large tomatoes, peeled and finely chopped	1/2-1 teaspoon fennel seeds
2 garlic cloves, minced	1/4 teaspoon salt

1. Preheat oven to 400°F. Heat oil in a Dutch oven over medium-high heat; add onion and cook until tender. Remove from heat; stir in tomatoes, garlic, basil, fennel and salt.

2. Bake, covered, for 1 hour, or until thick and bubbly, stirring occasionally. Taste and adjust the seasonings before serving. Makes 1 1/2 cups.

Keystone Fresh Peach Salsa

3 tomatoes, cut in quarters

1 Mayan Sweet* onion,
cut in quarters

1 green bell pepper,
cut in quarters

1-2 jalapeño peppers,
cut in quarters

3 tablespoons cider vinegar

1 tablespoon paprika

1 tablespoon black pepper

1 tablespoon salt, or to taste

1 teaspoon garlic powder

1 teaspoon sugar

1 teaspoon celery seed

1/2 teaspoon ground cumin

1/8 teaspoon hot pepper
sauce, or to taste

2 1/2 cups diced Sunny
South** peaches

1 1/2 cups brown sugar,
or to taste

1. In a food processor, pulse tomatoes, onion,
bell pepper and jalapeño peppers until coarsely
chopped. Add vinegar, paprika, pepper, salt, garlic
powder, sugar, celery seed, cumin and hot sauce;
pulse briefly to combine.

2. Mix together peaches and brown sugar. Stir the
salsa mixture into the peaches. Serve with corn
tortilla chips. Makes about 15 servings.

*Substitute Walla Walla River or Plantation Sweet onions.

**Brands may vary by region; substitute a similar product.

Dole Pineapple Salsa

1 20-ounce can Dole
Pineapple Chunks or
Crushed Pineapple,
drained, 1/4 cup
juice reserved

1/2 cup finely chopped
Dole* red bell pepper

1/4 cup finely chopped
Dole* green bell pepper

1 tablespoon chopped
Dole* green onion

2 teaspoons chopped fresh
cilantro or parsley

2 teaspoons chopped
jalapeño pepper

1 teaspoon grated lime peel

1. Combine pineapple, reserved juice, bell
peppers, onion, cilantro, jalapeño and lime
peel in a small bowl.

2. Serve salsa at room temperature or slightly
chilled with grilled chicken breasts or fish fillets.
Makes 6-8 servings.

Tip: Pineapple salsa can also be served as
a dip with tortilla chips or spooned over
quesadillas or tacos.

*Brands may vary by region; substitute a similar product.

Rain Forest Ceviche

2 pounds diced Rain Forest*
tilapia fillets

4 cups fresh lime juice

1 cup ginger ale

1 red bell pepper,
finely chopped

1 green bell pepper,
finely chopped

1 red onion, finely chopped

1 white onion,
finely chopped

1 tablespoon
minced garlic

Pinch of ground cumin

Salt and pepper

Minced chile

Minced cilantro

1. Combine all ingredients in a large bowl, seasoning
to taste with salt, pepper, chile and cilantro.

2. Refrigerate for at least 1 hour or overnight.

3. Serve chilled with crackers. Makes 6-8 servings.

*Brands may vary by region; substitute a similar product.

Foxy Foods Cauliflower and Broccoli Salad with Peanut-Chili Dressing

Foxy Foods, of Salinas, California, represents farmers growing premium-quality vegetables in the fertile fields of California and Arizona. A company progressive in its methods and conservative in its practices, Foxy Foods offers items that are healthful, nutritious and continuously checked for food safety.

1/3 cup bottled chili sauce	3 cups Foxy* cauliflower florets
1/3 cup crunchy peanut butter	
3 tablespoons water	3 cups Foxy* broccoli florets
1 1/2 tablespoons honey	
1 teaspoon fresh lemon juice	2 green onions, thinly sliced
1/2 teaspoon bottled hot pepper sauce	1 1/2 tablespoons chopped salted peanuts

1. Prepare the dressing by whisking together chili sauce, peanut butter, water, honey, lemon juice and hot pepper sauce.

2. In simmering water, blanch cauliflower for 2 minutes; remove and rinse in cold water; drain. Repeat with broccoli.

3. In a large bowl, toss together blanched vegetables and dressing. Sprinkle with green onions and peanuts. Makes 6 servings.

Brands may vary by region; substitute a similar product.

In 1988 two young entrepreneurs started Alpine as a small importer of berries and asparagus. Today, Alpine is one of the world's premier growers of mangoes, asparagus and grape tomatoes. With great pride, they offer these family recipes for you and your family to enjoy.

Alpine Fresh Mango Salsa

This delicious salsa can be served with tortilla chips, but it is also excellent with chicken, fish or pork. Its lively taste and color will jazz up your meal.

4 large Alpine* mangoes, chopped	1 large onion, finely chopped
Juice of 3 limes	1 teaspoon salt
1 bunch cilantro, finely chopped	1/2 teaspoon pepper

Toss mangoes with lime juice in a large bowl. Add cilantro, onions, salt and pepper. Makes 8 servings.

Brands may vary by region; substitute a similar product.

Alpine Italian Santa Grape Tomato Salad ◄

2 pounds Alpine Santa Variety* grape tomatoes	3 tablespoons red wine vinegar
1/2 cup julienned fennel	1/3 cup extra-virgin olive oil
1/2 cup diced fresh mozzarella	1 tablespoon chopped parsley
	Pinch of crushed red pepper
	Salt and pepper

1. Combine tomatoes, fennel and mozzarella.

2. Whisk together vinegar, olive oil, parsley and red pepper.

3. Combine the dressing with the salad. Season to taste with salt and pepper. Makes 6 servings.

Brands may vary by region; substitute a similar product.

Alpine Asparagus Parmesan ▼

1 bunch (2.2 pounds) Alpine* asparagus	3 tablespoons soft white bread crumbs
2 1/2 tablespoons olive oil	5 tablespoons grated Parmesan cheese

1. Preheat oven to 350°F. Toss asparagus in olive oil; place in a large greased baking dish. Sprinkle with bread crumbs and Parmesan.

2. Bake for 20 minutes, or until the top is lightly browned. Makes 6 servings.

Brands may vary by region; substitute a similar product.

Seald Sweet Fresh Grapefruit and Spinach Salad

1 10-ounce package
   spinach leaves, washed,
   stemmed and torn

3 cups sectioned
   Seald Sweet fresh
   Florida grapefruit

1 red bell pepper, cut into
   short, thin strips

1/2 cup sliced green onions

1/2 cup honey-Dijon or fat-
   free Italian salad dressing

1/4 cup bacon bits

Croutons

1. In a large bowl, combine spinach, grapefruit, bell pepper and green onions. Toss salad with dressing.

2. Arrange salad on 4 serving plates. Sprinkle with bacon bits and croutons. Makes 4 servings.

Tip: Cut a fresh Florida grapefruit in half starting at the stem. Place knife at the stem and cut each half into 4 to 6 equal wedges. Lay each wedge on its side and carefully cut the peel from the fruit. Cut each wedge in half.

DNE World Fruit Orange and Cucumber Salad

Orange juice plus a little mint makes a refreshing, low-fat dressing for this salad or other favorite salad combos.

1 large head Boston or
   Bibb lettuce

3 medium Florida oranges,
   peeled, halved, thinly
   sliced and seeded

1 large cucumber, thinly sliced

1/4 cup frozen Florida orange
   juice concentrate, thawed

2 tablespoons white
   wine vinegar

1 tablespoon salad oil

1 tablespoon honey

1 tablespoon snipped fresh
   mint or 1/2 teaspoon
   dried mint, crushed

Freshly ground black pepper

1. Line 6 salad plates with lettuce. Arrange orange and cucumber slices in circles on lettuce.

2. For the dressing, in a screw-top jar combine thawed concentrate, vinegar, salad oil, honey, mint and a dash of pepper. Cover and shake well.

3. Drizzle over salads. Makes 6 servings.

Dole Miami Beach Chicken Salad

1 1/2 cups Dole* Pineapple Juice, divided	1 pound Dole* fresh asparagus, cooked
4 boneless, skinless chicken breast halves	2 cups sliced Dole* peaches or Dole plums mixed with Dole grapes
1 cup vanilla yogurt	
3 tablespoons mango chutney	1 package (12 ounces) Dole* Salad Blend
1 teaspoon grated lemon peel	

1. Pour 1 cup juice into a glass dish. Add chicken. Cover; refrigerate 30 minutes.

2. Stir together remaining juice, yogurt, chutney and lemon peel; set aside.

3. Grill chicken, brushing with marinade, for 5 minutes, or until completely cooked. Discard marinade.

4. Arrange chicken, asparagus and fruit over salad on 4 plates. Serve with yogurt dressing. Makes 4 servings.

Brands may vary by region; substitute a similar product.

OSO Sweet Onion Salad with Sweet Onion-Orange Vinaigrette

OSO Sweet onions are grown in the foothills of the Andes Mountains in Chile, where the rich volcanic soil, ideal climate and pure water provide the perfect conditions for growing a "world class" sweet onion. This refreshing salad, perfect for entertaining, combines juicy navel oranges and fresh OSO Sweet onions.

SWEET ONION SALAD	SWEET ONION-ORANGE VINAIGRETTE
1 large head Boston lettuce, torn	3 tablespoons orange juice
2 cups fresh spinach, torn	1/4 cup minced OSO Sweet onion
3 large navel oranges	2 tablespoons white wine vinegar
1 OSO Sweet onion, peeled	
3 red apples, cored and diced	2 teaspoons Dijon-style mustard
1 star fruit, sliced thin, optional	2 teaspoons honey
2 tablespoons sesame seeds, toasted	1/3 cup salad oil

1. FOR THE SALAD: Put torn greens in a large salad bowl. Peel oranges over a medium bowl to catch juices, and cut along sections. Add orange sections to the greens, reserving juice for the vinaigrette. Mince 1/4 cup of the onion; reserve for the vinaigrette. Cut remaining onion into thin slices. Add onion, apples and star fruit to salad. Garnish with sesame seeds.

2. FOR THE VINAIGRETTE: In a bowl, whisk together orange juice, onion, vinegar, mustard and honey. Gradually whisk in oil until well blended.

3. Toss salad well with Sweet Onion-Orange Vinaigrette. Makes 6 servings.

Nathalie Dupree

Nathalie Dupree, the epitome of Southern grace and charm, advises all cooks to give themselves permission to spend as much time practicing a new dish as someone would take learning to hit a hole in one.

Grits with Cream and Cheese ▲

This really luscious, creamy, cheesy dish is an incredibly delicious accompaniment to a roast or an elegant meal.

1 cup heavy cream mixed with 2 cups milk	Salt
3/4 cup quick grits	Freshly ground white pepper
2 tablespoons butter	1 cup freshly grated imported Parmesan cheese

1. In a heavy saucepan, bring cream and milk to a simmer. Add grits, stirring, and return to a boil.

2. Reduce heat, cover and cook for 7 minutes, stirring occasionally. If the grits begin to separate and turn lumpy, add a bit of water to keep it creamy.

3. Remove from heat, add butter and salt and pepper to taste; stir in cheese. This can be made ahead and reheated over low heat or in a microwave. Makes 4 servings.

Refrigerator Biscuit Mix ▸

This biscuit mix is ideal for a busy cook. It will keep for several months in a tightly covered container in the refrigerator. Simply combine one part milk or buttermilk with two parts mix for any quantity of biscuits for 6 to 60.

10 cups self-rising flour	4 teaspoons baking powder
3 teaspoons salt	2 cups shortening

1. Sift together flour, salt and baking powder. With a pastry cutter, 2 knives or your fingers, cut in the shortening until it resembles a coarse meal. Store in the refrigerator in an airtight container.

2. Preheat oven to 500°F. Measure out 2 1/2 cups biscuit mix. Add 1 1/4 cups milk or buttermilk. Mix just until it forms a wet dough.

3. Turn out onto a lightly floured surface and knead gently 3-4 times. Roll or pat the dough to 1/2-inch thickness. Using a 2-inch cutter, cut the dough into 12 rounds. Place on an ungreased cookie sheet with their sides barely touching.

4. Bake until golden, about 8-10 minutes. Makes 12 biscuits.

Charred Brussels Sprouts, Carrots, Onion and Garlic ◂

Baked and caramelized Brussels sprouts are quite different from steamed or boiled. They have a nutty flavor with a crisp center. The charred garlic, onions and carrots enhance the sprouts with their color and caramelized flavor.

1 pound Brussels sprouts, X cut in the bottom and outer layers removed	3-6 tablespoons olive oil
	Salt
6-8 garlic cloves, peeled	Freshly ground black pepper
2 medium onions, cut in wedges	1-2 tablespoons fresh lemon juice
2 carrots, cut in sticks	3 tablespoons chopped fresh parsley

1. Preheat oven to 425°F. Toss Brussels sprouts, garlic, onions and carrots with olive oil and arrange in an oiled pan in a single layer. Bake 30 minutes, stirring occasionally, or until the vegetables are crisp-tender and charred.

2. Season to taste with salt and pepper. Squeeze lemon juice over the vegetables and sprinkle with parsley. Makes 6-8 servings.

Nathalie Dupree shares her recipe for Chocolate Pecan Tarts on page 180.

SIDE DISHES

Bill's Baked Beans

1 7-pound can baked beans	1 tablespoon Worcestershire sauce
1 45-ounce bottle barbecue sauce	2 tablespoons mustard
1/2 large onion, chopped	1 dash hot sauce or more
1/2 green bell pepper, chopped	1/2 cup brown sugar
	3 tablespoons bacon bits
	4 slices bacon

1. Preheat oven to 350°F. Mix beans with barbecue sauce, onion and bell pepper in a large baking pan or 4-quart casserole. Stir in Worcestershire sauce, mustard, hot sauce, sugar and bacon bits. Taste and adjust seasonings.

2. Top with bacon. Bake for 1 hour.
Makes 25 servings.

Tip: Use a Costco aluminum half-sheet pan, 10x12x2.5 inches. This recipe freezes well.

Bill Green, Duluth, Georgia

Marsha Passmore, Plant City, Florida

Marsha's Corn Soufflé Casserole

1 stick margarine, melted	1 15 1/4-ounce can whole kernel corn
1 cup sour cream	1/4 cup chopped onion
2 eggs, beaten	1/2 teaspoon salt
1 8 1/2-ounce box corn bread mix	Paprika
1 15 1/4-ounce can cream-style corn	

1. Preheat oven to 350°F. Combine margarine, sour cream and eggs in a bowl.

2. Beat in corn bread mix. Stir in corns, onion and salt.

3. Pour into a greased 8-by-8-inch pan. Bake for 45-60 minutes, or until lightly browned. Sprinkle with paprika. Makes 6-8 servings.

FROM THE
COSTCO
Wine
EXPERT

Sipping Wine with Seafood

David Andrew, Costco's global wine director, says, "Fish is my favorite food, but some wines can easily overpower its delicate range of flavors. Aim for something light and fresh that will let the flavor of the fish shine." As with all foods, the method of preparation will affect how well wines accompany them, but here are a few wines that should work with fish no matter what the preparation:

Sauvignon Blanc: *New Zealand varieties are particularly good—really zesty and grassy.*

Sancerre and Pouilly-Fumé: *Also made from Sauvignon Blanc, these are excellent all-around fish wines.*

White Bordeaux: *This is a blend of Sauvignon Blanc and Semillon in varying proportions. The Semillon adds richness to the Sauvignon, a combination that can stand up to richer fish and sauces. I particularly like it with smoked salmon, but it has never met a fish it didn't like.*

Muscadet-Sur-Lie: *The classic oyster wine from the mouth of the River Loire in France also works well with lighter fish preparations.*

Chablis: *This pure, mineral-edged Chardonnay from northern Burgundy is great with mussels and oysters.*

New World Chardonnay: *Richer fish dishes call for weightier wines, and many New World Chardonnays fit the bill nicely. It's best to avoid overly oaky styles, which may overpower the fish.*

Pinot Grigio: *A good all-around wine, this has a neutral character that makes it very flexible.*

Australian Riesling: *It's bone dry with lime-juice acidity, making it the perfect choice for a wide variety of fish.*

Pinot Noir: *Yes, it's okay to drink red wine with fish! Pinot Noir works particularly well with salmon, but try it with grilled fish or anytime you're having fish and just want to drink red.*

Camanchaca
Florida Orange Salmon ▸

4 Camanchaca* salmon portions (6-8 ounces each)	2 shallots, chopped
	1/2 cup dry white wine
Salt and pepper	1/2 cup fresh squeezed orange juice
4 tablespoons butter	3 tablespoons honey

1. Season salmon with salt and pepper. Melt butter in a large saucepan over medium-high heat. Add shallots and cook about 2 minutes.

2. Add salmon and sear about 2 minutes on each side. Add wine, orange juice and honey.

3. Reduce the heat to low and cook for 8-10 minutes, stirring and turning salmon. Season sauce with salt and pepper to taste. Makes 4 servings.

*Brands may vary by region; substitute a similar product.

Mrs. Dash Grilled Citrus Halibut ◂

This delicious main course is not only low in sodium and fat, but also full of zesty, buttery flavor. It's especially good hot off the outdoor grill.

2 tablespoons Mrs. Dash Original Blend	3 tablespoons lime juice
2 teaspoons Molly McButter Natural Butter Flavor Sprinkles	3 tablespoons Dijon-style mustard
	3 tablespoons olive oil
1/4 cup lemon juice	1 pound halibut, cut into 4 equal pieces

1. Combine first 6 ingredients in a resealable plastic bag. Add halibut and seal bag. Marinate in the refrigerator for at least 30 minutes.

2. Remove halibut and discard marinade. Grill on medium-high heat 4-5 minutes per side, or until fish flakes easily. Makes 4 servings.

Fishery Products Tilapia Tacos with Tropical Fruit Salsa

1/2 cup chopped mango	2 teaspoons grated lime peel
1/2 cup chopped papaya	1 teaspoon ground cumin
1/2 cup chopped pineapple	1 teaspoon dried oregano
1/4 cup chopped red onion	1/2 teaspoon chili powder
1/4 cup chopped cilantro	1 teaspoon salt
1/4 cup chopped red bell pepper	2 teaspoons black pepper
2 tablespoons lime juice	6 5-ounce Fishery Products* tilapia fillets
1/2 teaspoon ground cumin	Tortillas
Salt and pepper	

1. Combine mango, papaya, pineapple, onion, cilantro and bell pepper in a medium bowl. Stir in lime juice and cumin. Season to taste with salt and pepper.

2. Mix lime peel, cumin, oregano, chili powder, salt and pepper together. Rub on tilapia fillets. Place fillets on greased foil; broil for 8 minutes, or until internal temperature is 145°F.

3. Arrange fish on warm tortillas and top with salsa. Makes 6 servings.

Brands may vary by region; substitute a similar product.

Mountain Stream Caribbean-Style Tilapia

1 1/2 pounds Mountain Stream* tilapia fish fillets	1 1/2 teaspoons grated orange peel
Salt and pepper	1/2 teaspoon grated lemon peel
Ground nutmeg	1/2 teaspoon grated lime peel
1/4 teaspoon Jamaican jerk seasoning	4 orange slices
	4 lemon slices

1. Preheat oven to 400°F. Place fillets in a lightly buttered baking dish. Sprinkle with salt and pepper, nutmeg and jerk seasoning. Sprinkle citrus peel on top and cover with foil.

2. Bake for 15 minutes, or until internal temperature at the thickest part of fillets is 145°F. Garnish with fresh orange and lemon slices. Makes 4 servings.

Brands may vary by region; substitute a similar product.

FROM THE
COSTCO
Seafood
EXPERT

Tilapia Facts

Bright gold, red, green or white, tilapia is also called sunfish and sometimes St. Peter's fish, as it's thought to be the legendary fish that multiplied to feed the masses in biblical times. Why is it a favorite fresh fish in the South? According to Jeff Lyons, Costco's seafood expert, there are several reasons:

✔ The white flesh has a sweet and delicate flavor and is slightly firm to the bite.

✔ It is a lean, versatile fish that can be baked, broiled, sautéed or steamed.

✔ It is excellent in many Cuban, Caribbean and Hispanic dishes.

✔ The farm-raised fillets are boneless and skinless and are always available.

Delta Pride Grilled Catfish with Citrus Marinade

Delta Pride U.S. farm-raised catfish, with its mild taste and lean, firm flesh, is catching on across the country. Delta Pride's fish are raised in clay-bottom ponds filled with pure water from deep aquifers and fed a grain-based, high-protein diet to ensure good flavor and a light, even texture. Delta Pride is the only catfish processor in the country with full-time USDA inspectors.

4 Delta Pride U.S. farm-raised catfish fillets	1 teaspoon chopped garlic
1/4 cup orange juice	1/4 teaspoon cracked black pepper
2 tablespoons soy sauce	1 tablespoon chopped fresh parsley
1 tablespoon lemon juice	
2 tablespoons vegetable oil	

1. Rinse fillets, pat dry and place in a shallow glass dish.

2. Combine remaining ingredients and pour over fillets. Chill for 1-3 hours.

3. Grill fillets over high heat for 3-4 minutes on each side, or until fish flakes easily with a fork or internal temperature is 145°F. Makes 4 servings.

Heinz Tomato Ketchup Tuna Creole

This speedy recipe relies on pantry staples, so it's easy to make when you can't decide what to fix for dinner. Creole cookery reflects the full-flavored combination of the best of French, Spanish and African cuisines.

1 4-ounce can sliced mushrooms, drained, reserving liquid	1 tablespoon cornstarch
Oil	1/2 cup Heinz Tomato Ketchup
1/4 cup chopped onion	1/8 teaspoon hot pepper sauce
1/4 cup chopped green bell pepper	1 9-ounce can tuna, drained
	Hot cooked rice

1. Add water to reserved mushroom liquid to measure 1 cup.

2. Heat oil in a small saucepan over medium-high heat; cook mushrooms, onion and bell pepper until tender-crisp.

3. Dissolve cornstarch in reserved mushroom-water; stir in ketchup and hot sauce; add to vegetables.

4. Cook over medium heat, stirring, until thickened. Gently stir in tuna until heated through. Serve over rice. Makes 3 servings.

Fish House Foods

There's no easier meal than a prepared entree from the Costco Deli. These ready-to-cook dishes are created on the premises using quality ingredients. Choose from meatloaf, manicotti, rotisserie chicken, spinach salad, chicken Caesar salad, rolled flank steak with portobello mushrooms and more. Here are two easy embellishments for the delicious stuffed salmon.

Fish House Foods Service Deli
Stuffed Salmon–Italian Style

½ cup pesto

½ cup mayonnaise

1 package Kirkland Signature stuffed salmon entrée

½ cup bread crumbs

Freshly grated Parmesan cheese

1. Mix pesto to taste and mayonnaise in a small bowl; spread over each fillet.

2. Sprinkle bread crumbs over pesto. Top with Parmesan.

3. Bake according to the package instructions. Makes 3-4 servings.

Fish House Foods Service Deli
Stuffed Salmon–Cajun Style

1 package Kirkland Signature stuffed salmon entrée

1 cup Cajun seasoning mix

Olive oil

1. Flatten stuffing into salmon portions.

2. Dredge fillets generously in Cajun seasoning on both sides (more seasoning will increase spiciness).

3. Heat a large ovenproof skillet over medium-high heat. Add olive oil.

4. Carefully place seasoned fillets in the hot skillet, stuffing side down. Cook for approximately 3-5 minutes.

5. Turn over, cook for approximately 3-5 minutes more or cook according to the package instructions. Makes 3-4 servings.

Richmond New Zealand Farm-Fresh
Cajun Ground Beef Kebabs

1 pound ground beef	Olive oil
1 medium onion, chopped fine	1 long cucumber, peeled, chopped
1 tablespoon salt	Salt
1 tablespoon Cajun spice mix	2 garlic cloves
	3/4 pint Greek-style yogurt
1/2 cup chopped parsley	White pepper
1 tablespoon water	

1. Knead together ground beef, onion, salt, spice mix, parsley and water for 2-3 minutes, until the meat becomes sticky.

2. Form the meat into sausage shapes; thread on kebab sticks. Brush with oil; grill until golden brown and internal temperature is 140°F.

3. PREPARE DIPPING SAUCE: Sprinkle cucumber liberally with salt, place in a sieve and let drain for 30 minutes. In a bowl, mash garlic to a paste in 1/4 teaspoon salt. Add yogurt, cucumber and pepper to taste. Makes 4 servings.

ConAgra Foods
Ragin' Cajun Jambalaya

Southern Creole cooking favors tomatoes, rice, peppers, onions and spices. ConAgra Foods takes a classic dish and creates a spicy skillet sensation in 30 minutes.

Pam No Stick Cooking Spray	1 1/2 cups uncooked long-grain rice
1 pound smoked sausage, cut in 1/2-inch slices	2 10-ounce cans Rotel* Original Diced Tomatoes with Green Chilies
1 pound boneless, skinless chicken breasts, cut in strips	
1 medium onion, diced	3 cups Butterball* Chicken Broth
2 garlic cloves, minced	1 6-ounce can Hunt's Tomato Paste

1. Coat a deep cast-iron skillet or Dutch oven with cooking spray and heat on medium-high. Add sausage, chicken, onion and garlic; cook until browned, stirring frequently.

2. Add rice; cook for 5 minutes, or until golden brown.

3. Stir in tomatoes, chicken broth and tomato paste; bring to a boil. Cover, reduce heat to low and cook for 20 minutes, or until rice is tender. Stir to blend. Makes 8 servings.

Brands may vary by region; substitute a similar product.

Charlie's Steak with Garlic Mushrooms and Onions

Charlie Winters and his wife, Lynn, prefer boneless steaks cut from the tenderloin. Restaurants sell this as a filet mignon or Chateaubriand. T-bone is the bone-in steak from the same section.

1 pound butter, room temperature	1/2 pound mushrooms, sliced
1/2 garlic head, peeled and minced	1 pound beef tenderloin
1/4 cup dry white wine	Salt and freshly ground pepper
1/4 cup chopped fresh parsley	Garlic powder
1/4 teaspoon ground pepper	1 teaspoon crushed red pepper
1 large onion, sliced	Dash of sherry

1. PREPARE GARLIC BUTTER: Combine butter, garlic, wine, parsley and pepper in an electric-mixer bowl; mix on low speed until thoroughly blended. This mixture freezes well.

2. Melt 2 tablespoons garlic butter in a large skillet over medium-high heat. Add onion and sauté until golden. Add mushrooms and cook lightly. Transfer to a plate and keep warm. Drain and wipe pan.

3. Season meat to taste with salt, pepper, garlic powder and crushed red pepper. Melt 1 tablespoon garlic butter in the same skillet over medium-high heat. Add meat and cook on all sides until browned and the internal temperature is 130°F, for medium-rare. Remove the meat.

4. Return mushrooms and onions to the pan; add sherry, stirring to blend. Slice meat into 4 pieces and top with additional garlic butter. Serve with mushrooms and onions. Makes 4 servings.

FROM THE
COSTCO
Meat
EXPERT

Best Cuts for Grilling

Costco sells USDA Choice or higher, yield grades 1, 2 or 3. These steaks feature extra butchering value, with 1/4-inch trim, connective tissue removed, no bone chips, cuts or seams. Cuts from the loin section are the most tender, says vice president Charlie Winters, and marbling fat adds flavor. Grill or broil to 130°F for medium-rare:

✔ **Boneless:** New York strip, rib-eye or top sirloin steak (rib-eye is often listed on restaurant menus as Delmonico, Spencer or beauty steak)

✔ **Bone-in:** T-bone steak or thick-cut pork chops

Emeril's Grilled Chicken Salad

3 tablespoons Emeril's Original Essence*	1/2 cup chopped red bell pepper
1 pound boneless chicken breasts	1/2 cup corn kernels
1 cup mayonnaise	1/2 cup black beans
1/3 cup chopped cilantro	1/4 cup sliced scallions
2 tablespoons milk	Toasted bread slices or lettuce

1. Rub 2 tablespoons Essence on chicken breasts. Grill for 15 minutes, or until internal temperature is 160°F.

2. Combine remaining Essence, mayonnaise, cilantro, milk, bell pepper, corn, beans and scallions. Chop grilled chicken and stir into mixture.

3. Serve on toasted bread slices or lettuce leaves. Makes 4 servings.

Brands may vary by region; substitute a similar product. Recipe courtesy of Emeril's Food of Love Productions 2002.

Gold Kist Farms
Lively Lime-Grilled Chicken

Gold Kist is the nation's second-largest chicken company. With a tradition of quality begun in 1933, these family farmers are dedicated to producing the finest, freshest chicken anywhere. Gold Kist Farms is 100 percent all-natural chicken—nothing added.

10 ounces hot jalapeño jelly	1 cup loosely packed cilantro leaves
6 ounces frozen limeade concentrate, thawed	6 Gold Kist Farms* boneless, skinless split chicken breasts
5 garlic cloves	

1. Puree jelly, limeade, garlic and cilantro in a food processor; reserve 2/3 cup. Coat chicken with remaining marinade; refrigerate 30 minutes.

2. Remove chicken from marinade. Heat marinade to boiling. Preheat grill.

3. Grill chicken over medium heat, basting with boiled marinade, 5-6 minutes on each side, or until tender, with an internal temperature of 160°F.

4. Serve chicken with reserved sauce. Makes 6 servings.

Brands may vary by region; substitute a similar product.

America's Kitchen Chicken Pot Pie
Dinner Idea

The perfect accompaniment to America's Kitchen Chicken Pot Pie is a crisp green salad with fresh herbs that balances the creamy richness of the pie.

1/4 cup olive oil	Fresh chopped parsley, tarragon or thyme
1 tablespoon red wine vinegar	America's Kitchen Chicken Pot Pie, prepared according to package directions
1/2 teaspoon garlic powder	
Salt and pepper	
1 12-ounce package mixed salad greens	

1. Whisk oil and vinegar together in a small bowl. Stir in garlic powder. Season to taste with salt and pepper.

2. Toss dressing with salad greens. Sprinkle herbs on top. Serve with chicken pot pie. Makes 6-8 servings.

Minute Maid Almond Tea Cake with Orange Glaze

After more than 50 years, the Minute Maid Company has developed great expertise in juice nutrition and taste. They were the first company to introduce a calcium-fortified orange juice and the first to fortify with vitamin D.

3 tablespoons milk	3/4 teaspoon baking powder
3 large eggs	1/4 teaspoon salt
1 teaspoon almond extract	3/4 cup butter, at
1 1/2 cups sifted cake flour	room temperature
3/4 cup sugar	2 cups Minute Maid
	Premium Orange Juice

1. Heat oven to 350°F. Butter three 3-by-5-inch tea-loaf pans and dust with flour.
2. Whisk together milk, eggs and almond extract. Sift together flour, sugar, baking powder and salt into an electric-mixer bowl. Add butter and half the egg mixture to the dry ingredients and beat to combine. Scrape down the sides of the bowl and add remaining egg mixture, beating to combine.

3. Spoon batter into prepared pans and smooth surfaces with a spatula. Bake for about 40 minutes, or until a toothpick or cake tester inserted in the center comes out clean. Let cakes cool for about 10 minutes on a wire rack. Turn out of pans and cool completely.

4. Meanwhile, pour orange juice into a small saucepan and set over medium heat. Let simmer until the liquid is reduced by half and is thick and syrupy, about 40 minutes. Remove from heat. Cool and pour over the cakes. Makes 3 small loaves, or 15 servings.

FROM THE EMPLOYEE'S KITCHEN

Piper's So Simple Peanut Butter Cookies

You don't have to be on a popular diet to enjoy these flour-free cookies. The peanut butter flavor is pleasing, and the crunchy texture will surprise you.

1 cup peanut butter,	1 cup packed brown sugar
smooth or crunchy	1 egg

1. Preheat oven to 350°F. Beat all ingredients together with an electric mixer or a fork. Drop on a cookie sheet by the tablespoonful. Flatten with a fork.
2. Bake for 10-12 minutes, or until golden brown. Cool on the cookie sheet for 1 minute before removing to a rack to cool. Makes 18 cookies.

Piper Montague, Ravensdale, Washington

Nathalie Dupree

Candles and flowers and a roaring fire have their places in seduction. But perhaps the best seduction is this rich chocolate and pecan filling in its delicate crust. The fabulous shortcrust pastry in these tarts sturdily holds the chocolaty, caramely pecan filling, but melts in your mouth with a hint of cinnamon.

Chocolate Pecan Tarts ▾

1 1/4 cups all-purpose flour	1/4 cup semisweet chocolate chips
1/4 cup sugar	
1/4 teaspoon ground cinnamon	2 large eggs
1/3 cup butter, softened	1 cup coarsely chopped pecans
1/3 cup dark corn syrup	2 tablespoons all-purpose flour
1/4 cup sugar	1/2 teaspoon vanilla extract
1/4 cup butter	Dark or white chocolate curls, pecan halves or confectioners' sugar

1. Preheat oven to 350°F. Combine flour, 1/4 cup sugar and cinnamon in a medium bowl. With 2 knives, cut in softened butter until coarse crumbs form. Divide the mixture among four 1/2-inch-deep by 3 1/2-inch-round fluted tart pans with removable bottoms; press evenly on the bottoms and sides of the pans.

2. Stir corn syrup and 1/4 cup sugar in a small saucepan over medium heat until sugar dissolves and the mixture boils. Remove from heat and stir in butter and chocolate chips until melted and smooth.

3. Beat eggs in a large bowl with a whisk or fork until frothy; add the chocolate mixture in a slow, steady stream, beating constantly. Stir in pecans, 2 tablespoons flour and vanilla.

4. Pour the filling into the prepared tart shells and bake 25 minutes, or until the filling is set in the center and slightly puffed.

5. Cool in the pans on a wire rack. Remove the sides of the tart pans and release the tarts. Serve decorated with chocolate curls and pecans or a sprinkling of confectioners' sugar. Makes 4 servings.

Pillsbury Triple Chocolate Ice Cream Pie ▴

1 18-ounce package Pillsbury Refrigerated Chocolate Chip Cookie dough	1 pint vanilla ice cream, softened
	1 cup hot fudge sauce
1 pint chocolate chip ice cream, softened	

1. Preheat oven to 350°F. Press cookie dough evenly in the bottom of an ungreased 9- or 10-inch pie plate or springform pan. Bake for 14-18 minutes, or until golden brown. Chill.

2. Spread chocolate chip ice cream over cookie crust. Freeze 30-60 minutes, or until firm.

3. Spread vanilla ice cream over chocolate chip layer. Drizzle hot fudge sauce over ice cream. Freeze 2-3 hours before serving. Makes 6-8 servings.

Cheesecake Extras

Jean-Yves Mocquet, in the research and development area of Costco's bakery department, says there are many ways to serve a cheesecake from Costco.

Next to chocolate, cheesecake is perhaps the most decadent of desserts. With its rich taste and creamy texture, it is a year-round favorite. And it's easily dressed up to satisfy all tastes. Berry toppings are always popular, whether blueberries, strawberries and raspberries or a combination. Mangoes, guavas and apples are delicious as well. Change the topping to accommodate seasonal fruits.

Of course, cheesecake served sans topping allows the flavors of the sweetened sour cream and border of non-dairy whipped topping to come through. Plain cheesecake can be served with a garnish, such as lemon peel or sliced strawberries, or on a plate dusted with confectioners' sugar. Drizzle melted chocolate over plain cheesecake for an added taste treat.

Costco's cheesecake serves approximately 16 guests. For equal portions, cut the cheesecake into quarters and then slice each of the quarters into four pieces. Uneaten portions can be stored in the refrigerator for up to five days.

Mango Coulis

2 whole mangoes, peeled, pitted, and chopped

Juice of one lemon

2/3 cup water

1/2 cup sugar

1. Combine chopped mango, lemon juice, water and sugar in a saucepan. Bring the mixture to a boil. Reduce to a simmer and cook for 5 minutes, or until the fruit is very tender.

2. Pour the mixture into a food processor and puree until smooth. Spread on top of cheesecake.

Nutella
Black-and-White Cheesecake

Nutella is the chocolaty hazelnut spread that can be eaten with a variety of foods and enjoyed at any time of the day. Created in Italy, Nutella is perfect at snack-time or in recipes for kids and adults alike.

8 ounces cream cheese, softened	3/4 cup Nutella,* warmed slightly
1/4 cup sugar	1 purchased chocolate cookie piecrust
2 cups heavy cream, divided	

1. Beat cream cheese and sugar with an electric mixer for 2 minutes, or until light and fluffy.

2. In another bowl, whisk 1/2 cup heavy cream with Nutella until smooth. Whip remaining heavy cream until soft peaks form.

3. Fold half of the whipped cream into the cream cheese and half into the Nutella mixture. Alternately spoon the two batters into the piecrust, creating layers. Refrigerate for at least 1 hour. Makes 9 servings.

Tip: Warm Nutella in a bowl in a microwave on high for 5 seconds. Or heat in a saucepan on the stove top over low heat until creamy.

Brands may vary by region; substitute a similar product.

Fordel Tropical Melon Sorbet

1/3 cup fresh lime juice or more	1 cup sugar or more
1/3 cup orange liqueur or orange juice	1/2 teaspoon salt
1 tablespoon fresh lemon juice	1 ripe medium Fordel* cantaloupe or 1/2 Fordel honeydew, pureed (about 4 cups)

1. Combine lime juice, orange liqueur, lemon juice, sugar and salt in a saucepan. Bring to a simmer and stir until sugar dissolves. Remove from the heat and cool. Chill for at least 1 hour in a cake pan.

2. Add melon puree to the syrup. Taste and adjust flavors, adding more lime juice or sugar. Flavors will be less intense when the mixture is frozen.

3. Freeze in an ice-cream maker according to manufacturer's directions or in a cake pan, beating well twice at 2-hour intervals. Makes 6-8 servings.

Brands may vary by region; substitute a similar product.

FROM THE MEMBER'S KITCHEN

Kathleen's Grapefruit Pie or Parfaits

This tangy dessert, submitted by Kathleen James of Surprise, Arizona, can also be served without the crust in a footed dessert bowl, topped with whipped cream.

3-5 large pink grapefruit, sectioned, seeded, membranes removed	1/2 cup fresh orange juice and pulp
1/3-1/2 cup sugar, depending on sweetness of grapefruit	1/2 cup water
	6 ounces heavy cream, whipped, or 2 cups whipped dessert topping
1 1/4-ounce envelope unflavored gelatin	1 9-inch graham cracker piecrust
1/8 teaspoon salt	

1. Drain sections briefly and refrigerate.

2. Mix sugar, gelatin and salt in a medium, non-aluminum saucepan. Stir in juice and water and let stand 1 minute. Stir over medium heat until gelatin is dissolved. Place in refrigerator until slightly thickened.

3. Gently fold 1/2 cup of gelatin mixture into the whipped cream or dessert topping.

4. Drain grapefruit sections again, then mix them into the remaining gelatin mixture and pour into pie shell or parfait glasses.

5. Top with whipped mixture and then chill until firm. Makes 6-8 servings.

Tip: Omit the crust and chill grapefruit mixture in a footed dessert bowl with cream on top.

Vie de France Orchard-Fresh Shortcake

1 Vie de France butter croissant	1/2 cup fresh berries
Confectioners' sugar	Honey, warmed in microwave
1/4 cup whipped cream or non-dairy topping	

1. Using a sharp serrated knife, cut a lengthwise 1-inch-deep V in the top of the croissant. Sprinkle generously with confectioners' sugar. Spread a layer of whipped cream in the trench.

2. Rinse berries and pat dry. If using strawberries, cut in half. Arrange berries on the whipped cream. Brush the berries with hot honey.

3. Refrigerate immediately to set the honey. Serve chilled. Makes 1 serving.

Martinelli's Summer Caribbean Punch

The Martinelli family of Watsonville, California, takes advantage of its Sparkling Cider to enhance this cool summer punch that will please any palate.

2 16-ounce cans frozen orange juice concentrate	1 quart water, chilled
1 12-ounce can frozen lemonade concentrate	3 bananas, peeled
3 bottles (25.4 ounces) Martinelli's Sparkling Cider, chilled	1 pint fresh raspberries
	2 pints fresh strawberries, hulled
1 quart cranberry juice cocktail, chilled	1 cup sugar, optional
	2 oranges, sliced
1 quart fruit punch, chilled	2 limes, sliced
	1 lemon, sliced

1. Combine orange juice concentrate, lemonade concentrate, sparkling cider, cranberry juice cocktail, fruit punch and water. (Do not add water to frozen orange juice and lemonade as directed on cans; use only the concentrate.)

2. In a blender, puree bananas, raspberries and strawberries with some of the punch mixture. Strain the mixture to remove seeds if desired. Stir into punch.

3. Add sugar to taste. Stir until sugar is dissolved. Garnish with orange, lime and lemon slices. Makes approximately 2 gallons of punch, or 32 8-ounce servings.

Apple & Eve Ruby Red Sunrise

Ruby Red grapefruit juice is a grapefruit lover's dream. This smooth, surprisingly sweet beverage is loaded with 130 percent of your daily vitamin C requirement and has no artificial flavors or preservatives.

1 1/2 cups Apple & Eve* Ruby Red Grapefruit Juice Cocktail	1 large ripe banana
	2 scoops orange sherbet and vanilla ice cream blend
1/3 cup pineapple juice	2 cups ice cubes

1. Place grapefruit juice, pineapple juice, banana and sherbet/ice cream in a blender.

2. Add ice to fill the blender. Blend until smooth and frosty. Add more or less ice for desired consistency.

3. Garnish with pineapple or orange slice. Makes 6-8 servings.

Tip: For a healthier option, substitute low-fat ice cream or frozen yogurt.

Brands may vary by region; substitute a similar product.

Kirkland Signature Chilled Mocha Drink

Trendy and appealing, this coffee-on-ice drink can be enjoyed for its energy boost, to beat the heat, as a refreshing afternoon break or for dessert.

1 1/2 cups brewed double-strength Kirkland Signature 100% Colombian or Decaf Arabica coffee	1/4 cup chocolate syrup
	1/8 teaspoon vanilla extract
	Ice cubes

1. Chill coffee; store in a covered container to retain freshness.

2. Mix coffee, chocolate syrup and vanilla until well blended. Pour into tall glasses filled with ice. Makes 2 servings.

Bounty
of the
north

The prairies and the sea share their wealth

THE IROQUOIS FIRST NATION has been credited with the word canada, *meaning village or community. Today, Canada is a very large, diverse "village" stretching over 10 provinces and three territories. Likewise, its cuisine is full of diversity, encompassing the specialties of numerous First Nation tribes and those of immigrants from around the world.*

To the far west on the Pacific coast lies British Columbia, a region full of food experimentation and a cuisine that fuses the cooking techniques of First Nation tribes and Europeans with Asian flavorings and local ingredients. Salmon, black cod, halibut, grapes, huckleberries, hothouse tomatoes, hazelnuts, potatoes, mushrooms, wild game and wines highlight the menu.

The heartland prairie provinces of Alberta, Saskatchewan and Manitoba are rich in pioneering history. Settlers created hearty, portable dishes that are still popular today: roasted meats, steamed puddings, berry jams, cabbage rolls, borscht (beet soup) and sausages. Wild rice, mushrooms, freshwater fish and game such as bison and rabbit are abundant, as are root vegetables, grains and berries.

For centuries, the citizens of Ontario have farmed and tended vineyards and orchards. In this region, Yukon Gold potatoes were first bred, McIntosh apples were discovered and ice wine made from frozen grapes gained international status. Cattle ranches, cider mills, cranberry bogs, fish-smoking houses and wineries dot the landscape. In trendy, cosmopolitan Toronto, ethnic cuisine abounds. Here a food lover can find authentic German sausage, molasses shoofly pie, apple fritters, baked beans, scones, oat bread, smoked fish and cipaille, or sea pie (a layered meat pie).

Quebec's multifaceted, multicultural cuisine is built on a history of long winters and strong ties to France. Venison and quail, waterfowl, nuts, sturgeon, eel, root vegetables, buckwheat, pork, goats, lamb and indigenous corn, beans, squash and maple syrup are the essence of the land's gastronomic fare. Recipes proliferate for onion soups, fish chowders, country patés, pickled vegetables and ketchup aux tomates rouges (chili sauce).

Foods from the Atlantic provinces of Newfoundland, Nova Scotia, Prince Edward Island and New Brunswick center around one-pot meals of boiled beef and root vegetables, stews, chowders and sea harvests. Dried cod is said to have originated in this rugged land. Cod, lobster, snow crab, sea scallops and clams are dietary staples, as are dried peas, root vegetables, lingonberries, oats, beef, maple syrup and molasses. Zest is added with chowchow (a spicy mixture of green tomatoes, salt, onions, vinegar, brown sugar and pickling spices), chutney, sauerkraut and mincemeat.

Canadian Costco warehouses stretch from coast to coast. While many items in the warehouses are similar to those found in the United States, there are a number of regional specialties: poutine (a dish of French fries, warm gravy and melted cheese curds served at Costco Food Courts in eastern Canada), Clamato (tomato clam juice), peameal bacon (Canadian bacon) and cheese curd (East Coast only), Saskatoon berry jam, BeeMaid honey, Alberta beef, back bacon (akin to ham) and Quebec maple syrup. |O|

Switzerland Cheese
Walliser Tomatenfondue

2 tablespoons butter

1 garlic clove, finely chopped

1 medium onion, finely chopped

3 tomatoes, peeled and diced

1 cup dry white wine

18 ounces Gruyère Switzerland cheese, shredded

11 ounces Emmentaler Switzerland cheese, shredded

4 teaspoons cornstarch

3 tablespoons kirsch (brandy)

White pepper

Nutmeg

Marjoram, optional

Oregano, optional

Baguette cut in 1-inch cubes for dipping or raw vegetables such as broccoli or mushrooms

1. Melt butter in a fondue pot over medium heat. Add garlic, onions and tomatoes; cook briefly; add wine.

2. Add cheese and bring to a simmer, stirring constantly. Combine cornstarch and kirsch (brandy) and add to the simmering ingredients. Continue to stir until very smooth. Add pepper and nutmeg to taste. Add marjoram and oregano to taste if desired. Serve with bread or vegetables for dipping. Makes 4 servings.

Tip: To prepare the diced tomatoes, make 4 slices through the skin and plunge into boiling water very quickly. Cool off in cold water, peel, cut in half, squeeze the seeds out and dice the tomatoes.

Ocean's Hot Crab and Artichoke Dip

1 8-ounce package cream cheese, softened

2 6-ounce cans Ocean's Crabmeat with Leg Meat*

1 1/2 cups marinated artichoke hearts, chopped

1/2 cup mayonnaise

1 cup grated Parmesan or mozzarella cheese

1/4 cup finely chopped red bell pepper

1/4 cup finely chopped yellow bell pepper

Baguette, crackers or raw vegetables

1. In a medium casserole, blend cream cheese, crab, artichokes, mayonnaise, cheese and peppers until creamy.

2. Heat in microwave for 2-3 minutes. Remove and stir. Can also be heated in an ovenproof dish at 350°F for 15-20 minutes, or until hot and bubbly.

3. Serve with sliced baguette, crackers or raw vegetables. Makes 6-8 servings.

Brands may vary by region; substitute a similar product.

Tanimura & Antle

Harvested by hand to ensure consistent size, appearance and quality, Tanimura & Antle lettuce is then packed immediately in the field and shipped within minutes of harvest to cooling facilities to maintain field freshness.

Tanimura & Antle
Chinese Chicken Salad

Shred iceberg lettuce for salads or use whole leaves as wrappers for spring rolls or other mixtures. Wash and dry gently just before using.

1/2 cup red wine vinegar	*1 head Tanimura & Antle iceberg lettuce, thinly shredded*
1 tablespoon dry mustard	
1 tablespoon soy sauce	
3 tablespoons hoisin sauce	*1/2 cup diagonally sliced scallions*
1 tablespoon hot chili oil	
1/2 cup toasted sesame oil	*1/2 cup coarsely chopped cilantro*
1/2 cup canola oil	*2 cups fried rice sticks*
4 boneless chicken breasts, marinated in purchased teriyaki sauce, grilled and cut or torn into slivers	*1/4 cup toasted sesame seeds*
	1/4 cup chopped roasted peanuts
	Fresh cilantro sprigs

1. In a mixing bowl, whisk together vinegar, mustard, soy sauce, hoisin sauce and chili oil. Slowly drizzle in sesame and canola oils while continuing to whisk.

2. Toss chicken, lettuce, scallions and cilantro with the dressing. Garnish with rice sticks, sesame seeds and peanuts. Top with cilantro sprigs. Makes 6 servings.

Francoise's Endive and Walnut Salad

8 endives

1/2 cup walnuts

4 tablespoons good-quality oil (chestnut or walnut oil, if possible)

2 tablespoons good-quality red wine vinegar

1 1/2 tablespoons Dijon-style mustard

Salt

Pepper

1. Rinse endive leaves, pat each to dry and cut the leaves into squares. Place in a salad bowl with walnuts.

2. In a separate bowl, combine oil, vinegar, mustard, and salt and pepper to taste, until emulsified.

3. Toss endive and walnuts with dressing. Makes 6 servings.

Francoise Moreau, Ottawa, Ontario

BC Hot House
Tomato Mango Basil Salad

This salad makes a colorful addition to any table with an unusual trio of flavors that work well together.

6 large BC Hot House* tomatoes, sliced 1/2 inch thick

2 large ripe mangoes, peeled and sliced in thin wedges

1 cup packed fresh basil, cut in thin strips, reserving several leaves for garnish

Olive oil

1. Arrange tomatoes in overlapping circles to cover a large round platter.

2. Intersperse mango wedges among tomatoes.

3. Sprinkle with basil. Drizzle with olive oil. Garnish with reserved basil leaves. Makes 10-12 servings.

Brands may vary by region; substitute a similar product.

Marcy's Hungarian Scalloped Potatoes

Marcy Goldman, author of *The Best of BetterBaking.com*, says, "I got this recipe years ago from a cousin who made it to please her Hungarian-born husband when they were first married. It is simply outstanding."

8-10 red potatoes, boiled, cooled and sliced	1/2 cup freshly grated Parmesan cheese
Salt, pepper and paprika	4 scallions, minced fine
2 large spicy dry sausages, diced, about 1 cup	1 cup shredded Cheddar cheese
1 cup sour cream or yogurt	Bread crumbs and/or additional Parmesan for dusting
1/2 cup unsalted butter, melted	
4-6 hard-boiled eggs, crumbled or sliced, optional	1 cup milk

1. Preheat oven to 350°F. Arrange a layer of sliced potatoes in a large casserole. Sprinkle generously with salt, pepper and paprika. Toss on some of the sausage, dollops of sour cream, melted butter, hard-boiled eggs, Parmesan and scallions. Continue layering, ending with potatoes.

2. Sprinkle the final layer with Cheddar, paprika and bread crumbs and/or Parmesan; pour milk through gaps in the dish (this will keep it moist).

3. Bake for about 45 minutes, or until the top is bubbling and golden. Let rest 10 minutes before serving. Freezes well, or make a day ahead and bake when ready to serve. Makes 8-10 servings.

Marcy Goldman, Montreal, Quebec

Money's Mushroom Quiche

Money's mushrooms are canned fresh from the growing houses. The Fresh Pack seal assures you that these mushrooms were packed immediately after harvest.

1 9-inch piecrust	1/2 teaspoon coarsely ground black pepper
2 tablespoons butter	
2 garlic cloves, chopped	1 teaspoon dried tarragon
1 large onion, thinly sliced	3 tablespoons chopped fresh parsley
2 10-ounce cans sliced Money's* mushrooms, drained	2/3 cup whipping cream
	2 eggs
1/2 teaspoon garlic salt	

1. Preheat oven to 400°F. Prick the piecrust bottom all over with a fork. Place a circle of foil or parchment paper on the bottom; cover with dried beans or pastry weights. Bake for 15-20 minutes, or until the fluted edge is golden. Remove paper and weights; continue baking until the bottom is also browning. Lower oven temperature to 325°F.

2. Melt butter in a heavy skillet over low heat; cook garlic, onion and mushrooms for 3-4 minutes, stirring occasionally, or until browned. Spread in the baked crust.

3. Beat together garlic salt, pepper, tarragon, parsley, cream and eggs. Pour over mushroom mixture in crust. Place on a baking sheet; bake for about 40 minutes, or until browned and slightly puffy. Cool for 5 minutes before cutting into wedges. Makes 6 servings.

*Brands may vary by region; substitute a similar product.

FROM THE MEMBERS' KITCHENS

Carol and Diane's Turnip Soup with Maple Syrup

Carol Lambourne and Diane Madill of Edmonton report that this recipe is a favorite with guests. One man asked what kind it was. When they replied, "Turnip," he exclaimed, "This is the lowly turnip?" Yes, this is the lowly turnip—and you will love it!

½ cup butter	3 tablespoons maple syrup
1 medium onion, finely chopped	Salt and pepper
3 garlic cloves, minced	1 cup whipping cream
4 cups diced turnip	Sour cream
8 cups canned chicken broth	Chopped chives

1. Melt butter in a large skillet over low heat; cook onion and garlic until onion is tender but not browned. Add turnips and broth and simmer over low heat for 1 hour, or until turnips are tender.

2. Strain vegetables and puree with 1 cup of the broth in a food processor. Return this to the rest of the broth. Add maple syrup.

3. Season to taste with salt and pepper. Stir in cream and reheat. Serve in bowls with a dollop of sour cream and chopped chives. Makes 6-8 servings.

Sandi Richard, Cochrane, Alberta

FROM THE FOOD PROFESSIONAL

Sandi's Vegetable Tortellini Soup

Sandi Richard, author of *Cooking for the Rushed*, says, "Here's a recipe that's a hit with children and adults alike. It also happens to be very healthy and takes only a few minutes to whip up."

1 medium onion, finely chopped	2 cups frozen mixed vegetables
1 large celery stalk, finely chopped	1 teaspoon crushed red pepper
1 quart chicken broth	1 cup water
1 24.5-ounce jar mushroom-flavor pasta sauce	4-5 cups cheese tortellini
2 teaspoons minced garlic	Grated low-fat Parmesan cheese
2 teaspoons Italian seasoning	Whole-wheat crackers

1. Place onion and celery in the center pot of a slow-cooker. Add chicken broth, pasta sauce, garlic, Italian seasoning, vegetables and crushed red pepper. Pour the water into the empty sauce jar, give it a shake and add it to the pot. Stir, cover and store the center pot overnight in the refrigerator.

2. In the morning, return the center pot to the slow-cooker; cover and set at low heat.

3. In the evening, add tortellini to the pot and set the timer for 15 minutes.

4. Sprinkle each serving with Parmesan and serve with whole-wheat crackers. Makes 4-6 servings.

ENTRÉES

Anne's Grilled Salmon with Citrus, Ginger and Coriander Perfume

Anne Desjardins is the award-winning chef and owner of l'Eau a la Bouche (translated as "mouthwatering" in French), a hotel-restaurant located in St.-Adèle, Quebec.

Grated peel of 1 lime	3 tablespoons minced fresh cilantro, divided
2 teaspoons fresh lime juice	
Grated peel of 1 orange	3 tablespoons minced fresh ginger
2 teaspoons fresh orange juice	Hot pepper sauce
2 tablespoons toasted sesame seeds	Salt
	4 thick 6-ounce salmon fillets
2 scallions, minced, divided	Coarse sea salt

1. Mix together lime peel and juice, orange peel and juice, sesame seeds, half of the scallions, half of the coriander, ginger, hot pepper sauce and salt to taste. Marinate salmon fillets in half the mixture for 1 hour in the refrigerator.

2. Grill over medium-high heat on a micro-perforated aluminum plate without turning fillets, basting with the rest of the marinade mixture, until the internal temperature is 145°F.

3. Sprinkle fillets with sea salt and garnish with remaining scallions and cilantro. Makes 4 servings.

Anne Desjardins, St.-Adèle, Quebec

Mary Lou Green, Teeswater, Ontario

Mary Lou's Stuffed Sole

8 scallions, chopped	1/2 cup freshly grated Parmesan cheese
4 tablespoons butter, divided	
8 ounces baby shrimp	Salt and pepper
8 ounces crabmeat	2 pounds sole fillets
2 tablespoons bread crumbs	Butter, cut in small pieces
1/2 cup crushed crackers	

1. Preheat oven to 350°F. Cook scallions in 1 tablespoon butter in a large skillet over medium heat until translucent. Stir in shrimp and crab; remove.

2. Mix bread crumbs, crackers and Parmesan in a large bowl. Season to taste with salt and pepper.

3. Melt remaining butter in the same skillet over low heat; turn off the heat. Dip each fillet in butter and then in crumbs.

4. Spoon shrimp mixture on top of each fillet. Roll up fillets and place in a buttered baking dish. Sprinkle with the remaining crumbs and dot with butter. Bake for 20-30 minutes, or until the crumbs are toasted and the fish flakes. Makes 6-8 servings.

Anne's Pork Tenderloin with Spices and Maple Syrup

This recipe is just as delicious with chicken.

1 tablespoon sunflower oil	8 drops of hot pepper sauce or more
2 tablespoons balsamic vinegar	1 teaspoon blend of star anise powder, ground black pepper and ground pink peppercorns
1 tablespoon apple juice or other fruit juice	
2 tablespoons soy sauce	2 pork tenderloins, about 1 1/4 pounds each
2 small scallions, minced	
1 garlic clove, minced	2 tablespoons maple syrup
1 teaspoon grated fresh ginger	

1. Combine oil, vinegar, apple juice, soy sauce, scallions, garlic, ginger, hot pepper sauce and spice blend. Marinate tenderloins in half of the mixture for at least 2 hours.

2. Grill meat over medium-hot embers until browned and almost done, with an internal temperature of 150°F. Add maple syrup to the remaining marinade and baste the meat, taking care not to let the flames burn it. Makes 4 servings.

Anne Desjardins, St.-Adèle, Quebec

Anne's Mustard and Herb Steak

1 tablespoon vegetable oil	1/2 teaspoon salt
5 tablespoons Dijon-style mustard	4 10-ounce boneless beef strip loins
1 teaspoon balsamic vinegar	Coarse sea salt and freshly ground pepper
2 teaspoons herbes de Provence	

1. Combine oil, mustard, vinegar, herbes de Provence and salt. Brush half of this mixture onto both sides of the meat at least 1 hour before cooking.

2. Sear the meat on both sides over high heat. Continue cooking over a medium flame, brushing with the remaining mustard mixture.

3. Cook meat to 130°F for medium-rare, remove from the grill and set aside for a few minutes before serving. Sprinkle with sea salt and pepper to taste. Makes 4 servings.

DESSERTS

Andrée Lemire, Hull, Quebec

Andrée's Maple Syrup Pie

2 cups brown sugar	Pinch of salt
2 tablespoons all-purpose flour	1 purchased or homemade single 8-inch pie shell, uncooked
1/4 cup heavy cream	
2 eggs, beaten	Whipped cream
1/2 cup maple syrup	

1. Preheat oven to 350°F.

2. Mix brown sugar and flour in a large bowl.

3. Beat in cream, eggs, maple syrup and salt. Pour mixture into pie shell.

4. Bake for 35 minutes, or until the filling is firm and the crust is golden. Serve with whipped cream. Makes 6-8 servings.

Marcy's Country Plum Tart

More a pastry than a pie or tart, this treat impresses everyone and stays fresh-looking and good-tasting for days.

TART PASTRY	1 cup sugar
3 cups all-purpose flour	2 teaspoons fresh lemon juice
1 cup cold unsalted butter, cut into small pieces	1 teaspoon raspberry or plum vinegar
1/2 teaspoon cinnamon	1 teaspoon balsamic vinegar
1/2 cup cold heavy cream	1/8 teaspoon cinnamon
1 tablespoon sugar	1 tablespoon all-purpose flour
1 teaspoon salt	1 tablespoon cornstarch
FILLING	Confectioners' sugar for dusting
2 1/2 pounds small plums, quartered and pitted	

1. For the pastry, combine flour, butter and cinnamon in a large bowl. Using a pastry cutter or your fingers, cut or rub the butter into the flour until the mixture resembles a coarse meal. Make a well in the center and add cream, sugar and salt. Stir to make a rough mass. If the dough seems too dry, add 1 or 2 tablespoons of water.

2. Transfer to a lightly floured surface and knead very gently for a few seconds to smooth out the dough. Pat the dough into a disk and wrap well in plastic. Refrigerate for at least 1 hour or as long as overnight.

3. For the filling, combine all the ingredients in a large bowl and toss to blend.

4. Transfer the dough to a floured surface and divide in half. Wrap one-half in plastic and place in the freezer. Roll out the second half into a 10-inch round to fit the bottom of a lightly greased 9- or 10-inch pie pan; roll out and press the scraps into the sides of the pan and trim the edges.

5. Mound the filling in the pastry shell.

6. Preheat oven to 400°F. Remove the dough from the freezer. Using the large holes of a box grater, shred the dough into a bowl. If the dough is too cold to work with, let it warm for 10-15 minutes. Sprinkle the shredded dough over the fruit.

7. Place the pan on a baking sheet lined with parchment paper and bake for 15 minutes. Lower the oven temperature to 375°F and bake for another 20-30 minutes, or until the juices begin to bubble and the crust is lightly browned. Transfer to a wire rack and let cool completely. Before serving, dust with a very generous shower of confectioners' sugar. Makes 8-10 servings.

Marcy Goldman, Montreal, Quebec

More *than* mole

Variety is the spice in today's Mexican cuisine

EXTRAORDINARILY DIVERSE TOPOGRAPHY *and climate set the stage for Mexican cuisine. Grown in 14 separate vegetation zones ranging from volcano-dotted seas of grass (savannas) to thorny forests of acacia trees pelted by tropical rains, the foods of Mexico speak of endurance. It is here that corn, varietal beans, peanuts, sweet potatoes, squashes, pumpkins, tomatoes, chiles, vanilla and cocoa have taken hold and flourished.*

To the south, the Yucatan Peninsula and the Isthmus of Tehuantepec offer foods wrapped in banana leaves, hot habanero chiles, and seafood such as shark, octopus and red snapper. Farther north, exotic fruits such as mangoes and pomegranates grow. In Puebla, considered the birthplace of Mexican cuisine, the crowning achievements are mole poblano, *a national dish that contains chocolate and chiles, and* chiles en nogada, *which are stuffed with meats,*

fruits and nuts, covered in a walnut cream sauce and topped with pomegranate seeds.

The Pacific coast of Mexico brings shrimp, scallops, cheeses, lemons, limes and rice to the table. The frontier lands bordering the United States and the country's interior high fertile plateaus add the rustic cuisine of the vaqueros (cowboys). The standards here are dishes made with adobado marinades (chiles, spices and vinegar), barbacoa (outdoor-style slow cooking in deep pits), Caesar salads, papitas al ajo (potatoes with garlic), carne asada (grilled beef) and pozole, the famous red, green and white stew representing the colors of the Mexican flag, made with pork, hominy, tomatoes and avocado.

Mexico is also the land where a tortilla—made of corn in the south and wheat in the north—is the bread, plate and spoon. A pot of beans cooking on the back burner is the common denominator everywhere.

Costco's Mexican warehouses now number 23 (see www.costco.com's warehouse locator for information and locations), and more are in the works. Popular food products in the warehouses are the basics of Mexican cuisine: sugar, milk, corn oil, chocolate and canned tuna fish. Also readily available are national favorites such as mole, canned pozole and chiles, frozen tacos, prepared guacamole, Spanish-style rice (paella), bacalao (codfish), romeritos (a pungent herb blended with mole and shrimp), pan de muerto (a traditional round loaf), rosca de reyes (a crown-shaped sweet bread), spicy salsas and fresh chile poblano.

While it is still the custom of most Costco members here to cook Mexican at home and save international cuisine for special-occasion restaurant dining, new food trends are making inroads. Demand is increasing for fresh regional food choices, especially produce, as well as the healthier dietary options of natural and fat-free products and olive oil. ⑩

Campbell's
Poblano Chili Pepper Dip ◀

3 tablespoons cream cheese	2 tablespoons chopped onion
1 14.7-ounce can Campbell's Poblano Chili Pepper Cream*	Salt and pepper
	Tortillas, cut in triangles and fried
Chopped fresh cilantro	Carrot, celery, jícama and cucumber sticks

1. In a bowl, whip cream cheese until soft, then add chili pepper cream and blend thoroughly.

2. Stir in cilantro and onion. Season to taste with salt and pepper.

3. Accompany with tortillas or vegetables. Makes 6 servings.

Available in Mexican markets with imported canned products.

Marine Harvest Salmon Ceviche ▶

1 medium onion, diced	1 1/4 cups freshly squeezed lemon juice
1 1/2 pounds Marine Harvest skinless salmon fillet, diced	3 tablespoons high-quality vegetable oil
1/2 red bell pepper, diced	Salt and pepper
2 green onions, finely chopped	Lemon or lime slices
3 tablespoons finely chopped cilantro	Crackers and hot sauce

1. Place onion in a sieve, sprinkle with salt and let stand for 10 minutes. Rinse onion in boiling water and let cool.

2. In a nonreactive bowl, thoroughly mix salmon, bell pepper, green onions, cilantro, lemon juice, oil, and salt and pepper to taste. Add diced onion. Marinate for at least 4 hours, or preferably overnight, in a cold part of the refrigerator.

3. Garnish with lemon or lime slices. If desired, serve with crackers and hot sauce. Makes 4 servings.

Roberto's Chipotle Shrimp ◀

½ medium onion, chopped	1 7.5-ounce can tomato puree
1 garlic clove, chopped	Salt
1 chipotle pepper, chopped	1 shot of tequila
½ stick margarine, divided	1 pound 23/30-count shrimp

1. Cook onion, garlic and chipotle in half the margarine in a small skillet over medium heat until soft.

2. Stir in tomato puree; season to taste with salt. Add tequila and some water.

3. Cook shrimp in remaining margarine in a large skillet over medium heat until pink. Stir in the sauce to combine. Makes 3-4 servings.

Roberto Cabrera, Mexico City, Mexico D.F.

SOUP

Jesús' Cream of Poblano Soup ▶

5 poblano chiles, roasted, seeded and deflamed, if desired	1 stick butter
	2 tablespoons cornstarch
2 12-ounce cans evaporated milk, divided	4 small summer squashes, finely chopped
1 ½ teaspoons chicken stock powder	Kernels from 2 ears of sweet corn
White pepper	¼ pound Manchego cheese, grated

1. Combine chiles in a blender with 1 can of milk and chicken stock powder. Season to taste with white pepper.

2. Melt butter in a casserole over low heat; add cornstarch and cook, stirring, until it is browned; add the chile mixture, stirring constantly. Add the remaining can of milk, squash and corn. Bring to a boil and simmer, stirring constantly, about 4 minutes, or until corn and squash are tender.

3. Sprinkle with grated cheese. Makes 5 servings.

Tip: If the chiles are too hot for your taste after roasting, boil them, changing the water three times.

Jesús Cabral Valdes, Polanco, Mexico D.F.

Maria's Chili Peppers Stuffed with Sweet Corn ▶

Kernels from 3 ears of corn

3 14-ounce cans condensed milk

5 eggs

1 teaspoon baking powder

1/2 teaspoon salt

10 poblano chiles, roasted and seeded

2 cups cooked pinto beans, seasoned and pureed with a bit of water

Heavy cream

Grated Manchego cheese

1. Combine corn, condensed milk, eggs, baking powder and salt in a blender; puree.

2. Stuff chiles with the corn mixture. Wrap the chiles in foil and steam for 30 minutes, or until the stuffing is firm.

3. Remove the foil and arrange the chiles on a plate; spoon bean sauce over chiles, add a splash of cream and sprinkle with cheese. Makes 10 servings.

Maria de Lourdes Estebanez, Coapa, Mexico D.F.

Mario Díaz Carrillo, Xalapa, Veracruz

Mario's Stuffed Plantains ◀

Easy to prepare, this inexpensive, nutritious dish can be eaten hot or at room temperature. Plantains are usually available worldwide year-round.

4 plantains

1/2 pound crumbled panela cheese (fresh cheese)

All-purpose flour for dredging

Butter or oil

Heavy cream

Cooked white rice

1. Cut unpeeled plaintains in slices. Put in a pot of hot water and bring to a boil. Simmer until soft. Drain and cool.

2. Peel the slices and mash to form a dough; flatten into tortilla shapes with a hand press or with your hands. Sprinkle with cheese and roll up to form a log shape. Pinch the ends closed. Dredge the logs in flour.

3. Cook in hot butter in a large skillet over medium heat until browned. Pour a splash of cream on each log and serve with rice. Makes 4 servings.

Tip: Instead of panela, stuff plantains with chicken, minced meat, beans or cream cheese. Bake instead of frying.

Gabriela's Bacalao Vizcaína (Semi-dry Codfish) ▼

1 pound salt cod
(Norway bacalao)

1 cup olive oil, divided

2 garlic cloves,
finely chopped

1 white onion, chopped

1/4 cup chopped parsley

2 cups finely chopped
fresh tomatoes

2 cups canned tomato puree

Salt and pepper

1 pound small red potatoes,
baked and peeled

1/2 cup sliced almonds

2 tablespoons capers

1/2 cup pitted green olives

6 yellow chiles,
roasted and chopped

1/2 cup black raisins

1/2 cup chopped canned
red bell pepper

White bread

1. Soak fish overnight in 1/2 gallon of water, changing the water several times. Drain and simmer fish in water, uncovered, for 15 minutes. Cool in the water. Crumble the fish, removing the bones.

2. In a large pan, heat 1/2 cup olive oil over medium heat; add the fish and cook, stirring, for 5 minutes. Transfer to a paper-towel-lined plate; cover with foil to keep warm. In the same pan, heat the remaining oil over medium heat. Add garlic and onions; cook, stirring, until tender, about 5 minutes. Add parsley and cook about 2 minutes more.

3. Add tomatoes and tomato puree; cook, stirring, for 2 minutes. Season to taste with salt and pepper. Reduce the heat to low and cook, stirring occasionally, for 20 minutes.

4. Add fish, potatoes, almonds, capers, olives, yellow chiles, raisins and red bell peppers. Reduce the heat to low, cover and simmer about 20 minutes. Serve with white bread. Makes 4 servings.

Gabriela Mendoza, Mexico City, Mexico D.F.

Mexican Ingredients

Adobo sauce: A paste or sauce made from chile peppers, vinegar and other seasonings.

Ancho chile pepper: The sweetest of the dried chiles and the most popular for its rich, earthy flavor. Frequently combined with other chiles to make mole sauces, it is the dried version of poblano.

Chipotle chile pepper: A ripe (and red) jalapeño pepper that has been dried by smoking over mesquite wood, giving a distinctive flavor to many dishes. It is frequently found canned in adobo sauce.

Chorizo: A spicy fresh pork sausage typically used in small quantities in beans, eggs, soup and paella. Spanish chorizo differs from the Mexican version in that it is smoked and typically seasoned with smoked paprika.

Guajillo chile pepper: One of the most commonly used chiles in salsa, sauces, soups and stews, valued for its distinctive fruity, berry flavor. It is the dried version of mirasol.

Jalapeño chile pepper: A well-known pepper that can be used raw when green or when fully ripened and red. It is also used roasted in cooking. Ripened and dried jalapeños are called chipotles.

Longaniza: A spicy pork sausage made in all Hispanic countries that can be fresh or smoked. Spelling variations include longganisa, linguisa and linguica.

Manchego cheese: Nutty, golden, semi-firm sheep's milk cheese served as a snack or dessert with fruit or quince paste; it's also good for cooking.

Panela cheese: A fresh, crumbly cheese similar to Greek feta that is sprinkled in salads, tacos and burritos and is used in cooking.

Pasilla chile pepper: A dried chile with a rich, hot flavor that is generally ground and used for sauces. It is also used in its fresh form, chilaca.

Poblano chile pepper: A dark green chile with a mild to hot flavor. It is most commonly used for stuffing because of the thickness of the flesh, but is also found in sauces. Ripe red poblanos are dried and are then called ancho.

El Monterey Mexican Grill
Charbroiled Chicken Quesadillas ▶

3/4 cup heavy cream

1 8-ounce can refried beans

1/2 cup red chile/enchilada sauce – tomato-free

1 1/2 tablespoons chicken base

1/2 teaspoon ground cumin

2 cups shredded iceberg lettuce

1/2 cup shredded green cabbage

1/4 cup shredded red cabbage

4 green onions, thinly sliced

1/4 cup cilantro leaves, thinly sliced

5 El Monterey* Mexican Grill Charbroiled Chicken Quesadillas**

2 Roma tomatoes, chopped

1 large avocado, peeled and cubed

1 cup shredded cotija cheese

1. Combine cream, beans, chile/enchilada sauce, chicken base and cumin in a blender. Blend until creamy. Cook in a saucepan over medium heat, stirring occasionally, or in the microwave, covered, for 2 minutes.

2. Mix lettuce, cabbage, green onions and cilantro in a bowl.

3. Cook quesadillas in a lightly greased pan on medium heat, flipping frequently with a spatula, until golden brown. Arrange on a serving plate.

4. Unfold the hot quesadillas enough to spoon bean sauce onto the chicken and cheese filling; next add the lettuce mixture, tomatoes and avocado. Sprinkle with generous amounts of shredded cheese. Makes 5 servings.

*Brands may vary by region; substitute a similar product.
**1 (35-ounce) package of El Monterey Mexican Grill Charbroiled Chicken Quesadillas contains 10 quesadillas.

Eugenia Pulido, Mexico City, Mexico D.F.

Mishel's Beef Tinga ◀

1/4 pound chorizo sausage, chopped

1 onion, chopped

1 pound loin of beef, boiled and shredded

3 pickled chipotle chiles, chopped, sauce reserved

Salt and pepper

12 tostadas (flat, crisp corn tortillas)

1. Cook chorizo and onion in a large skillet over medium heat until the onion is softened and the sausage is cooked thoroughly.

2. Stir in beef and the chipotles with a bit of the sauce. Season to taste with salt and pepper. Arrange on top of tostadas. Makes 6 servings.

Gabriela's Valenciana Paella ▸

½ cup olive oil

4 chicken thighs

4 pork loin chops

6 chorizo

5 breakfast sausage links

¼ cup chopped onion

1 tablespoon chopped garlic

⅓ pound squid

¼ cup tomato puree

1 teaspoon paprika

6 clams

¼ pound peas

¼ pound green beans

¼ pound red bell pepper, cut in slices

7 cups water

½ cup red wine

1 tablespoon powdered chicken broth

1 tablespoon powdered fish broth

1 tablespoon garlic powder

1 tablespoon onion powder

1 tablespoon celery powder

⅛ teaspoon Spanish saffron

1 pound rice

4 New Zealand mussels

7 26/30-count shrimp, without heads

1. In a paella pan or large skillet, heat olive oil over medium heat; cook chicken, pork, chorizo and breakfast sausage until browned on all sides. Add chopped onion and garlic. Cook until softened.

2. Add squid and cook for 8 minutes, stirring constantly. Add tomato puree and paprika; cook for 10 minutes more. Add clams, peas, green beans and bell pepper.

3. Stir in water and wine and heat to a simmer; stir in powdered chicken and fish broth and garlic, onion and celery powders. Stir in saffron. Stir in rice. Simmer for 15 minutes.

4. Place mussels and shrimp on top.

5. Reduce heat to low; cover and simmer for about 40 minutes, or until rice is tender. Makes 6 servings.

Gabriela Mendoza, Mexico City, Mexico D.F.

Diego's Hunger Killer (Matahambre) ▶

Oil

2 pounds pork loin chops

Garlic salt

Black pepper

2 pounds spicy pork
    sausage (longaniza),
    removed from casing

1 pound potatoes, half-boiled,
    coarsely chopped

3 sweet red peppers,
    seeded and chopped

1 onion, coarsely chopped

1 pound grated Edam cheese

Chopped jalapeño peppers

1. Heat oil in a large ovenproof skillet over medium heat; cook pork until lightly browned. Cool slightly and cut into small cubes; season to taste with garlic salt and black pepper. Drain the fat from the pan.

2. Add sausage, potatoes, red peppers and onion to the skillet; cook over medium heat until the vegetables are soft. Stir in the pork cubes.

3. Sprinkle cheese on top; broil until cheese melts. Sprinkle with jalapeños to taste.
Makes 6-12 servings.

Diego Rodrigo Díaz de la Fuente, Xalapa, Veracruz

High Praise for Pozole

In the Nahuatl language, pozolli means froth. When the largest and whitest maize (corn) grains (called cacahuazintle) are boiled, they open like flowers, forming froth. This way of cooking maize is pre-Hispanic, with a somewhat gory origin. As narrated by Fray Bernardino de Sahagún in his General History of Things in New Spain (Historia General de las Cosas de la Nueva España), during festivities honoring the god Xipe, Moctezuma was sent a pozole containing the thigh of a sacrificed prisoner.

In our times, pozole is a dish found throughout Mexico. It is served in many restaurants and prepared in every home. Considered an infallible hangover remedy, it is a predawn classic for revelers that no longer requires human sacrifice.

David's Poultry and Pork Red Pozole ▶

David Carlos Stanton, Aguascalientes, Aguascalientes

1 6.6-pound can
    Teasdale pozole corn

1 large onion, chopped

1 head garlic, chopped

¼ cup chicken stock powder

Salt

2.2 pounds Kirkland
    Signature pork loin, cut
    in 1-inch pieces

4 chicken breasts

4 ancho chiles

4 guajillo chiles

Lime wedges, chopped
    pequín chiles, sliced
    radishes, coarsely
    chopped onion,
    oregano and tostadas

1. Rinse pozole corn in cold water, place in a large pot and cover with water. Add onion, garlic, chicken stock powder and salt and bring to a boil; simmer about 30 minutes.

2. Add pork and chicken; simmer until tender.

3. Remove meat, shred and return to the pot.

4. In a small pot, boil ancho and guajillo chiles in water to cover for 30 minutes, or until they color the water slightly red. Remove the veins and seeds and puree in a blender with enough of the pozole water to make a sauce. Pour the sauce into the pozole until it colors a little red, or to your taste.

5. Season to taste with salt. Pass seasonings and garnishes at the table: lime wedges, pequín chiles, radishes, chopped onion, oregano and tostadas. Makes 6-12 servings.

Gaspar's Adobado Pork Loin ▶

2 large garlic cloves	1 medium onion, cut in quarters
40 black peppercorns	4 pasilla chiles, seeded
Salt	1 tablespoon vinegar
2 pounds Kirkland Signature pork loin, cut in 1-inch cubes	1 teaspoon dried thyme
Oil	1 teaspoon dried sweet marjoram
1 quart milk	1 bay leaf
1 tomato, cut in quarters	Cooked red rice

1. Puree garlic and peppercorns with a pinch of salt in a food processor. Toss with pork cubes. Cook in a pressure cooker or on a stove top over low heat for 30 minutes, or until no longer pink.

2. Heat a small amount of oil in a large skillet over medium heat and cook the pork cubes until golden; remove pork from the skillet.

3. Add milk to the skillet, stirring to remove all the brown bits from the bottom. Add tomato, onion, chiles, vinegar, thyme, marjoram and bay leaf.

4. Cover the skillet and cook over low heat for 10 minutes, or until the vegetables are tender. Season to taste with salt. Puree in a food processor.

5. Drizzle over the pork cubes. Taste and adjust the seasonings. Serve with red rice. Makes 4 servings.

Gaspar Zamora Armenta, Celaya, Guanajuato

DESSERT

Gabriela Estebanez, Coapa, Mexico, D.F.

Gabriela's Cheese Flan ◀

1 12-ounce can evaporated milk	1 8-ounce package cream cheese
1 14-ounce can condensed milk	1/2 cup sugar
5 eggs	2 tablespoons water

1. Puree evaporated milk, condensed milk, eggs and cream cheese in a blender.

2. Brown the sugar with the water in a heavy pan over low heat to obtain a clear caramel; pour the melted sugar into a flat flan can.

3. Pour the milk mixture over the sugar in the can and cover with foil. Cook over barely simmering water in a double boiler for 45-60 minutes, or until set; or bake at 325°F in a water bath for 1 hour, or until set.

4. Unmold the flan onto a plate. Makes 6-8 servings.

Pub food *to* pudding

UK *cuisine favors commonsense comfort food*

AN EMPIRE OF EXTRAORDINARY *culinary offerings is an apt description for the lands of England, Wales, Scotland and Northern Ireland. It is here that teas and chutneys from Ceylon (Sri Lanka) share the kitchen with Indian mulligatawny (curried) soup, Scottish haggis (stuffed sheep's stomach), roast beef and Yorkshire pudding, steamed Sussex pond pudding, Stilton cheese and Cumberland sauce.*

The Brits, full of practicality, tradition and passion for savory delights, steer their palates toward wholesome tender meats, fresh fish and seasonal vegetables. The irregular, craggy coastline and numerous rivers and lakes offer a plethora of finfish such as cod, haddock, whiting, herring (preferably salted and smoked for kippers), sole, salmon, pike, perch and trout as well as lobster, crab, clams, mussels, oysters and scallops. Beef, most notably Aberdeen Angus, lamb, wild game, poultry, new potatoes, tiny peas, young carrots, cucumbers, onions, parsnips, cabbage, cereals, cheeses and fruits such as berries and apples round out the basic pantry. Not to be forgotten are English ales and Scottish whiskies.

The best known and best loved of all English gastronomic and social institutions is afternoon tea time, generally from 4 to 6 p.m. There's nothing more uniquely tied to England than this daily custom, whether it's just pausing for a simple cup of tea and a cucumber sandwich or gathering with friends for a spread of petite thinly sliced sandwiches, delicate cakes and pastries, scones, butter, jams, marmalade, lemon curd, clotted cream and berries served on china—always accompanied by a pot of tea.

The English and Scottish Costcos (see www.costco.com's locator for information and locations) are finely tuned to the desires of their members. Very popular at the moment are the ready-to-cook meals, as well as locally produced food, particularly in the fresh categories, and olive oil. Costco's prepared foods speak of international cuisine with a typically British flair. Look for lamb shanks, pork Normandy, beef bourguignon, sausage and mash, and mild curry dishes such as lamb rogan josh and chicken korma.

Of course, food diversity abounds within United Kingdom Costcos. Find haggis, sliced sausage meat and Scotch pies in Scotland's warehouses, red hard cheese (as opposed to white) in warehouses in the north of England, Banks's bitter beer in the Birmingham Costco, and mushy peas (canned) in Leeds. Also not to be missed is spotted dick (a suet pudding with sultanas and raisins), mince pies (a sweet mix of dried fruit usually served in a puff pastry case), chicken tikka massala (a mild curry dish that actually originated in the United Kingdom), sausage rolls (seasoned sausage meat inside a puff pastry case), Wensleydale (a moist, crumbly cheese made for Costco in a small region of Derbyshire) and Marmite (a concentrated yeast extract paste).

Costco basics are also big sellers, with fresh Kirkland Signature chicken breasts, ground beef, Scottish sirloin steak and lamb chump steaks, lagers, beer and granulated sugar rounding out the warehouses' top 10 food and beverage list. Just don't expect to find corn dogs, flavored bagels or cinnamon rolls. |◎|

Rita's Asparagus and Red Pepper Vol-au-Vents ▼

4 red bell peppers, roasted, peeled and seeded

1 medium onion, chopped

Olive oil

2 garlic cloves, chopped

6 ounces vegetable stock

8 fresh asparagus spears

1 packet puff pastry

1 egg, beaten

4 slices bacon, chopped and cooked crisp

Lemon juice

1. Preheat oven to 350°F. Cut peppers into quarters and reserve the best 8 pieces.

2. Cook onion in olive oil in a large skillet over medium heat until soft; stir in garlic and 8 pieces of pepper. Puree; return to the skillet and stir in vegetable stock. Simmer for 10-15 minutes.

3. Blanch asparagus in boiling water for 1 minute. Before assembly, grill to warm and make grill marks.

4. Roll out pastry and cut into 4 circles 4 inches in diameter; cut 4 more circles 1 1/2 inches in diameter. Brush with beaten egg. Place on a baking sheet and bake for 15 minutes, or until golden brown.

5. To assemble, place a large pastry round on a serving plate; spoon a little sauce on top. Add 2 pieces of reserved red pepper, 2 asparagus spears, another spoonful of sauce and bacon. Top with a small pastry circle. Drizzle olive oil and lemon juice decoratively around the plate. Makes 4 servings.

Rita Carter, Bedford, Bedfordshire

Marine Harvest Salmon Mousse ▲

Marine Harvest is the largest producer and supplier of farmed salmon and a pioneer in research and development in the farming of new species.

1 cup milk

1 small onion, sliced, divided

1 medium carrot, sliced, divided

2 bay leaves, divided

4 black peppercorns, divided

Salt and pepper

1/4 cup white wine

1 tablespoon lemon juice

12 ounces Marine Harvest salmon

1 level tablespoon powdered gelatin

2 tablespoons butter

2 tablespoons flour

5 tablespoons mayonnaise

1 cup heavy cream, whipped to soft peaks

Fresh dill

Lemon slices

1. Place milk in a small saucepan with half the onion and carrot, 1 bay leaf and 2 peppercorns. Bring slowly to a boil. Remove from heat, cover and leave to infuse for 30 minutes. Strain milk. Season to taste with salt and pepper.

2. Meanwhile, place the remaining onion and carrot, 1 bay leaf, 2 peppercorns, wine, lemon juice and 5 tablespoons of water in a shallow pan. Bring to a boil and add salmon. Reduce heat, cover salmon with a piece of buttered greaseproof paper and let simmer for 10-15 minutes. Remove poached fish and separate flakes. Let cool.

3. Boil salmon liquor to reduce by half and strain into a bowl. Season to taste with salt and pepper.

4. Sprinkle gelatin into 3 tablespoons cold water.

5. Melt butter in a saucepan and stir in flour. Cook for 1 minute, then gradually stir in the strained milk. Continue cooking, stirring, until the sauce thickens. Stir in the softened gelatin and the salmon liquor and set aside to cool.

6. Carefully stir the flaked salmon into the gelatin mixture. Transfer to a food processor. Add mayonnaise and pulse for a few seconds.

7. Place the salmon mixture in a large bowl and fold in whipped cream. Season to taste with salt and pepper.

8. Pour into a mold lined with oiled plastic wrap; refrigerate for 2 hours, or until set. Unmold and, if desired, garnish with finely chopped fresh dill and lemon slices. Serve with crackers or toast points. Makes 6-8 servings.

Fresh Salmon Tips

Costco's farm-raised Atlantic salmon is a leading seller in warehouses from Korea to Mexico. The reason? These fresh salmon fillets are boneless and skinless, with all pin bones, belly fat and silver skin removed.

Freshness and quality are the key criteria of the Costco Fresh Meat and Fish department, notes seafood expert Jeff Lyons. "We closely control each link in the logistics chain, including the environmental standards of our producers."

"We want only the finest farming technology, combined with the purest waters. This allows us to offer a superior-quality salmon fillet. Only after that do we look at price."

Grilling

Salmon, along with tuna and mackerel, has a high natural oil content that makes it a good choice for grilling.

- ✔ *Select fillets at least 1/2 inch thick for grilling*
- ✔ *Allow 6 to 8 ounces per serving*
- ✔ *Grill over medium heat for gentle cooking without charring*

Leftovers

Cooking a large salmon fillet may result in useful leftovers that will keep for several days properly wrapped in the refrigerator.

- ✔ *Make salmon cakes*
- ✔ *Liven up omelets, quiches, casseroles*
- ✔ *Combine with linguine in cream sauce*
- ✔ *Toss chunks with salad greens in vinaigrette*

FROM THE FOOD PROFESSIONAL

Frank's Pasta e Fagioli ▼

"This is probably my all-time favorite soup," says Frank Bordoni, a professional chef and caterer. It is hearty enough to serve on its own with a chunk of warm Italian-style bread for a main meal. It is an old family recipe that can be eaten hot or cold—perfect for any time of the year!

Olive oil

1 onion, chopped

2 garlic cloves, minced

2 carrots, chopped

1 celery stalk, chopped

1 pinch oregano

2 cups cooked
    borlotti beans*

1 cup finely
    shredded cabbage

1 1/2 quarts vegetable
    stock or more

1 28-ounce can chopped
    plum tomatoes

Salt and pepper

1 pound small dried pasta,
    cooked according to
    package directions

1 tablespoon chopped
    fresh basil

Grated Parmesan cheese

1. Heat olive oil in a large soup pot; cook onion, garlic, carrots and celery over medium heat until vegetables are soft.

2. Stir in oregano, beans and cabbage. Add vegetable stock and tomatoes. Bring soup to a boil and simmer until all the vegetables are thoroughly cooked. Season to taste with salt and pepper.

3. Stir in the cooked pasta. Sprinkle basil and Parmesan on each bowl of soup.

Makes 6-8 servings.

*These Italian beans are tan with red and black streaks and are called cranberry beans in the United States.

Frank Bordoni, Northwood, Middlesex

SIDE DISH

Kamini's Lentil Daal ◀

1/2 cup lentils	4 fresh curry leaves, optional*
Salt	1 cup canned
2 tablespoons oil	chopped tomatoes
1 teaspoon cumin seeds	1 teaspoon curry powder
2 garlic cloves, crushed	1 tablespoon ground coriander
1 teaspoon ground ginger	Cooked basmati rice
1 green chile, minced	or naan bread

1. Simmer lentils with salt in 1 1/2 pints of water in a medium saucepan for 30 minutes, or until soft.

2. Heat oil in a saucepan over medium heat and add cumin seeds. When the seeds start to pop, add garlic, ginger, chile and curry leaves and fry for a few seconds.

3. Stir in tomatoes, curry powder and coriander; simmer for 5 minutes.

4. Stir in lentils; simmer for 5 minutes, or to the thickness desired. Add more boiled water to thin the sauce if necessary. Serve with rice or naan (Indian flat bread). Makes 2-4 servings.

Fresh green curry leaves are available in Indian markets; the dried variety do not add much flavor.

Kamini Shah, Wembley, Middlesex

ENTRÉES

Pam's Lancashire Hot-Pot ▶

2 pounds lamb shoulder blade chops	Salt and pepper
2 onions, sliced	1 1/4 cups stock
1 pound potatoes, peeled and sliced	Oil

1. Preheat oven to 325°F. Trim any excess fat off the chops and place in a casserole. Add onions and potatoes in layers, finishing with potatoes; season well with salt and pepper. Pour in stock and brush potatoes with oil.

2. Cover and bake for 2 hours, or until the meat is tender. Remove the cover, increase the heat to 425°F and bake until potatoes have browned. Makes 4-6 servings.

Pam Broadhurst, Watford, Hertfordshire

Janet Binbasii, Bushey, Hertfordshire

Janet's Steak and Kidney Pie

8 ounces lamb, pig
   or ox kidney, cut in
   1-inch cubes

2 pounds stewing steak,
   cut in 1-inch chunks

2 tablespoons flour

3 tablespoons oil

1 large onion, chopped

1/2 cup red wine

1/4 cup beef stock

1 tablespoon
   Worcestershire sauce

Salt and pepper

PIE CRUST

3/4 cup flour

Pinch of salt

1/4 cup lard or shortening

1/4 cup margarine

2 tablespoons or
   more cold water

1 egg, beaten with water

1. Coat kidneys and steak in flour. Heat oil in a large flameproof casserole over medium heat, add meat to the pan a few pieces at a time and cook until browned all over. Remove the pieces as they brown, adding more oil if required.

2. When all the meat is browned, reduce the heat and add onion to the pan; cook until it is almost tender, stirring occasionally.

3. Stir in wine, stock, Worcestershire sauce and browned meat and bring to a boil. Reduce heat, cover and simmer for 2 hours, or until the meat is tender. Season to taste with salt and pepper.

4. Sift 3/4 cup flour and salt into a large bowl. Cut fat into small pieces and add it and the margarine to the flour. Rub into the flour between the fingertips until the mixture looks like fine bread crumbs; add water and stir with a round-bladed knife until the dough begins to stick together in lumps. Wrap the pastry in parchment paper and refrigerate for at least 30 minutes.

5. Preheat oven to 400°F. Spoon the meat into a 9-by-2-inch pie dish and place a pie funnel* in the center.

6. Roll the pastry out into a circle 2 inches larger than the dish; cover the pie dish with the pastry and trim; brush the pastry with egg and water; make a slit in the center with a knife to let steam escape.

7. Bake for about 40 minutes, or until the crust is golden brown and the filling is hot. Makes 6 servings.

*A pie funnel or pie bird is a baker's tool that lets steam escape from a piecrust and helps hold up the crust.

Anytime for Lamb

Costco is converting more and more members into lamb fans by offering a good selection of top-quality cuts that fit the times, notes Costco vice president Charlie Winters. Lamb is delicious, different and easy to cook.

✔ Chops are real fast food, cooking in minutes on the grill or stove top.

✔ Rack of lamb is a celebration feast that cooks remarkably quickly on the grill or in the oven.

✔ Leg of lamb requires roasting in the oven, which takes a little longer, but it feeds a crowd.

✔ Boneless leg unfurled, or butterflied, is perfect for grilling medium-rare.

✔ Shoulder chops are brilliant in a slow-cooker.

Lamb is also versatile. It is at home with the flavors of many cuisines. If you're in the mood for Mediterranean, rosemary and garlic seem to have been created to go with lamb. It's the same with Indian curries or Southwestern American chili. Classic Sunday dinner with rice and dried-fruit accents is always another option for lamb.

Asian-Australian Barbecue

Here's another international cooking idea from Australia, where homegrown, grass-fed lamb is plentiful and gaining recognition around the world for taste and tenderness.

Grill loin chops over high heat for about 2 minutes on each side, or until they begin to turn brown. Baste with an Asian-style sauce made with equal parts soy sauce and peanut oil seasoned with grated fresh ginger and sugar. Cook the chops for about 2 minutes more on each side, or until the internal temperature is 130°F, for medium-rare. Serve with more sauce on the side.

Smucker's Strawberry Tarts ◄

Smucker's has been bringing you the goodness of jams, jellies and preserves for more than 100 years. Create your own dessert by using your favorite flavor for this recipe. As you've no doubt heard, "With a name like Smucker's, it has to be good."

12 unbaked 3-inch pastry shells	1/4 teaspoon almond extract
2 eggs, well beaten	1 cup Smucker's* Strawberry Preserves
2 cups sour cream	Toasted slivered almonds
1/2 teaspoon vanilla extract	

1. Preheat oven to 350°F. Place pastry shells on a cookie sheet.

2. Combine eggs, sour cream and vanilla and almond extracts; blend well. Fold in Smucker's Strawberry Preserves.

3. Spoon filling into pastry shells. Sprinkle tops with almonds.

4. Bake for 25-30 minutes, or until the filling is set. When cool, refrigerate at least 2 hours before serving. Makes 12 servings.

Brands may vary by region; substitute a similar product.

Frank's Cherry Clafouti ▶

This is a traditional French dessert, best served warm so that the full flavor of the cherries comes through. In winter, pears or apples can be used instead.

Homemade or purchased pastry for 9-inch pie pan or tart pan with a removable bottom	3 ounces milk
	3 ounces heavy cream
	1 teaspoon vanilla extract
1/2 cup sugar	1 tablespoon kirsch
4 large eggs	1 pound ripe fresh cherries, stemmed and pitted

1. Preheat oven to 400°F. Roll out the pastry on a lightly floured surface; place it in a lightly greased 9-inch pan. Bake for 15 minutes.

2. Place sugar, eggs, milk, cream, vanilla and kirsch in a large bowl and mix thoroughly.

3. Arrange cherries in the prebaked pastry; pour the egg mixture over the cherries.

4. Bake for 20-25 minutes, or until the filling is lightly golden and set. Makes 6-8 servings.

Frank Bordoni, Northwood, Middlesex

Walkers Scottish Flan ◀

2 packets (5.3-ounce) Walkers* Shortbread Cookies	3 cups raspberries, divided
	1 cup blueberries, divided
¼ cup almonds, finely chopped	1 cup heavy cream
	½ cup sour cream
½ teaspoon cinnamon	1 tablespoon confectioners' sugar
1 stick (½ cup) unsalted butter, melted	1 tablespoon brown sugar, optional

1. Crush shortbread in a food processor or a strong plastic bag. Place in a bowl and mix with almonds, cinnamon and butter. Press firmly onto the bottom and sides of a 10-inch tart pan with a removable bottom. Refrigerate for at least an hour.

2. Carefully remove the bottom of the tart pan and place on a serving plate; scatter half the raspberries and blueberries over the shortbread crust.

3. Whip cream until it stands in soft peaks; stir in sour cream and confectioners' sugar. Spoon over berries.

4. Scatter remaining berries over the cream and sprinkle with brown sugar. Serve immediately or store in the refrigerator for a few hours. Makes 6 servings.

Note: Flan can also be prepared in a 10-inch baking dish and sliced to serve.

Brands may vary by region; substitute a similar product.

Pam's Jam Sponge Pudding ▶

½ cup butter or margarine, softened	Few drops of vanilla extract
½ cup superfine* sugar	¾ cup self-rising flour
2 eggs, beaten	2 tablespoons jam
1 tablespoon milk	Custard sauce

1. Cream together butter and sugar until pale; add eggs, milk and vanilla a little at a time and beat well.

2. Sift half the flour into the mixture and fold in with a large spoon; sift and fold in the rest of the flour.

3. Spread the jam in the bottom of a greased 4-cup mold or small casserole; spoon the pudding mixture on top of the jam; cover with parchment paper and tie in place with string.

4. Place the mold in a large saucepan half full of boiling water, cover and steam for 1½ hours. Turn the pudding onto a warm plate and serve with custard sauce. Makes 4-6 servings.

Pulse granulated sugar in a food processor several times to make it superfine.

Pam Broadhurst, Watford, Hertfordshire

Tastes of tradition

Sweet and savory add spice to the mystical East

SOUTH KOREA IS A COUNTRY of cold, dry winters, hot, rainy summers, spiny mountainous terrain and deeply indented coastlines. The people, descendants of the hardy Mongolian race, have had to learn to adapt, which is why the land's cuisine is dominated by rice, hearty vegetables and grains, and a large variety of seafood.

Three quintessential ingredients, three essential sauces and seven palate sensations best describe this healthy, low-fat cuisine. Garlic, green onions and hot peppers are almost always present. They are most commonly offered in the form of kimchi, a spicy-hot fermented condiment made of vegetables such as napa cabbage, Korean radish and/or cucumber, plus hot chili and garlic.

Sauces center on kanjang (soy sauce), toenjang (fermented soybean paste) and kochujang (red hot pepper paste). Palate sensations encountered during a traditional meal, most particularly dinner, include: 1) Hot to burning hot, from the liberal use of hot peppers; 2) Sweet, from grain syrups and fruits; 3) Salty, most commonly from soy

sauce or salt; 4) Sour, from grain vinegars, herbs and certain fruits; 5) Bitter, from ginger, ginseng, berries, seeds and certain vegetables and herbs; 6) Astringent, from unripe persimmon; and 7) Nutty, from pine nuts, chestnuts, walnuts, ginkgo nuts or sunflower, pumpkin or sesame seeds.

The sea is an abundant resource, offering fish of all shapes and sizes, squid, octopus, clams, crabs, oysters, mussels, seaweed and kelp.

Noodle or one-dish meals such as bibimbap (steamed rice with assorted vegetables) can be served for lunch or special occasions. Stews such as tchim (braised dishes), jeongol (hot-pot dish served in broth and traditionally cooked in a casserole on a fire at the dining table) and kui (grilled dishes) are popular side dishes. Bulgogi, made of thin strips of marinated, grilled beef (sometimes chicken, pork or octopus is substituted for beef and prepared in a spicy sauce such as kochujang), is considered Korea's signature dish, as is pajon, a scallion pancake. Bap (steamed rice) is usually presented as part of the main course, often acting as a buffer for spicier dishes. After the meal, tea or fruits are served.

Costco shoppers will find a plentiful supply of basic items for a Korean meal in all warehouses, as well as a vast array of foods from other lands. (See www.costco.com's warehouse locator for information and location of all South Korea warehouses.)

Top South Korea Costco warehouse items are meat, rice and flatfish sashimi. Other popular products are mixed grains, frozen dumplings, Chinese cabbage, ramen and kimchi. All vegetables are 100 percent domestic. On the rise are fast and easily prepared foods, as well as imported items such as seedless grapes, oranges, pure fruit juices, olive oil, mixed grains, clam chowder, spaghetti sauce, cheese, chocolate and health foods. Not to be overlooked are Costco's own private label Kirkland Signature items such as extra-fancy mixed nuts, walnuts, meats and variety muffins. And of course you'll always find Costco's famous hot dog and soda! 〖◉〗

Donna's Kimchi Chee Gai ◄

Donna's husband, Fritz, who served two years in the military in Korea, taught her to make this dish.

1 tablespoon dark sesame oil	1 12-ounce package extra-firm tofu, cubed
1 teaspoon toasted sesame seeds	1/2 cup cold water
	Cooked rice
1/2 pound boneless pork, cut in 1/2-inch cubes	Seaweed, optional*
1 14-ounce jar kimchi*	

1. Combine oil, sesame seeds and pork in a 2-quart saucepan. Cook over medium heat until pork is no longer pink inside.

2. Stir in kimchi, tofu and water. Simmer, covered, for 1-3 hours. The mixture will not thicken; the flavor will be richer the longer it cooks. Serve over rice. Makes 4 servings.

Serving Variation: Mix with rice and wrap in toasted seaweed. To toast the seaweed on a gas stove, skim it over the flame at medium heat.

Kimchi and seaweed are available at Asian grocery stores or in the produce section of many specialty stores.

Donna Krieser, Overgaard, Arizona

Hee's Radish Ramen ►

This soup is simple enough to prepare quickly and is surprisingly delicious.

5 slices daikon radish	1 teaspoon chopped spring onion
1 package ramen noodles	

1. Cut radish slices into narrow strips.

2. Cover radishes with water and bring to a boil in a medium saucepan over high heat.

3. Stir in ramen; cook until tender; add spring onion. Makes 1 serving.

Hee Jung, Seoksong-ri, Jeonan-myeon, Gongju

FROM THE MEMBER'S KITCHEN

Hee's Hot Pepper and Radish Kimchi ◀

Hee Jung says, "Although its origin remains unclear, this is a very special and fresh summer dish that came to be on our table. Relatives visit our home just to taste it." While working on the tough decision of which bulgogi was the tastiest, the *Cooking the Costco Way*'s tasters in the U.S. found this recipe to be a refreshing palate cleanser.

1 large daikon radish, about 7 ounces, grated	2 teaspoons sugar
	1 teaspoon salt
1 teaspoon minced garlic	MSG
1 tablespoon shredded spring onions	2.2 pounds unripe hot peppers, sliced open, stemmed and seeded
1 tablespoon shredded carrots	
1 tablespoon shredded leeks	

1. Mix daikon, garlic, spring onions, carrots and leeks with sugar. Add salt and MSG to taste.

2. Stuff the peppers with mixed vegetables.

3. Put into a kimchi container.* Add filtered water equal to 1 1/2 times the volume of ingredients.

4. Mature for 1 or 2 days at room temperature before refrigerating. Makes enough for 1 week.

*A kimchi container is a large nonreactive container, a ceramic crock or glass jar.

Hee Jung, Seoksong-ri, Jeonan-myeon, Gongju

Hae-Kyeong Kim, Nokbeon-dong, Eunpyeong-gu, Seoul

FROM THE MEMBER'S KITCHEN

Hae-Kyeong's Beef Roasted on an Iron Plate ▲

Butter	2 king oyster mushrooms*, sliced
1 pound beef, sliced thin	1 7-ounce package green bean sprouts
4 ounces scallops	
1 potato, sliced	Black pepper
1 onion, sliced	Steak sauce, mustard or salt and sesame oil
1 green bell pepper, sliced	
1 7-ounce package winter (enoki) mushrooms, sliced	

1. Put a pat of butter in a heated large frying pan.

2. Add beef, scallops, potato, onion, green pepper and mushrooms, stirring rapidly.

3. Add sprouts; cover and cook over medium heat until vegetables are crisp-tender. Season with black pepper to taste. Serve with steak sauce, mustard or salt and sesame oil. Makes 4 servings.

*King (eryngii) oyster mushrooms are a tasty large cultivated variety of the oyster family with firm, meaty texture and a tender stem that is valued, not discarded.

FROM THE
COSTCO
Meat
EXPERT

Best Beef for Korean Cooking

To be successful with recipes that feature thinly sliced beef cooked quickly over high heat, Costco meat buyer Doug Holbrook suggests naturally tender cuts such as:

✔ Rib-eye steak
✔ Beef tenderloin tip
✔ Chuck-eye roll
✔ New York strip steak
✔ Tri-tip

The most economical cut to use with these recipes is tri-tip. It is easier to slice meat thin when it is partially frozen. Wrap it carefully in plastic and freeze for 1-2 hours, or until firm but not frozen solid.

Slicing meat across the grain will make any cut seem more tender because it shortens the meat fibers. Meat cut with the grain will seem chewy.

The secret of bulgogi, the famous Korean meat dish, is in the marinade. Costco selected CJ, maker of the best-selling bulgogi sauce in Korea, to introduce their product to the U.S. market. It works well with beef, pork or chicken. Use it as a marinade or basting sauce for a rich barbecue flavor with Asian flair.

CJ Korean Bulgogi (Barbecued Beef) ▶

This is a rendition of the Korean favorite by the maker of a popular sauce.

1 1/4 pounds beef loin (chuck roast or chuck eye roll)	1 cup or more Bulgogi Korean Sauce of CJ*
1/4 cup thinly sliced leek	Vegetable oil
1/2 cup finely chopped onion	1 teaspoon toasted sesame oil
2 tablespoons thinly sliced oyster mushroom	

1. Slice beef into pieces about 1/8 inch thick. Combine beef, leek, onion and mushrooms with bulgogi sauce; set aside for 30 minutes.

2. Heat oil to hot in a large skillet over high heat; add the beef mixture, stirring rapidly to cook quickly. Stir in sesame oil. Makes 4 servings.

*Brands may vary by region; substitute a similar product.

Elliott's Korean Barbecue (Bulgogi)

Here is a new American version of the Korean classic. This old family recipe started with a grandmother in Korea, was passed on to a mother who lives in Hawaii and has been refined by Californians Elliott Lum and his wife, Linda, over the years. They report great results with the tri-tip roasts from Costco.

1 1/3 cups soy sauce	2 stalks green onion, finely chopped
3/4 cup sugar	
1/2 cup toasted sesame oil	3 inches or more fresh ginger, peeled, sliced and finely chopped
2 tablespoons toasted sesame seeds	
1/2 teaspoon black pepper	4 pounds tri-tip roast, sliced across the grain in 3/16-inch slices
2 tablespoons chopped garlic	
	Rice and kimchi

1. Combine soy sauce, sugar, oil, sesame seeds, pepper, garlic, onion and ginger in a bowl, stirring until sugar is dissolved.

2. Put the sauce in a 1-gallon resealable freezer bag. Add the meat in batches, massaging the bag before adding more to ensure uniform marination. Refrigerate for 3-8 hours, turning the bag over several times.

3. Grill the slices for a few minutes on each side over medium heat. Test the first few samples to ensure that the meat is cooked but not overcooked.

4. Serve with rice and kimchi as an entrée. Makes 8-10 servings.

Tip: Thread on skewers for grilling to serve as an appetizer.

Elliott Lum, Carlsbad, California

Jung-Min's Clam Curry Rice

2-4 tablespoons curry powder	1 onion, cut in 1/2-inch cubes
Vegetable oil	1 carrot, cut in 1/2-inch cubes
Butter	1 green bell pepper, seeded and cut in 1/2-inch cubes
1 tablespoon crushed garlic	
1/4 cup clam meat, rinsed in salt water and drained	1 hot red pepper, seeded and cut in 1/2-inch cubes
2 potatoes, cut in 1/2-inch cubes	Cooked rice

1. Mix curry powder to taste with enough water to make a thin paste, stirring until there are no lumps.

2. Heat equal amounts of vegetable oil and butter in a pan. Cook garlic over low heat, stirring until fragrant. Stir in half of the clam meat.

3. Add potatoes, onions and carrots. Cook and stir. Add water to cover, bring to a boil and simmer until vegetables are fully cooked.

4. Stir in curry paste, the remaining clam meat and green and red peppers; cook until peppers are tender. Serve with rice. Makes 2 servings.

Jung-Min Yang, Geumgok-dong, Bundang-gu, Seongnam

J A P A N

The art of food

Delicious simplicity defines an ancient culture

J APANESE CUISINE IS AN INTERTWINING of form and function. At its center are the freshest of seasonal ingredients. In fact, seasonality is considered by many to be the soul of this island nation's cuisine.

Dishes are prepared to perfection and artfully presented. Heavy sauces and extended cooking times are rare. It's common to present small portions of various dishes with contrasting colors, textures, taste sensations and shapes.

The land dictates the nature of the foods served. Rugged mountains dominate the landscape of the Japanese island chain (Honshu, Hokkaido, Kyushu, Shikoku and numerous smaller islands), and the population is packed into dense urban corridors, making good farmland scarce. Hardy, fast-growing rice, with a six-month harvest cycle, and grains such as buckwheat, used to make noodles (most commonly soba), have therefore become the mainstays.

In fact, most Japanese believe that a meal is not complete without rice. It can be cooked simply and offered in a bowl as a side dish, enhanced with ingredients such as curry for kare raisu, *fried*

(introduced from China) or intricately prepared as sushi. It should be noted that sushi is usually cold cooked rice dressed with vinegar and shaped into bite-sized pieces and topped with raw or cooked fish, or formed into a roll with fish, egg or vegetables and wrapped in seaweed.

Foods from the sea are another important aspect of Japanese cuisine. The Pacific Ocean and Sea of Japan surround the islands, offering up a variety of exotic marine life, such as salmon, spiny fish, bonito (related to tuna), eel, octopus, monkfish, abalone, scallops, oysters, shrimp, seaweed and sea urchin roe. Seafood is eaten raw (sashimi) as well as dried, boiled, grilled, deep-fried and steamed.

Fruits such as mandarins and tangerines, which are indigenous to Japan, and the freshest of vegetables are presented as close to their natural state as possible.

Not to be missed is tempura, derived from a 16th-century Portuguese delicacy. The freshest seafood and vegetables are coated with tempura batter and deep-fried to perfection. Tempura is, of course, always artfully presented.

The demand for fresh local items as well as international foods has led the Japanese Costco warehouses to provide products for a variety of food palates. (See www.costco.com's warehouse locator for information and location of all Japan warehouses.) Topping the warehouse food list are U.S. beef chuck flap steak, koshihikari rice, sushi family 48-piece combo, dinner rolls and mineral water. Miso (fermented soybean paste), soy sauce, sauces and marinades, and dry products such as mushrooms, seaweed and tofu are also popular.

Members in Tokyo and other urban centers tend to have tastes that are more international, whereas those who live in the south or in rural areas of Japan are focused more on regional food. However, no matter where the member shops, health and food safety is an issue that Costco takes seriously. Given a national move toward healthier eating, many of Costco's Japanese suppliers now provide their names and photographs on labels. 📷

Naoko's Marinated Salmon Marine ▶

1 onion, thinly sliced

1/2 pound boneless, skinless salmon fillet

1/2 lemon, thinly sliced

Olive oil

Vinegar

1. Spread onion slices over salmon in a container with a lid. Top with lemon slices.

2. Mix equal amounts of olive oil and vinegar, enough to generously coat the salmon but not cover.

3. Cover and refrigerate for 2-5 days before serving. Thinly slice the salmon and serve with the onion slices from the marinade. Makes 2 servings.

Naoko Shiki, Amagasaki City, Hyogo Ken

SOUP

Naoko's Miso Soup ◀

3 cups water

1 ounce seaweed, chopped

1 10-ounce package tofu, cut in small cubes

1 potato, cut in small cubes

1/4 cup miso (bean paste)

1-2 green onions, chopped

1. Bring water and seaweed to a boil in a saucepan over high heat. Add tofu and potato; cook over low heat for 10-15 minutes, or until the potato is tender.

2. Stir in miso. Sprinkle with onions. Makes 2-3 servings.

Miso

Derived from fermented soybeans, miso is extremely nutritious, offering protein, fiber, vitamins, enzymes and anti-oxidants. Miso soup begins the day in Japan and miso will appear throughout the day in soups, sauces and marinades. One tablespoon in a cup of hot water is an energizing afternoon beverage.

SALAD

Aki's Rice Salad ▶

This refreshing vegetable combination is a casual presentation of sushi without the nori seaweed wrapper.

1/4 cup salad oil	1/4-1/2 cup shredded cheese
1 tablespoon lemon juice	2 cups cooked rice
Salt and pepper	8-12 lettuce leaves
1 cucumber, chopped	8-12 slices salmon, smoked or fresh
2 slices baked ham, chopped	
1/4 Japanese radish, chopped	1/4 onion, thinly sliced
1 tomato, chopped	Lemon juice

1. Whisk together oil and lemon juice. Season to taste with salt and pepper.

2. In a bowl, combine cucumber, ham, radish and tomato. Stir in cheese and rice. Toss with lemon juice dressing.

3. Arrange lettuce on plates. Top with salmon, onion and a spoonful of rice. Season with a splash of lemon juice if desired. Roll up the lettuce leaf to eat. Makes 2-3 servings.

Aki Morimoto, Kobe City, Hyogo Ken

ENTRÉES

Emily Kinai, Chiba City, Chiba Ken

Emily's Tai Fish with Sweet and Sour Sauce ◀

1 1/2 cups water, divided	3 tablespoons cornstarch
1 8-ounce can pineapple tidbits or chunks	1/2 teaspoon salt or more
	1 teaspoon MSG, optional
1/2 cup pineapple juice	1 whole tai fish or red snapper
1 teaspoon minced garlic	
2 tablespoons soy sauce	Salt and pepper
2 tablespoons lime juice	Flour
1 medium-sized green bell pepper, cut in strips	Oil for deep-frying

1. Place 1 cup water in a saucepan. Add pineapple, pineapple juice, garlic, soy sauce and lime juice. Bring to a boil and simmer for 5 minutes over low heat. Stir in green pepper strips.

2. Combine cornstarch with 1/2 cup water; add to pineapple mixture, stirring constantly for 3 minutes over low heat. Season to taste with salt and MSG.

3. Season fish with salt and pepper; dredge fish in flour. Pour 1 inch of oil into a large skillet and heat to 350°F. Cook fish until golden on both sides. Pour sauce over fried fish. Makes 4 servings.

Marine Harvest

Fish forms a vital part of a healthy, balanced diet. It also tastes good, is easy to cook and is versatile. Marine Harvest supplies first-class farmed fish products to customers in more than 70 countries.

Marine Harvest
Oriental Grilled Salmon

1 tablespoon soy sauce	1 teaspoon finely minced garlic
1 tablespoon rice wine vinegar	2 scallion bulbs, crushed
1 tablespoon toasted sesame oil	4 Marine Harvest salmon portions (6 ounces each)
1 teaspoon finely minced fresh ginger	

1. Whisk together soy sauce, vinegar, sesame oil, ginger, garlic and scallions and pour onto salmon. Marinate for 30-60 minutes in the refrigerator.

2. Grill for approximately 5 minutes on each side, or until salmon flakes apart evenly with a fork. Makes 4 servings.

Essential Japanese Flavorings

Shoyu is a Japanese pure soy sauce, used in cooking and as a condiment at the table. Chinese soy sauce is not a satisfactory substitute for shoyu's distinctive flavor. Koikuchi shoyu (regular shoyu) is the most widely used kind. Other Japanese soy sauces are tamari (wheat-free) and usukuchi shoyu (lighter and saltier than regular).

Dashi is a stock base made from dried kelp and dried bonito flakes. It is used in many dishes and is the heart of miso soup, a staple of the Japanese diet. Concentrated powdered and liquid varieties are commonly used instead of home-made. Other popular bases for dashi are shiitake mushrooms and sardines.

Miso is fermented soybean paste, which adds a rich, salty flavor to Japanese salad dressings, pickles and soup.

Sake, the sacred rice wine of Japan, is served with great ritual, usually warm. It also has many uses in cooking.

Mirin, sweetened rice wine, is used only in cooking.

Rice vinegar is a delicate ingredient in many Japanese dishes, sauces and salads.

Other more well-known ingredients that create the special flavors of Japanese cuisine include citrus fruits, fresh ginger, Japanese basil, mustard, hot red pepper, Szechwan pepper and wasabi.

Akira's Tonkatsu (Deep-Fried Pork Cutlet) ▾

Fried pork cutlet has been a favorite of the Japanese people since the era of the Meiji Restoration in the late 19th century. *Ton* means pork in Japanese, and *katsu* means cutlet, an approximation of the word "cut."

4 6-ounce boneless pork sirloin cutlets	6 cabbage leaves, cut in fine strips
White pepper	2 teaspoons Japanese mustard
1 cup flour	Lemon slices
1 egg, beaten	Tonkatsu sauce or barbecue sauce
2 cups bread crumbs	
Oil for deep-frying	

Akira Sakuma, Katori Gun, Chiba Ken

1. Season pork with white pepper to taste. Roll the cutlets in flour, dip in egg and roll in bread crumbs.

2. Pour oil into a fryer about 1 inch deep; heat to 350°F, or until a 1/2-inch cube of bread turns golden after 1 minute. Cook the cutlets for about 4 minutes, or until golden brown on both sides. Remove carefully and drain on a rack or paper towels.

3. Arrange cabbage on plates and top each serving with 1/2 teaspoon mustard. Arrange the fried cutlet by the cabbage and top with a lemon slice. Serve with tonkatsu sauce. Makes 4 servings.

Swift

Swift & Company is a leading supplier of fresh beef and pork under the Swift Premium and Swift brands. Swift pork tenderloins offer convenience in quick cooking on the grill or stove top or in the oven. The sweet flavor of pork is versatile in many cuisines and is a natural choice for barbecue around the world.

Swift Asian BBQ Pork Tenderloin ◄

2 pounds Swift pork tenderloin, trimmed	1 tablespoon hot pepper sauce
MARINADE:	*DIPPING SAUCE:*
1/3 cup apple juice	1 cup lightly packed fresh cilantro
4 garlic cloves, chopped	1 cup lightly packed fresh mint
2 tablespoons soy sauce	
2 tablespoons oyster sauce	1/4 cup water
1 tablespoon toasted sesame oil	2 tablespoons unseasoned rice vinegar
2 teaspoons five spice powder	2 teaspoons sugar
1/2 teaspoon dried thyme	1 garlic clove, minced
2 tablespoons dark brown sugar	1 tablespoon hot pepper sauce

1. Combine marinade ingredients in a covered bowl or zipper-lock bag. Add pork to marinade. Marinate for at least 2 hours, or overnight.

2. Combine all dipping sauce ingredients in a food processor and pulse until finely chopped. This can be made ahead and stored in the refrigerator.

3. Grill marinated pork over medium heat for 15-18 minutes, turning and basting often, or until it reaches an internal temperature of 160°F.

4. Let pork stand 5-10 minutes before slicing. Serve with dipping sauce. Makes 4 servings.

Michael Toshio Cuisine
Oyako-tori Donburi ▲

Michael Toshio Cuisine strives to create delicious authentic products that are also convenient. *Oyako* means "mother and child," reflecting the chicken and egg in the recipe. This is a popular dish served at Japanese restaurants in individual rice bowls *(donburi)*.

2 tablespoons vegetable oil	1/2 cup chopped green onions
1/2 onion, sliced	3/4 cup chicken broth
12 skewers Michael Toshio Cuisine Gourmet Yakitori,* thawed	3/4 packet teriyaki glaze (included in package), thawed
6 shiitake mushrooms, sliced	5 eggs, beaten
	4 cups cooked rice

1. Heat oil in a large skillet or wok over medium-high heat; cook onion until soft.

2. Add skewers, mushrooms, green onions and chicken broth; simmer for 5 minutes.

3. Stir in teriyaki glaze; simmer for 3 minutes.

4. Mix in eggs and simmer until cooked. Serve over rice in soup bowls. Makes 4 servings.

Brands may vary by region; substitute a similar product.

DESSERT

Takako's Green Tea Crepe ▽

Adzuki beans, typically small dark red beans, can be used fresh, dried for sprouts or ground into meal. Naturally sweeter than many beans, they are used in desserts as well as savory dishes.

1 cup water	3/4 cup vanilla ice cream
1 tablespoon green tea powder, or more to taste	3/4 cup canned adzuki beans, sweetened
1 tablespoon rice flour (shiratamako)	3/4 cup whipped cream flavored with green tea powder
3/4 cup pancake mix	

1. Combine water and green tea powder; combine rice flour and pancake mix; stir enough water-tea mixture into pancake mix to make a thin batter.

2. Pour a small amount of batter into a hot greased skillet over medium-high heat, tipping the pan to spread the batter as thinly as possible. When bubbles form, flip and cook briefly on the other side until lightly browned. Remove and cool slightly.

3. Scoop a generous spoonful of ice cream onto each crepe; sprinkle with adzuki beans and make a roll.

4. Garnish with whipped cream. Makes 2-4 servings.

Tip: Garnish with sliced bananas.

Takako Iwatsu, Amagasaki City, Hyogo Ken

Flavors
of the
Orient

Simple, rustic dishes meet in a mix of cultures

T AIWAN'S CULINARY STYLE *reflects centuries of immigration and trade, and is a mixture of foods from Chinese provinces with an overlay of Japanese culture. Lighter flavors, natural sweetness, color and nutritional value are prized.*

Today, typically Taiwanese foods include preserved radishes, chiles, parsley, peanuts, black beans and Asian basil. Hot-pot meals using either a wok or a clay pot are prepared with pork meatballs, fish cakes, seafood, Chinese mushrooms, tofu and sliced meats or bok choy enhanced by chicken stock and sauces.

Some of the finest tea fields in the world are found on the island, thanks to its rich soil, mild climate and plentiful sunlight. Dense forests and mountainous terrain are well

suited for pigs and goats. Rice, duck, fish and leafy vegetables are abundant.

Favorite ingredients include sweet potatoes, asparagus, taro, cabbage, tofu, eggs and mustard greens. Garlic-infused chili sauce, soy sauce and rice wine add jolts of flavor. Fermented rice pudding, sweet wraps made of red bean paste, and fresh watermelon, pineapple or banana often complete the traditional meal.

Not to be missed are roasted duck, steamed sea perch, braised shark fins, broiled prawns with chili sauce, steamed pork in lotus-leaf packets, stewed pork balls, fried beef with oyster oil, spring onions with mutton, cabbage with dried shrimp, Szechuan-style sautéed tofu, sliced chicken and abalone soup, and beef with hot pot sauce.

Costco's Taiwanese warehouses (see www.costco.com's warehouse locator for information and locations) place equal emphasis on regional products and international favorites. Members are cosmopolitan, with many having attended schools in the United States and Europe, and as a result preferences often lean toward Western, Japanese, Korean and Thai as well as local foods.

"Good for your health" food items sell well in the warehouses because most Taiwanese believe that good food is essential to one's well-being. Healthy foods are considered a way of life here and not just a new trend.

It is no wonder then that the "favorites" list in the warehouses is such an eclectic affair: Campbell's clam chowder, olive oil, nacho cheese Doritos, black wheat juice, sesame yam tea mix, barista-style rich lattes, frozen sashimi fish fillets, dumplings, Korean seaweed and kimchi, cranberry juice, dried cranberries, tomato juice, grape seed oil, Japanese yams and Chinese pork buns. 🍽

APPETIZER

Jasmine's Dragon on the Snow

1 tablespoon egg white

2 teaspoons cornstarch

1/3 teaspoon salt

1/2 pound medium
tiger shrimp, shelled
and deveined

1 large sheet of rice paper
or rice noodles

Sesame oil

Salt

1 cup vegetable oil

3 tablespoons ketchup

1/2 tablespoon chili oil

1 tablespoon wine

1/2 teaspoon salt

1/2 teaspoon sugar

1/3 cup water

2 teaspoons cornstarch

1/4 teaspoon sesame oil

1/2 tablespoon chopped garlic

1 teaspoon chopped ginger

1 tablespoon chopped
green onion

1. Combine egg white, cornstarch and salt in a
bowl; add shrimp and toss to coat thoroughly.
Refrigerate for at least 20 minutes.

2. Cut the fresh rice paper into strips; rinse
with hot water for 3 seconds. Drain and mix
with a little sesame oil and salt. Arrange on
a serving plate.

3. Heat oil in a large skillet or wok to 320°F.
Fry the shrimp for about 15 seconds. Remove
the shrimp and all but 1 tablespoon of the oil
from the skillet or wok.

4. Combine ketchup, chili oil, wine, salt, sugar,
water, cornstarch and sesame oil in a small
bowl to make a paste.

5. Heat oil over high heat, then stir-fry garlic,
ginger and green onion.

6. Stir ketchup mixture into garlic-ginger mixture
until the sauce boils; add shrimp and stir-fry
until thoroughly hot and coated with sauce.
Remove to a platter. Place shrimp on rice paper
strips. Makes 4 servings.

Jasmine Chang, Taipei, Taiwan

SOUP

Marine Harvest Oriental Noodle Soup with Atlantic Salmon

6 ounces buckwheat
noodles (soba)

8 cups clam juice (water
or vegetable soup base
can also be used)

12 fresh shiitake mushrooms

1 12-ounce bag shredded
broccoli slaw (or 2 cups
shredded cabbage)

2 tablespoons soy sauce

10 quarter-size ginger slices

2 teaspoons grated lemon peel

1-2 serrano or jalapeño
peppers, diced fine,
optional

1 1/2 pounds Marine Harvest
Atlantic salmon, cut in
1/2-inch chunks

Freshly ground pepper

2-3 teaspoons toasted
sesame oil

1 green onion, thinly sliced

6 tablespoons chopped
fresh cilantro

1. In a large pot, boil water and cook noodles
according to package directions (about 5 minutes),
being careful not to overcook. Drain quickly and
rinse under cool water to stop cooking process.

2. Put clam juice, mushrooms, broccoli slaw, soy
sauce and ginger in a large pot; boil for 5 minutes.
Stir in lemon peel and diced peppers.

3. Place salmon chunks in broth and cook gently
until fish is opaque, about 5 minutes.

4. Remove ginger slices. Add noodles to broth
and stir. Add ground pepper to taste.

5. Ladle soup into individual bowls. Place salmon
in the center of each bowl and drizzle with
sesame oil. Sprinkle with green onion slivers and
cilantro. Makes 4 servings.

Flav-R-Pac
Tangy Imperial Stir-Fry

1 tablespoon oil	2 pounds Flav-R-Pac* Imperial Stir Fry Vegetables, frozen
2 teaspoons minced garlic	
1 teaspoon crushed red pepper	1 sauce packet
	2 tablespoons honey
12 ounces boneless chicken, cut in small pieces	1 1/4 cups shredded basil leaves

1. Heat oil over high heat in a wok or skillet. Stir-fry garlic, red pepper and chicken until chicken is opaque. Remove from the pan.

2. Add frozen vegetables to the hot pan and cook 6-8 minutes, or until crisp-tender.

3. In a small bowl, combine sauce packet, honey and basil. Add cooked chicken and sauce to heated vegetables, tossing to coat; bring to a simmer. Makes 4 servings.

Brands may vary by region; substitute a similar product.

Trina Lu, Taipei, Taiwan

FROM THE EMPLOYEE'S KITCHEN

Trina's Scrambled Eggs with Tomatoes

This is a very quick, healthy home-cooked dish.

3-4 eggs	2 medium red tomatoes, each cut in 8 pieces
1-2 scallions, chopped	
1-2 tablespoons vegetable oil	Salt

1. Beat eggs in a bowl; stir in scallions.

2. Preheat a wok for about 1 minute over medium heat; add oil. When oil is medium hot, stir-fry tomatoes until soft.

3. Pour eggs into the wok; stir slightly to mix with tomatoes until eggs are about half done; turn eggs over and continue cooking to desired firmness.

4. Cut in several pieces. Season to taste with salt. Makes 4-6 servings.

Oils in Asian Cooking

Sesame oil comes in various forms. Oriental sesame oil, made from toasted sesame seeds, has a rich color, aroma and flavor. In Chinese and Korean dishes, it is usually used as a seasoning at the end of cooking. In Japan it's often blended as flavoring with other oils for deep-frying (tempura). Cold-pressed sesame oil, made from raw seeds, is clear, with no nutty flavor, and is popular in India for cooking, medicine and massage.

Peanut oil is ideal for deep-frying and stir-frying because it has a high smoke point. Asian peanut oil has a distinctive peanut flavor, whereas Western versions are virtually flavorless after refining.

Coconut oil is often used for deep-frying because it has a high smoke point.

Tan Hsu, Taipei, Taiwan

Melissa's Chinese Meat Sauce with Noodles

Melissa tells us, "I call this dish Chinese Spaghetti. It's very popular Chinese home-cooking, similar to spaghetti in Italy. I made this recipe many times over the years as a homesick student in Pittsburgh."

3 tablespoons oil	1 1/2-2 cups water or more
1 tablespoon minced garlic	Soy sauce and sugar
2 tablespoons minced green onion	1 tablespoon cornstarch mixed with 3 tablespoons water, optional
1/2 teaspoon minced fresh ginger	1 1/3 pounds fresh noodles, cooked and drained
10 1/2 ounces ground pork	
5-6 pieces pressed dried bean curd (yellow), diced	2 medium Chinese cucumbers, shredded
4 tablespoons soybean paste* or 2 tablespoons each regular and hot soybean paste	1 small carrot, shredded
	5 ounces bean sprouts, blanched 10 seconds and drained
2 tablespoons sweet soybean paste	Sesame oil

1. Preheat a wok; add oil. Stir-fry garlic, green onion and ginger over low heat until fragrant.

2. Add ground pork and bean curd and cook over medium-high heat, stirring frequently. When pork changes color, add soybean pastes and stir-fry for 1 minute.

3. Add enough water to cover all ingredients and bring to a boil; then reduce heat and simmer until the sauce thickens. Season to taste with soy sauce or sugar. (For a faster cooking time, simmer for 10-15 minutes and thicken with cornstarch mixture.)

4. Place noodles in a bowl; arrange some shredded cucumber, carrot and bean sprouts on top; pour meat sauce over and season with a few drops of sesame oil. Makes 4 servings.

Soybean pastes can be found in Asian grocery stores.

Tan's Short Ribs with Sa-cha Sauce

1 pound short ribs	1 teaspoon chopped garlic
1/3 teaspoon baking soda, optional	Salt
1 tablespoon cornstarch	2 tablespoons sa-cha sauce*
1 tablespoon soy sauce	1/2 tablespoon wine
1/4 teaspoon salt	1/2 tablespoon Worcestershire sauce
2 tablespoons water	1/4 teaspoon salt
5 tablespoons oil	1/2 teaspoon sugar
1 cup shredded onion	5 tablespoons water

1. Cut each short rib into 3 pieces. Combine baking soda, cornstarch, soy sauce, salt and water in a large bowl; add the ribs and rub in the seasonings; marinate ribs for at least 30 minutes.

2. Heat 4 tablespoons oil in a large skillet or wok to 320°F. Fry ribs piece by piece until browned and half cooked. Remove ribs to a heated casserole and drain off the oil.

3. Heat 1 tablespoon oil in a large skillet or wok over medium heat; stir-fry onion and garlic; season with salt. Pour over ribs.

4. Combine the sa-cha sauce, wine, Worcestershire sauce, salt, sugar and water in a small bowl. Add to the wok and bring to a boil, stirring.

5. Return the ribs to the wok; cover and cook for 30 seconds. Makes 4 servings.

Sa-cha sauce is soy-based, rich and spicy with chili and sesame. It is commonly used as a base for hot pots or as a condiment. It's available in Asian markets under many brands, such as Lee Kum Kee.

Melissa Yeh, Taipei, Taiwan

Hwa-Shen's Chicken Strips and Green Vegetables

3 teaspoons rice wine

1 teaspoon cornstarch

Salt

1 chicken breast, sliced in thin strips

3 tablespoons olive oil

10 1/2 ounces bean sprouts, heads and toes removed

MSG

10 1/2 ounces bok choy, sliced in half vertically, blanched

Olive oil

1. Combine wine, cornstarch and salt to taste; toss with chicken strips; set aside for 20 minutes.

2. Preheat a wok; add oil and stir-fry the chicken.

3. Add bean sprouts and salt and MSG to taste; cook, stirring constantly, until hot. Arrange on a plate. Surround chicken with bok choy, sprinkled with a dash of salt and oil. Makes 2-3 servings.

Hwa-Shen Lai, Taipei, Taiwan

DESSERT

Li-Shaun's Snowflake Cake

The Asian sensibility about eating relegates sweets to the non-essential category. A Western palate may find an Eastern dessert to be delicately flavored. This coconut-based flourless cake is subtly sweet, light and creamy.

2 cups milk

2 cups canned coconut milk

1 cup sugar

1 cup cornstarch

Coconut or peanut powder*

1. Combine milk and coconut milk in a saucepan. Reserve 1/3 in a bowl. Add sugar to the milk mixture in the saucepan and stir over medium heat until sugar is completely dissolved and milk comes to a boil. Reduce heat to low.

2. Add cornstarch to the reserved milk, stirring until dissolved. Slowly pour into the boiling milk, stirring until the mixture forms a paste.

3. Pour into a greased 6-cup mold or 8-inch square pan. Cool; refrigerate for about 3 hours, or until firm.

4. Cut into squares and sprinkle with coconut powder. Makes 4-6 servings.

*Coconut and peanut powders are available at Asian grocery stores in 4-ounce packages. Make your own at home by toasting and grinding in a food processor.

Li-Shaun Chang Chen, Kaohsiung, Taiwan

ACT II (CONAGRA FOODS RETAIL PRODUCTS COMPANY) *page 106*
5 ConAgra Drive
Omaha, NE 60515
www.conagrafoods.com

AGROLIBANO *page 51*
San Lorenzo
Valle, Honduras
Phone: 504-881-2256
Fax: 504-881-2186
www.agrolibano.hn/en
Cantaloupes, honeydews and watermelons

ALPINE *page 166, 167*
9300 N.W. 58th St., Suite 201
Miami, FL 33178
Phone: 305-594-9117
Fax: 305-594-8506
Mangoes, asparagus, raspberries, blueberries, blackberries, grape and heirloom tomatoes

AMERICA'S KITCHEN *page 178*
2150 Brandon Trail
Alpharetta, GA 30004
Phone: 770-754-0707
Fax: 770-754-0708
americaskitchen.com
Chicken Pot Pie

APIO, INC. *page 102*
P.O. Box 627
Guadalupe, CA 93434
Phone: 800-626-2746
Fax: 805-343-6295
www.apioinc.com
Broccoli florets, garden vegetables and sugar snap peas

APPLE & EVE *page 183*
2 Seaview Boulevard
Port Washington, NY 11050
Phone: 516-621-1122
Fax: 516-621-2164
appleandeve.com
Apple & Eve Ruby Red grapefruit juice cocktail, Apple & Eve power pouches and Apple & Eve variety pack

ARTHUR SCHUMAN INC. *page 56, 148*
40 New Dutch Lane
Fairfield, NJ 07004
Phone: 973-227-0030
Fax: 973-227-1763
www.arthurschuman.com
Cheeses: Parmigiano-Reggiano, Grana Padano, Pecorino Romano, Provolone and Asiago (shredded, grated and in wedges)

ATLANTIC VEAL & LAMB DBA PLUME DE VEAU *page 155*
275 Morgan Avenue
Brooklyn, NY 11211
Phone: 718-599-6400
Fax: 718-599-6404
ppeerless@atlanticveal.com
Veal cutlets and veal chops

AUSTRALIAN LAMB COMPANY, INC. *page 150, 151*
20 Westport Road, Suite 320
Wilton, CT 06897
Phone: 203-529-9200
Fax: 203-529-9101
www.auslamb.com
Southern Cross lamb, lamb chops, frenched racks and boneless legs

B & G FOODS *page 178*
4 Gatehall Dr.
Parsippany, NJ 07054
Phone: 973-401-6500
Fax: 973-630-6553
www.bgfoods.com
Emeril's, B&M, Accent, B&G, Maple Grove Farms and Polaner

BABÉ FARMS *page 53*
P.O. Box 6539
Santa Maria, CA 93456
Phone: 800-648-6772
Fax: 805-925-3897
Customerservice@babefarms.com
www.babefarms.com
Continental salad mix

BARILLA AMERICA *page 148*
1200 Lakeside Dr.
Bannockburn, IL 60015
Phone: 847-405-7500
Fax: 847-405-7505
www.barilla.com
Pasta and pasta sauce

BASIN GOLD COOPERATIVE *page 22*
2715 St. Andrews Loop, Suite C
Pasco, WA 99301
Phone: 509-545-4161
Fax: 509-545-4202
basingold.com
Potatoes and onions

BC HOT HOUSE FOODS INC. *page 24, 25, 188*
5355 152nd St.
Surrey, B.C. Canada V3S 5A5
Phone: 604-576-8525
Fax: 604-576-2115
www.bchothouse.com
Beefsteak tomatoes, tomatoes on the vine,
sweet bell peppers and long English cucumbers

BEAR CREEK COUNTRY KITCHENS *page 22*
325 W. 600th South
Heber City, UT 84032
Phone: 435-654-6415
Fax: 435-645-9100
www.bearcreekfoods.com
Premium soup mixes, complete entrees and pasta meals

BEE SWEET *page 72*
416 E. South Ave.
Fowler, CA 93625
www.beesweetcitrus.com
Full line of citrus produce

BELGIOIOSO CHEESE, INC. *page 143*
5810 County Road NN
Denmark, WI 54208-8730
Phone: 920-863-2123
Fax: 920-863-8791
www.belgioioso.com
Full line Italian cheese supplier

BIG VALLEY MARKETING *page 71, 135*
2301 Armstrong St. #211
Livermore, CA 94551
Phone: 925-245-3300
Fax: 925-294-8581
www.big-valley.com
Frozen fruit

BIRDS EYE FOODS *page 121*
90 Linden Oaks
Rochester, NY 14625-2808
585-383-1850
birdseyefoods.com
Birds Eye frozen vegetables, Voila, Nalleys chili and salsa

BOBOLI INTERNATIONAL *page 156*
3247 W. March Lane, Ste. 210
Stockton, CA 95219
209-473-3507
www.boboli-intl.com
Cream puffs, eclairs and frozen desserts

BORGES USA/STAR FINE FOODS *page 47*
559-498-2900
www.borgesusa.com
Olive oil, Spanish olives, artichokes, peppers,
capers and maraschino cherries

BOSKOVICH FARMS *page 54*
P.O. Box 1352
Oxnard, CA 93032
Phone: 805-487-7799
Fax: 805-487-5189
boskovichfarms.com
Spinach and green onions

BOUNTY FRESH LLC *page 51*
8550 N.W. 17th Street, Suite 100
Miami, FL 33126
Phone: 305-592-6969
Fax: 305-436-8969
www.bountyfresh.com
Cantaloupes, pineapples and mangoes

BRAD BARRY COMPANY, LTD *page 75*
14020 Central Avenue #580
Chino, CA 91710-5564
Phone: 909-591-9493
Fax: 909-627-3747
www.caffedvita.com
Instant cappuccino, chai latte tea mix and smoothie mix

BRAWLEY BEEF, LLC *page 69*
57 E. Shank Rd./P.O. Box 1211
Brawley, CA 92227
Phone: 760-351-2700
Fax: 760-351-2725
www.brawleybeef.com
Boxed beef and variety meats

BREWSTER HEIGHTS PACKING CO. *page 92*
908 Hwy 97
Brewster, WA 98812
Phone: 509-689-2521
Fax: 509-689-2033
Apples, pears and cherries

BROWN & HALEY *page 36*
P.O. Box 1596
Tacoma, WA 98401
Phone: 253-620-3000
Fax: 253-272-6742
www.brown-haley.com
Almond Roca, Accolade and Zingos

BUMBLE BEE SEAFOODS *page 148*
www.bumblebee.com

**BUTTERBALL (CONAGRA FOODS RETAIL
PRODUCTS COMPANY)** *page 176*
5 ConAgra Drive
Omaha, NE 60515
www.conagrafoods.com

CABOT CREAMERY COOPERATIVE *page 132*
One Home Farm Way
Montpelier, VT 05602
Phone: 802-229-9361
Fax: 802-371-1200
www.cabotcheese.com
Cheese–blocks, shredded, sliced; butter,
dips and sour cream

CALAVO GROWERS, INC. *page 50*
2530 Red Hill Ave.
Santa Ana, CA 92705
Phone: 949-223-1111
Fax: 949-223-1112
www.calavo.com
Avocados and papayas

CALIFORNIA AVOCADO COMMISSION *page 50*
38 Discovery, Suite 150
Irvine, CA 92618-3105
Phone: 949-341-1955
Fax: 949-341-1970
www.avocado.org
California avocado information, recipes and brochures

CALIFORNIA STRAWBERRY COMMISSION *page 78*
P.O. Box 269
Watsonville, CA 95077-0269
Phone: 831-724-1301
Fax: 831-724-5973
www.calstrawberry.com
California strawberries

CAMANCHACA INC. *page 172*
7200 N.W. 19th St., Suite 410
Miami, FL 33126
Phone: 800-335-7553
Fax: 305-406-2285
www.camanchacainc.com
Fresh Atlantic salmon

CAMPBELL'S DE MEXICO, S.A. DE C.V. *page 196*
Insugentes Sur No. 670. Segundo Piso.
Colonia Del Valle. 03100 Mexico, D.F.
Phone: 5255-54-48-57-00

CARDILE BROS. MUSHROOM PKG. INC. *page 142*
8790 Gap Newport Pike
Avondale, PA 19311
Phone: 610-268-2470
Fax: 610-268-8211
cardilebro@aol.com
White, portobello and shiitake mushrooms

CARTER THOMAS LLC *page 72*
250 W. Main St., Suite 200
Woodland, CA 95695
Phone: 530-662-8100
Fax: 530-662-7600
www.gotfruit.com
Bartlett pears, Mendocino Gold pears and gift baskets

CHRISTOPHER RANCH LLC *page 49*
305 Bloomfield Ave.
Gilroy, CA 95020
Phone: 408-847-1100
Fax: 408-847-5488
www.christopher-ranch.com
Garlic, shallots and ginger

CIBO NATURALS *page 32*
1914-A Occidental Ave. S.
Seattle, WA 98134
Phone: 206-622-1016
Fax: 206-622-7410
www.cibonaturals.com
Sauces, spreads, dips and toppings

CJ FOODS INC. (USA) *page 216*
5801 S. Malt Ave.
City of Commerce, CA 90040
Phone: 323-278-5200
Fax: 323-278-5252
Cjgourmet.com
Bulgogi marinade

CLEAR SPRINGS FOODS, INC. *page 96*
P.O. Box 712
Bahl, ID 83316
Phone: 208-543-4316
Fax: 208-543-5608
www.clearsprings.com
Rainbow trout

CLIFFSTAR CORPORATION *page 158*
One Cliffstar Ave.
Dunkirk, NY 14048-2800
Phone: 716-366-6100
Fax: 716-366-1067
cliffstar.com
Shelf-stable juice

CLOROX SALES CO. *page 141*
1221 Broadway
Oakland, CA 94612
800-537-2823
www.clorox.com
Bottled Hidden Valley, Dry Hidden Valley, Hidden Valley BBQ Ranch Dressing, KC Masterpiece BBQ sauce and KC Masterpiece marinade

COLUMBIA MARKETING INTERNATIONAL *page 36, 37*
2525 Euclid Ave.
Wenatchee, WA 98801
509-663-1955
www.cmiapples.com
Cherries and apples

COMITE DE PALTAS *page 50*
www.comitedepaltas.cl
Chilean Avocado Association

CONAGRA FOODS *page 63*
P.O. Box 2819
Tampa, FL 33601
Phone: 813-241-1500
Fax: 813-247-1782
www.conagraseafood.com

**CONAGRA FOODS
FOOD INGREDIENTS COMPANY** *page 138*
9 ConAgra Drive
Omaha, NE 68103
Phone: 800-851-9618
Fax: 402-595-4111
conagramilling.com
Wheat flour

CONAGRA FOODS RETAIL PRODUCTS COMPANY
page 68, 176
5 ConAgra Drive
Omaha, NE 60515
www.conagrafoods.com

CONCEPT 2 BAKERS *page 137*
7350 Commerce Lane
Minneapolis, MN 55432-3189
Phone: 800-266-2782
Fax: 763-574-2210
www.c2b.com
Artisan breads and rolls

CONTINENTAL MILLS *page 74*
18125 Andover Park West
Tukwila, WA 98188
800-457-7744
www.krusteaz.com

COUNTRYGOURMET FOODS, LLC *page 53*
71 McMurray Road, Suite 106
Pittsburgh, PA 15241
Phone: 412-854-9026
Fax: 412-854-9013
www.wolfgangpucksoup.com
Various Wolfgang Puck's hearty soups

COUNTRYSIDE BAKING CO., INC. *page 157*
1711 Kettering St.
Irvine, CA 92614
Phone: 800-478-4252
Fax: 949-851-9009
Info@countrysidebaking.com
Rugala and cookie dough

CRIDER, INC. *page 147*
1 Plant Ave.
Stillmore, GA 30464
Phone: 800-348-8449
Fax: 912-562-9286
www.cridercorp.com

CRISCO
(THE J.M. SMUCKER COMPANY) *page 95*
Strawberry Lane
Orrville, OH 44667
888-550-9555
www.smuckers.com

D'ARRIGO BROS. CO. OF CALIFORNIA *page 137*
383 W. Market Street
Salinas, CA 93901
831-753-5425
831-424-3136
www.andyboy.com
Romaine hearts

D'ORAZIO FOODS, INC. *page 149*
P.O. Box 243
Bellmawr, NJ 08099
Phone: 856-931-1900
Fax: 856-931-1907
www.dorazio.com
Frozen Italian pastas and entrées

DANNON COMPANY, INC. *page 107*
120 White Plains Road
Tarrytown, NY 10591
1-877-DANNONUS
www.dannon.com
Light'n Fit yogurt

DARE FOODS, INC. *page 46*
5 Bessom Street PMB #314
Marblehead, MA 01945-2328
781-639-1808
www.15minutestofame.com
Cookies and crackers

DEAN FOODS COMPANY *page 116*
2515 McKinney Ave., Suite 1200
Dallas, TX 75201
800-431-9214
www.deanfoods.com
Sour cream, cottage cheese and cream cheese

DEAN SPECIALTY FOODS GROUP *page 21*
857-897 School Place
Green Bay, WI 54303
Phone: 920-497-7131
Fax: 920-497-8058
deanfoods.com
Pickles, olives, sauces, syrups, nutrition beverages, non-dairy coffee creamer, prepared dips and instant breakfast drinks

DELANO FARMS COMPANY *page 44, 45*
10025 Reed Road
Delano, CA 93215
Phone: 661-721-1485
Fax: 661-721-2466
Table grapes

DELTA PRIDE CATFISH, INC. *page 174*
1301 Industrial Parkway/P.O. Box 850
Indianola, MS 38751
Phone: 800-421-1045
Fax: 662-887-5950
www.deltapride.com
U.S. farm-raised catfish

DIAMOND FRUIT GROWERS, INC. *page 20*
P.O. Box 185
Odell, OR 97044
Phone: 541-354-5300
Fax: 541-354-2123
www.diamondfruit.com
Fresh pears and fresh cherries (all varieties)

DNE WORLD FRUIT SALES *page 168*
1900 Old Dixie Highway
Fort Pierce, FL 34946
Phone: 772-465-1110
Fax: 772-465-1181
dneworld.com
Citrus

**DOLE FRESH FRUIT AND
VEGETABLE COMPANY** *page 70, 165, 169*
One Dole Drive
Westlake Village, CA 91362
Phone: 818-874-4000
Fax: 818-874-4527
www.dole.com
Dole bananas, pineapples, salads, asparagus, cauliflower, celery, lettuce, grapes and tree fruit

DOLE PACKAGED FOODS COMPANY *page 165, 169*
P.O. Box 5700
Westlake Village, CA 91359-5700
800-232-8888
www.dole.com

DOMEX MARKETING *page 20, 103*
151 Low Road
Yakima, WA 98908
Phone: 509-966-1814
Fax: 509-966-3608
www.superapple.com
Apples, cherries and pears

DON MIGUEL MEXICAN FOODS INC. *page 49*
P.O. Box 4062
Anaheim, CA 92806
Phone: 714-634-8441
Fax: 714-937-0493
www.donmiguel.com
*Lean Ole burritos, chicken mini tacos, beef mini tacos,
all white meat garlic chicken flautas, steak flautas,
chipotle chicken flautas and shredded beef tamales*

DOUGLAS FRUIT COMPANY *page 38*
110 Taylor Flats Road
Pasco, WA 99301
Phone: 509-547-2787
Fax: 509-545-4602
www.douglasfruit.com
*Red Delicious, Braeburn, Fuji, Granny Smith,
Gala and Pink Lady apples, yellow and white flesh
peaches and nectarines*

EARTHBOUND FARM *page 56*
1721 San Juan Highway
San Juan Bautista, CA 95045
800-690-3200
www.ebfarm.com

EMMPAK, AN EXCEL FOOD SOLUTIONS CO.
page 153
1515 W. Canal St.
Milwaukee, WI 53233
800-558-4242
www.excelmeats.com
*Fully cooked and marinated ready-to-cook beef,
pork and turkey*

ENACA INTERNATIONAL, LLC *page 64*
3900 N.W. 79th Ave., Suite 570
Miami, FL 33166
Phone: 305-599-8877
Fax: 305-599-2255
www.enaca.net
Fresh and frozen tilapia fillets and shrimp

EXCEL CORP. *page 124*
151 N. Main
Wichita, KS 67202
Phone: 877-596-4069
www.excelmeats.com

FERRERO U.S.A. INC. *page 181*
600 Cottontail Ln.
Somerset, NJ 08873
Phone: 800-FERRERO
Fax: 732-764-2700
www.ferrerousa.com
*Nutella hazelnut spread, Rocher fine hazelnut
chocolates, Tic Tac mints and Tic Tac silvers*

FISH HOUSE FOODS, INC. *page 175*
3285 Corporate View
Vista, CA 92083
Phone: 800-238-3482
Fax: 760-597-1271
Stuffed salmon

FISHERY PRODUCTS INTERNATIONAL *page 173*
18 Electronics Ave.
Danvers, MA 01923
Phone: 978-750-5416
Fax: 978-774-6692

FLETCHER'S FINE FOODS *page 31*
502 Boundary Blvd.
Algona, WA 98001
Phone: 253-735-0800
Fax: 253-333-6817
Bacon, ham and sausage

FORDEL INC. *page 182*
1000 Airport Blvd.
Mendota, CA 93640
Phone: 559-655-3237
Fax: 559-655-3895
fordelinc.com
Cantaloupe and honeydew

FOSTER FARMS *page 32, 33, 67*
1000 Davis St.
Livingston, CA 95334
800-255-7227
www.fosterfarms.com
Fresh and processed chicken and turkey products

FOUR STAR FRUIT INC. *page 44, 45*
P.O. Box 1990
Delano, CA 93216
661-725-0186
California grapes

FOWLER PACKING CO. *page 44, 45*
8570 S. Cedar
Fresno, CA 93711
Phone: 559-834-5911
Fax: 559-834-3336
fowlerpacking.com
California grapes

FRENCH'S *page 130*
1655 Valley Road
Wayne, NJ 07960
www.seasonalkitchen.com
*Frank's RedHot hot sauce, Cattlemen's barbecue sauce
and French's mustard*

FRESH NETWORK LLC *page 22*
495 Brunken Ave.
Salinas, CA 95902
Phone: 831-422-5400
Fax: 831-422-4268
www.freshnetwork.com
Baking potatoes

**GENERAL MILLS BAKERIES
& FOODSERVICE** *page 117*
One General Mills Blvd.
Minneapolis, MN 55426
800-767-5404

GENERAL MILLS, INC. *page 133, 180*
One General Mills Blvd.
Minneapolis, MN 55402
800-328-1144
www.generalmills.com
*Cheerios, Honey Nut Cheerios, Cinnamon Toast Crunch,
Bisquick, Fruit by the Foot, Gushers, Fruit Roll-ups,
Nature Valley granola bars, Pillsbury brand refrigerated
products, Yoplait yogurt and Progresso soups*

GEORGE WESTON BAKERIES INC. *page 138*
55 Paradise Lane
Bay Shore, NY 11706
800-842-9595
www.gwbakeries.com
Arnold, Thomas, Entenmann's and Boboli

GIORGIO FOODS, INC. *page 149*
P.O. Box 96
Temple, PA 19560
Phone: 610-926-2139
Fax: 610-926-7012
www.giorgiofoods.com
Mushrooms

GIUMARRA COMPANIES *page 50*
15651 Old Milky Way
Escondido, CA 92027
Phone: 760-480-8502
Fax: 760-489-1870
giumarra.com
Avocados

GLOBAL FISHING INC. *page 28, 29*
840 140th Ave. N.E.
Bellevue, WA 98005
Phone: 425-452-8188
Fax: 425-455-2156
www.globaltr.net
Red king crab

GOGLANIAN BAKERIES, INC. *page 18*
3401 W. Segerstrom
Santa Ana, CA 92704
Phone: 714-444-3500
Fax: 714-444-3800

GOLD KIST INC. *page 178*
244 Perimeter Center Pkwy. N.E.
Atlanta, GA 30346
770-393-5000
www.goldkist.com
*Chicken–fresh and further processed
(retail, food service and export)*

GOLD-N-SOFT (VENTURA FOODS, LLC) *page 59*
40 Pointe Drive
Brea, CA 92821
Phone: 714-257-3700
Fax: 714-257-3702
venturafoods.com
*Oils, shortenings, dressings, margarines,
soup bases and sauces*

GRACE BAKING CO. *page 121*
3200 G. Regatta Blvd.
Richmond, CA 94804
800-555-5755
www.gracebaking.com
Artisan breads

GRIMMWAY FARMS *page 57*
P.O. Box 81498
Bakersfield, CA 93380
Phone: 661-845-5200
Fax: 661-845-5221
www.grimmway.com
Carrots, full line of organic vegetables and citrus

GROWER DIRECT MARKETING LLC *page 72*
2097 Beyer Lane
Stockton, CA 95215
Phone: 209-931-7900
Fax: 209-931-7920
www.growerdirect.net
Cherries, asparagus, blueberries and apricots

HANNAH INTERNATIONAL FOODS *page 132*
1 Depot Lane/P.O. Box 458
Seabrook, NH 03874
Phone: 603-474-5805
Fax: 603-474-9292
hannahfoods.net
Bruschetta

HANSEN'S NATURAL *page 64*
1010 Railroad St.
Corona, CA 92882
800-HANSENS
www.hansens.com
Natural sodas, smoothies and energy drinks

HEBREW NATIONAL *page 121*
Two Jericho Plaza
Jericho, NY 11753-0249
516-949-7500
hebrewnational.com
Kosher hotdogs, Polish sausage and salami

H.J. HEINZ COMPANY *page 113, 132, 142, 147, 174*
357 6th Avenue
Pittsburgh, PA 15222
www.heinz.com

HELLMANN'S (UNILEVER BESTFOODS NORTH AMERICA) *page 48*
800 Sylvan Avenue
Englewood Cliffs, NJ 07632
800-418-3275
www.mayo.com
Lipton, Wish-Bone, Shedds Country Crock, Hellmann's, Bestfoods, Knorr, Skippy, Ragu, Lawry's, Bertolli and I Can't Believe It's Not Butter

HIGH LINER FOODS *page 146*
1 High Liner Ave.
Portsmouth, NH 03801
603-431-6865
www.highlinerfoods.com
Scallops, cod loins, breaded cod, mussels and breaded scallops

HOLTZINGER FRUIT COMPANY *page 32*
1312 N. 6th Avenue
Yakima, WA 98902
Phone: 509-457-5115
Fax: 509-248-1514
www.holtzingerfruit.com
Apples, cherries, pears and organics

HORMEL FOODS CORPORATION *page 69, 90*
1 Hormel Place
Austin, MN 55912
800-523-4635
www.hormel.com
Peloponnese olives, Hormel pepperoni, Hormel pre-cooked bacon slices, Old Smokehouse bacon, Spam, Stagg chili, Hormel chili, Dinty Moore stew, Marrakesh Express, El Torito foods and Hormel Premium crumbled bacon

HUNT'S (CONAGRA FOODS RETAIL PRODUCTS COMPANY) *page 176*
5 ConAgra Drive
Omaha, NE 60515
www.conagrafoods.com

INDEX FRESH, INC. *page 50*
P.O. Box 250
Bloomington, CA 92316
Phone: 909-877-1577
Fax: 909-877-0495
www.indexfresh.com
Avocados and Asian pears

J&J SNACK FOODS CORP. *page 85*
6000 Central Highway
Pennsauken, NJ 08109
888-JJSNACK
www.jjsnack.com
Minute Maid Soft Frozen Lemonade, SuperPretzel Soft Pretzels, Tio Pepe's Churros, Luigi's Real Italian Ice, Pretzel Fillers and Icee Squeeze Tubes

JELLY BELLY CANDY COMPANY *page 76*
One Jelly Belly Lane
Fairfield, CA 94533
707-428-2800
jellybelly.com
Jelly Belly jelly beans and other candies

JENNIE-O TURKEY STORE *page 90*
2505 Willmar Avenue S.W.
Willmar, MN 56201
Phone: 320-235-2622
Fax: 320-231-7100
Jennie-OTurkeystore.com
Various value-added turkey products

**JIF
(THE J.M. SMUCKER COMPANY)** *page 95*
Strawberry Lane
Orrville, OH 44667
888-550-9555
www.smuckers.com

THE J.M. SMUCKER COMPANY *page 210*
Strawberry Lane
Orrville, OH 44667
888-550-9555
www.smuckers.com

JON DONAIRE DESSERTS *page 35, 76*
12805 Busch Place
Santa Fe Springs, CA 90670
Phone: 562-946-6396
Fax: 562-946-3781
www.jondonaire.com
Baked New York cheesecake

KEEBLER/KELLOGG'S *page 91, 106*
One Battle Creek Square
Battle Creek, MI 49016
1-800-962-1413
www.kelloggs.com
Kellogg's cereals: Frosted Flakes, Frosted Mini-Wheats, Special K Red Berries, Smart Start, Fruit Harvest, Fruit Loops, Apple Jacks; Kellogg's Pop Tarts; Nutri-Grain bars; Rice Krispies Treats; Special K bars; Eggo waffles; Morningstar Farms breakfast patties; Kellogg's Snack Division crackers: CheezIts, Club Cracker, Krispy, Carr's, Austin Sandwich crackers; Kellogg's Snack Division cookies: Vanilla Wafers, Fudge Shoppe, Famous Amos and Pecan Sandies

KELSENBISCA, INC. *page 157*
510 Broad Hollow Road
Melville, NY 11747
Phone: 888-253-5736
Fax: 631-694-8085
www.kelsenbisca.com
Danish Butter cookies

KEYSTONE FRUIT MARKETING *page 165*
11 N. Carlisle St.
Greencastle, PA 17225
Phone: 717-597-2112
Fax: 717-597-4096
www.keystonefruit.com
Sweet onions and southern peaches

KING PAK POTATO CO. *page 94*
P.O. Box 22A
Edison, CA 93220
Phone: 661-366-3267
Fax: 661-366-0471
Potatoes: whites, reds, Yukon golds and russets

KINGSBURG APPLE SALES *page 71*
P.O. Box 38
Kingsburg, CA 93631
Phone: 559-897-2986
Fax: 559-897-4532
Sales@kingsburgapple.com
*Asian pears, pluots, Saturn peaches, white nectarines
and white peaches*

KIRSCHENMAN ENTERPRISES, INC. *page 44, 45, 94*
P.O. Box 27
Edison, CA 93220
Phone: 661-366-5736
Fax: 661-366-3825
Potatoes, watermelon, treefruit and California grapes

KRAFT FOODS NORTH AMERICA, INC. *page 102*
800-323-0768
www.kraftfoods.com

L&M NORTHWEST *page 103*
304 S. 1st St., Ste. A
Selah, WA 98942
Phone: 509-698-3881
Fax: 509-698-3922
www.lmcompanies.com
*Apples, pears, cherries, asparagus, potatoes, onions,
vegetables, melons and tropicals*

LAND O LAKES *page 116*
4001 Lexington Ave. N.
Arden Hills, MN 55126-2998
800-328-4155
www.landolakes.com
*Snack cheese, American cheese singles,
sour cream and cottage cheese*

**LAWRY'S (UNILEVER BESTFOODS
NORTH AMERICA)** *page 64*
800 Sylvan Avenue
Englewood Cliffs, NJ 07632
800-418-3275
www.lawrys.com
www.mymeals.com
*Lipton, Wish-Bone, Shedds Country Crock,
Hellmann's, Bestfoods, Knorr, Skippy, Ragu, Lawry's,
Bertolli and I Can't Believe It's Not Butter*

LEE BRANDS *page 57*
635 S. Sanborn Place, Ste. 19
Salinas, CA 93902
Phone: 831-796-4491
Fax: 831-775-0367
www.leebrands.com
Asparagus and green onions

LEGEND PRODUCE *page 51*
1269 Marie Street
Mendota, CA 93640
Phone: 559-655-1155
Fax: 559-655-3326
www.legendproduce.com
Cantaloupe, honeydew, mango and asparagus

LINDSAY OLIVES/BELL CARTER, INC. *page 46*
3742 Mt. Diablo Blvd.
Lafayette, CA 94549
Phone: 800-252-3557
Fax: 925-284-1954
lindsayolives.com
Ripe, Spanish and full line of specialty olive products

LING LING *page 59*
2395 American Avenue
Hayward, CA 94545
510-293-1838
www.ling-ling.com
Potstickers and crispy dumplings

**LIPTON (UNILEVER BESTFOODS
NORTH AMERICA)** *page 77*
800 Sylvan Avenue
Englewood Cliffs, NJ 07632
800-418-3275
www.liptont.com
*Lipton, Wish-Bone, Shedds Country Crock,
Hellmann's, Bestfoods, Knorr, Skippy, Ragu, Lawry's,
Bertolli and I Can't Believe It's Not Butter*

MACK FARMS, INC. *page 92*
P.O. Box 1077
Lake Wales, FL 33859
Phone: 863-678-0000
Fax: 863-678-0022
Potatoes

MANN PACKING COMPANY, INC. *page 53*
P.O. Box 690
Salinas, CA 93902
800-285-1002
www.broccoli.com
*Sugar snap peas, broccoli wokly, garden vegetables
and romaine hearts*

MAPLE LEAF CONSUMER FOODS *page 92*
7840 Madison Ave., Suite 135
Fair Oaks, CA 95628
Phone: 916-967-1633
Fax: 916-967-1690
www.mapleleaf.ca
Bacon and ham

MARCHO FARMS, INC. *page 155*
176 Orchard Lane
Harleysville, PA 19438
Phone: 215-721-7131
Fax: 215-721-9719
Veal

MARIANI PACKING COMPANY *page 65*
500 Crocker Drive
Vacaville, CA 95688
Phone: 800-672-8655
Fax: 707-452-2973
www.mariani.com
*Complete dried fruit line: dried plums, apricots, mixed
fruits, cranberries, tropical fruits, raisins, cherries and figs*

MARINE HARVEST *page 196, 206, 222, 228*
1600 S. Federal Highway, Suite 750
Pompano Beach, FL 33062
954-782-4015
www.marineharvest.com
www.nutreco.com

MARTINELLI'S *page 183*
P.O. Box 1868
Watsonville, CA 95076
Phone: 800-662-1868
Fax: 831-724-2910
www.martinellis.com
Sparkling cider and apple juice

MARTORI FARMS (KANDY) *page 55*
7332 E. Butherus Drive
Scottsdale, AZ 85260
Phone: 480-998-1444
Fax: 480-483-6723
Cantaloupes, honeydews and watermelons

MASTRONARDI PRODUCE *page 17*
2100 Road 4 East
Kingsville, Ontario N9Y 2E5
Phone: 519-326-1491
Fax: 519-326-8799
mastronardiproduce.com
Greenhouse tomatoes, peppers and cucumbers

MAZZETTA COMPANY, LLC *page 62, 63*
1990 St. Johns Ave.
Highland Park, IL 60035
Phone: 847-433-1150
Fax: 847-433-8973
www.mazzetta.com
Shrimp, lobster tails and orange roughy

**MCCORMICK & COMPANY, INC.
FOOD SERVICE DIVISION** *page 147*
226 Schilling Circle
Hunt Valley, MD 21031
Phone: 800-322-SPICE
Fax: 410-771-7512
www.mccormick.com/foodservice
Spices, herbs, seasonings and extracts

MCNEIL NUTRITIONALS *page 107*
15615 Acton Parkway #450
Irvine, CA 92618
Phone: 949-789-5508
Fax: 949-453-9406
www.splenda.com
Splenda no-calorie sweetener

MERCER RANCH *page 25*
46 Sonova Road
Prosser, WA 99350
Phone: 509-894-4773
Fax: 509-894-4965
www.mercerranch.com
Fresh carrots and sweet corn

MERISANT COMPANY *page 105*
10 S. Riverside, Suite 850
Chicago, IL 60606
Phone: 312-840-6000
Fax: 312-840-5400
www.equal.com
Equal sweetener packets and Equal Spoonful

METZ FRESH, LLC *page 63*
39405 Metz Road
King City, CA 93930
Phone: 831-759-4805
Fax: 831-775-0925
www.metzfresh.com
*Cello spinach, celery, green onions,
leeks, Brussels sprouts and stringless sugar peas*

MEYER FOODS *page 225*
4611 West Adams Street
Lincoln, NE 68524
Phone: 888-740-FOOD
Fax: 650-348-6149
www.michaeltoshio.com
Michael Toshio Cuisine and Gourmet Yakitori

MICHAEL FOODS *page 59*
401 Carlson Parkway, Suite 300
Minnetonka, MN 55305
877-727-3884
www.michaelfoods.com
Kirkland Signature Egg Starts

MILTON'S BAKING COMPANY *page 58*
3702 Via De La Valle, Suite 202
Del Mar, CA 92014
Phone: 858-350-9696
Fax: 858-350-0898
www.miltonsbaking.com
Healthy bread products

THE MINUTE MAID COMPANY *page 179*
2000 Saint James Place
Houston, TX 77056
713-888-5000
www.minutemaid.com
Fruit juices and drinks

MISSION PRODUCE *page 50*
P.O. Box 5267
Oxnard, CA 93031
Phone: 805-981-3655
Fax: 805-981-3662
www.missionpro.com

**MOLLY MCBUTTER
(ALBERTO CULVER SPECIALTY BRANDS)** *page 172*
2525 Armitage Ave.
Melrose Park, IL 60160
Phone: 708-450-3000
Fax: 708-450-2565
www.albertoculver.com
Mrs. Dash Seasoning and Molly McButter

MONEY'S MUSHROOMS PROCESSED DIVISION-CALKINS & BURKE LTD. *page 189*
800-1500 West Georgia Street
Vancouver, British Columbia
Canada V6G 2Z6
Phone: 604-669-3741
Fax: 604-669-9732
Mushrooms and pickled mushrooms

MONTEREY MUSHROOMS INC. *page 46*
260 Westgate Drive
Watsonville, CA 95076
Phone: 831-763-5336
Fax: 831-763-0700
www.montmush.com
Fresh, canned and marinated mushrooms

MONTEREY PASTA COMPANY *page 149*
1528 Moffett St.
Salinas, CA 93905
Phone: 831-753-6262
Fax: 831-755-0684
www.montereypasta.com
Gourmet pastas, sauces and baked sandwiches

MOTT'S USA *page 134*
6 High Ridge Park
Stanford, CT 06905
www.motts.com

MOUNTAIN STREAM INC. *page 173*
6800 N.W. 36th Ave.
Miami, FL 33147
866-691-7997
www.mountainstreamtilapia.com
Fresh tilapia fillets

MOUNTAIN VIEW FRUIT SALES *page 92*
4275 Ave. 416
Reedley, CA 93654
Phone: 559-637-9933
Fax: 559-637-9733
mountainviewfruit.com
Peaches, plums, nectarines, pluots, apricots and grapes

MOZZARELLA FRESCA, INC. *page 137*
1075 First Street
Benicia, CA 94510
Phone: 707-746-6818
Fax: 707-746-6829
sales@mozzarellafresca.com
www.mozzarellafresca.com
Fresh Italian Cheeses: mozzarella, ricotta and mascarpone

MRS. DASH
(ALBERTO CULVER SPECIALTY BRANDS) *page 172*
2525 Armitage Ave.
Melrose Park, IL 60160
Phone: 708-450-3000
Fax: 708-450-2565
www.albertoculver.com
Mrs. Dash Seasoning and Molly McButter

MULTIFOODS *page 104, 105*
111 Cheshire Lane
Minnetonka, MN 55305
800-866-3300
www.multifoods.com
Fun, fast and easy bakery products

NABISCO BISCUIT DIVISION
KRAFT FOODS NORTH AMERICA *page 93*
800-NABISCO (622-4726)
www.kraft.com
www.nabiscoworld.com

NANCY'S SPECIALTY FOODS *page 47*
6500 Overlake Place
Newark, CA 94560
Phone: 510-494-1100
Fax: 510-494-1140
www.nancys.com
Quiche, appetizers and party spirals

NAUMES INC. *page 156*
#2 Barnett St./P.O. Box 996
Medford, OR 97501
Phone: 541-779-9951
Fax: 541-772-3650
www.naumes.com
Cherries, Asian pears, pears and apples

NESTLÉ USA *page 75*
800 North Brand Blvd.
Glendale, CA 91203
818-549-6000
www.nestleUSA.com

NESTLÉ USA PREPARED FOODS COMPANY
HAND HELD FOODS GROUP *page 90*
20 Inverness Place East
Englewood, CO 80112
303-790-0303
Pocket Meals brand, Hot Pocket brand sandwiches and Lean Pocket brand sandwiches

NESTLÉ WATERS, NA *page 159*
777 N. Putnam Ave.
Greenwich, CT 06830
203-531-4100
www.perrier.com
Arrowhead, Ozarka, Ice Mountain, Deer Park, Zephyrhills, Poland Spring, Perrier and San Pellegrino

NEW STAR FRESH FOODS, LLC *page 143*
900 Work Street
Salinas, CA 93901
Phone: 831-758-7576
Fax: 831-758-7869
newstarfresh.com

NEW WORLD RESTAURANT GROUP INC. *page 139*
1687 Cole Blvd.
Golden, CO 80401
Phone: 303-568-8000
Fax: 303-568-8059
www.nwrgi.com

NEW YORK STYLE SAUSAGE CO. *page 152*
1228 Reamwood Ave.
Sunnyvale, CA 94089
Phone: 408-745-7675
Fax: 408-745-0680
nysdon@aol.com
www.nystylesausage.com
Italian sausage, breakfast sausage and basil garlic

NONNI'S FOOD COMPANY *page 157*
601 S. Boulder, #900
Tulsa, OK 74119
877-295-0289
www.nonnis.com
Nonni's biscotti

NORCO RANCH *page 25*
P.O. Box 910
Norco, CA 92860
Phone: 909-737-6735
Fax: 909-737-9405
Eggs

NORPAC/FLAVRPAC *page 229*
4350 S.W. Galewood St.
Lake Oswego, OR 97035
Phone: 800-733-9311
Fax: 503-699-0776
www.norpac.com
Petite peas, super sweet corn, broccoli Normandy, extra fine whole beans, triple berry blend, broccoli florets (small crowns) and Imperial stir-fry

THE NUNES COMPANY/FOXY FOODS *page 166*
P.O. Box 80006
Salinas, CA 93901
www.foxy.com
Romaine hearts, stringless snap peas, broccoli florets and garden vegetables

OCEAN FISHERIES LTD. *page 186*
13140 Rice Mill Road
Richmond, B.C. V6W 1A1
Phone: 604-272-2552
Fax: 604-272-5933
canned@oceanfish.com
www.oceanfish.com
Various salmon, tuna, crab and oysters

OCEAN SPRAY CRANBERRIES, INC. *page 156*
One Ocean Spray Drive
Lakeville-Middleboro, MA 02349
Phone: 508-946-1000
Fax: 508-946-7704
www.oceanspray.com
Cranberry Juice Cocktail and Craisins Sweetened Dried Cranberries

THE OPPENHEIMER GROUP *page 78*
11 Burbige St., Suite 101
Coquitlam, B.C. V3K 7B2
Canada
Phone: 604-461-OPPY (6779)
Fax: 604-468-4780
www.zesprikiwi.com
Zespri kiwifruit

ORCA BAY FOODS *page 84*
P.O. Box C-389664
Seattle, WA 98138-9664
Phone: 425-204-9100
Fax: 425-204-9200
www.orcabayfoods.com
Premium-quality frozen seafood

OREGON CHAI, INC. *page 38*
1745 N.W. Marshall
Portland, OR 97209
Phone: 503-552-2188
Fax: 503-796-0980
Sellchai.com
Oregon Chai tea original concentrate

PACIFIC FRUIT INC./BONITA BANANAS *page 79*
500 N. State College Blvd., Suite 560
Orange, CA 92868
Phone: 714-939-9939
Fax: 714-939-9906
Fresh bananas, pineapples and mangoes

PAM (CONAGRA FOODS RETAIL PRODUCTS COMPANY) *page 176*
5 ConAgra Drive
Omaha, NE 60515
www.conagrafoods.com

PHILLIPS FOODS, INC. *page 146*
1215 E. Fort Avenue
Baltimore, MD 21230
Phone: 888-234-CRAB (2722)
Fax: 410-837-8526
www.phillipsfoods.com
Backfin crabmeat and crab cakes

PREMIO FOODS, INC. *page 136*
50 Utter Ave.
Hawthorne, NJ 07506
Phone: 973-427-1106
Fax: 973-427-1140
www.premiofoods.com
Italian sausage and bratwurst

PRIMAVERA MARKETING *page 70*
P.O. Box 419
Linden, CA 95236
Phone: 209-931-9420
Fax: 209-931-9424
Primav2@attglobal.net
Apples, cherries and asparagus

PRIME TIME INTERNATIONAL *page 49*
86705 Avenue 54, Suite A
Coachella, CA 92236
760-399-4166
www.primetimeproduce.com
Seedless watermelons, red, yellow and green bell peppers, red, yellow and orange greenhouse peppers and tomatoes

PURATOS CORPORATION-US *page 104*
1941 Old Cuthbert Road
Cherry Hill, NJ 08034
Phone: 856-428-4300
Fax: 856-428-2939
Bakery ingredients

QUAKER *page 95*
555 West Monroe
Chicago, IL 60661
800-367-6287
www.quakeroatmeal.com
Quaker oatmeal, Tropicana juice, Gatorade,
Propel fitness water and Chewy granola bars

RAIN FOREST
AQUACULTURE PRODUCTS *page 165*
1000 Sawgrass Corporate Parkway, Suite 110
Sunrise, FL 33323
954-835-0988
Sales: 800-289-8452
www.tilapia.com
Tilapia fillets and fresh whole tilapia

READY PAC PRODUCE *page 55*
4401 Foxdale Avenue
Irwindale, CA 91706
Phone: 626-856-8686
Fax: 626-856-0088
Salads, fresh-cut fruits and vegetables

RICH-SEAPAK CORPORATION *page 120*
P.O. Box 20670
St. Simons Island, GA 31522
Phone: 800-654-9731
Fax: 912-634-3106
www.rich-seapak.com
Mozzarella cheese sticks, French toast sticks, onion
rings, breaded shrimp, appetizers, marinated & grilled
shrimp, crab cakes and clam strips

RICHMOND NEW ZEALAND
FARM FRESH *page 176*
3050 Saturn Street, Suite 102
Brea, CA 92821
Phone: 714-854-1590
Fax: 714-577-4924
www.richmondnz.com

ROTEL (CONAGRA FOODS RETAIL
PRODUCTS COMPANY) *page 176*
5 ConAgra Drive
Omaha, NE 60515
www.conagrafoods.com

RUIZ FOOD PRODUCTS *page 200*
P.O. Box 37
Dinuba, CA 93618
800-477-6474
www.elmonterey.com
Authentic frozen Mexican food

RUSSET POTATO EXCHANGE *page 94*
8550 Central Sands Road
Bancroft, WI 54921
715-335-8050
www.rpespud.com
Potatoes and onions

SAN FRANCISCO BAY GOURMET COFFEE *page 79*
1933 Davis St., Suite 308
San Leandro, CA 94577
Phone: 800-829-1300
Fax: 510-638-0760
www.sfbaycoffee.com
www.sfbcoffee.com
French Roast, Colombian Supremo, Decaf Gourmet
Blend and Hazelnut Crème

SARA LEE COFFEE & TEA *page 183*
990 Supreme Drive
Bensenville, IL 60106
www.superiorcoffeeshop.com
Kirkland Signature Colombian coffee,
Arabica Decaf coffee

SARA LEE FOODS *page 16*
Ball Park beef franks, Hillshire Farm Polska Kielbasa,
Hillshire Farm cocktail smokies, Hillshire Farm Deli
Select, Gallo salame chubs, Gallo sliced salame, Gallo
sliced lite salame, Galileo roasted garlic salame, Jimmy
Dean fresh sausage, Jimmy Dean sausage, egg and
cheese biscuits, Jimmy Dean Fresh Taste Fast sausage
links, State Fair corn dogs, Sinai Kosher mini bagel
dogs, Sinai Kosher beef polish sausage, Sinai Kosher
beef dinner franks, Sinai Kosher salami, Sinai Kosher
corn beef and Sinai Kosher pastrami

SAVEN CORPORATION *page 169*
3901 Highland Road, Suite G
Waterford, MI 48328
Phone: 248-706-1445
Fax: 248-706-1457
www.sweetonionsource.com
OSO Sweet onions

SCHREIBER FOODS, INC. *page 112*
425 Pine Street
Green Bay, WI 54301
Phone: 800-344-0333
Fax: 920-455-2700
www.schreiberfoods.com
Natural, process, specialty and cream cheese

SCHWAN'S CONSUMER BRANDS
NORTH AMERICA, INC. *page 143*
115 W. College Drive
Marshall, MN 56258
Freschetta, Red Baron, Sabatasso's, Minh,
Coyote Grill and Glacier Mountain Creamery

SEA WATCH INTERNATIONAL *page 134*
8978 Glebe Park Drive
Easton, MD 21601
Phone: 401-820-7848
Fax: 401-822-1266
www.seawatch.com
Chopped clams, clam strips and clam chowder

SEABOARD FARMS, INC. *page 122*
9000 W. 67th St., Suite 200
Shawnee Mission, KS 66202
Phone: 913-261-2600
Fax: 913-261-2626
www.prairiefresh.com
PrairieFresh Premium Pork

SEALD SWEET LLC *page 168*
P.O. Box 690152
Vero Beach, FL 32969-0152
772-569-2244
www.sealdsweet.com
Florida Citrus, various imported citrus and sweet onions

SHIITAKE-YA *page 51*
P.O. Box 7107
Huntington Beach, CA 92615-7107
www.shiitakeya.com

SHULTZ FOODS *page 91*
680 W. Chestnut St.
Hanover, PA 17331
Phone: 717-637-5931
Fax: 717-637-0487
World-class pretzels

SINGLETON (CONAGRA FOODS) *page 63*
P.O. Box 2819
Tampa, FL 33601
Phone: 813-241-1500
Fax: 813-247-1782
www.conagraseafood.com

SKAGIT VALLEY'S BEST PRODUCE *page 16*
P.O. Box 2328
Mount Vernon, WA 98273
Phone: 360-848-0777
Fax: 360-848-0778
svbest.com
Red, white and Yukon gold potatoes

SMITHFIELD PACKING COMPANY *page 154*
501 North Church Street
Smithfield, VA 23430
Phone: 757-357-4321
Fax: 757-357-1339

**SOUTH FLORIDA POTATO
GROWERS EXCHANGE** *page 92*
P.O. Box 901670
Homestead, FL 33034
Phone: 800-830-7783
Fax: 305-246-8900
Potatoes

STARBUCKS COFFEE COMPANY *page 39*
2401 Utah Avenue South
Seattle, WA 98134
206-447-1575
starbucks.com
Starbucks coffee

STEMILT GROWERS INC. *page 37*
123 Ohme Garden Road
Wenatchee, WA 98801
Phone: 509-662-9667
Fax: 509-663-2914
www.stemilt.com
Apples, pears, cherries and apricots

STEVCO INC. *page 44, 45*
9777 Wilshire Blvd., Ste. 619
Beverly Hills, CA 90212
Phone: 661-392-7134
Fax: 661-397-1361
grapegift.com
Table grapes

SUGAR FOODS CORPORATION *page 159*
950 Third Avenue
New York, NY 10022-2705
Phone: 212-753-6900
Fax: 212-753-6988
www.sugarfoods.com

SUN WORLD INTERNATIONAL *page 54*
52-200 Industrial Way
P.O. Box 1028
Coachella, CA 92236
Phone: 760-398-9300
Fax: 760-398-9413
www.sun-world.com
info@sun-world.com
California grapes, California plums, sweet colored peppers, grapefruit, lemons and seedless watermelon

SUNKIST GROWERS *page 119*
14130 Riverside Drive
Sherman Oaks, CA 91423
818-986-4800
www.sunkist.com
Navel oranges, Valencia oranges, moro oranges, lemons, grapefruit, pummelos, Fairchild tangerines, minneola tangerines and satsuma mandarins

SUNNYCOVE CITRUS *page 47*
440 Anchor Avenue
Orange Cove, CA 93646
Phone: 559-626-4085
Fax: 559-626-7210
www.sccitrus.com
Citrus

SUNWEST FRUIT CO. INC. *page 71*
755 E. Manning Ave.
Parlier, CA 93648
Phone: 559-646-4400
Fax: 559-646-3232
www.sunwestfruit.com
Tree-ripe peaches, plums, nectarines and navel oranges

**SWANSON BROTH
CAMPBELL SOUP COMPANY** *page 116*
Camden, NJ 08103
800-44-BROTH
www.swansonbroth.com
www.holidaycentral.com

SWIFT & COMPANY *page 124, 224*
1770 Promontory Circle
Greeley, CO 80634
800-727-2333

SWITZERLAND CHEESE MARKETING, INC. *page 186*
704 Executive Blvd.
Valley Cottage, NY 10989
Phone: 800-628-5226
Fax: 845-268-2480
www.switzerland-cheese.com
Emmentaler and Le Gruyere Switzerland

TANIMURA & ANTLE *page 52, 55, 187*
P.O. Box 4070
Salinas, CA 93912
800-772-4542
www.taproduce.com
Romaine hearts, head lettuce, Caesar salad and garden salad mix

TARANTINO WHOLESALE FOODS *page 140, 141*
2707 Boston Ave.
San Diego, CA 92113
Phone: 619-232-7585
Fax: 619-696-0093
Tarantino mild Italian sausage, hot Italian sausage and breakfast sausage

TILLAMOOK COUNTY CREAMERY ASSOCIATION *page 66*
P.O. Box 313
Tillamook, OR 97141
Phone: 503-842-4481
Fax: 503-815-1309
www.tillamookcheese.com
Cheese and ice cream

TOP BRASS MARKETING *page 23*
P.O. Box 1270
Shafter, CA 93263
Phone: 661-746-2148
Fax: 661-746-3643
Potatoes

TRAPPER'S CREEK SMOKING COMPANY, INC. *page 19*
5650 B. Street
Anchorage, AK 99518
Phone: 907-561-8088
Fax: 907-561-8389
www.trapperscreek.com
Smoked kippered wild king salmon

TREE TOP, INC. *page 79*
P.O. Box 248
Selah, WA 98942
Phone: 509-697-7251
Fax: 509-698-1453
www.treetop.com
Apple juice, frozen apple juice, blended juices and apple sauce

TRIDENT SEAFOODS CORP. *page 29*
5303 Shilshole Ave. N.W.
Seattle, WA 98107
Phone: 800-SEALEGS
Fax: 206-782-7246
www.tridentseafoods.com
Alaskan Seafood

TRINITY FRUIT SALES CO. *page 55*
9493 N. Fort Washington Rd., Suite 102
Fresno, CA 93720
Phone: 559-433-3777
Fax: 559-433-3790
trinityfruit.com
Cherries, blueberries, stone fruit, grapes, apples and kiwi

TYSON FOODS INC. *page 101*
2210 West Oaklawn Drive
Springdale, AR 72762
www.tyson.com
Poultry, beef and pork

VALLEY PRIDE SALES, INC. *page 16*
15356 Produce Lane
Mount Vernon, WA 98273
Phone: 360-428-2717
Fax: 360-428-3601
Red and white potatoes, blueberries, raspberries and mini pumpkins

VENTURA FOODS, LLC *page 59*
40 Pointe Drive
Brea, CA 92821
Phone: 714-257-3700
Fax: 714-257-3702
venturafoods.com
Oils, shortenings, dressings, margarines, soup bases and sauces

VIE DE FRANCE YAMAZAKI INC. *page 182*
2070 Chain Bridge Road, #500
Vienna, VA 22182
Phone: 800-446-4404
Fax: 703-847-0969
Bakery products and desserts

WALKERS SHORTBREAD, INC. *page 211*
170 Commerce Drive
Hauppauge, NY 11788
Phone: 631-273-0011
Fax: 631-273-0438
www.walkersshortbread.com
Scottish shortbread cookies

WALLACE FARMS *page 16*
P.O. Box 405
Burlington, WA 98233
Phone: 360-757-0981
Fax: 360-757-7783
www.wallacespuds.com
Red, white, yellow and purple potatoes, organic red, yellow and purple russet potatoes

WESSON (CONAGRA FOODS RETAIL PRODUCTS COMPANY) *page 68*
5 ConAgra Drive
Omaha, NE 60515
www.conagrafoods.com

WEST PAK AVOCADO, INC. *page 50*
42322 Avenida Alvarado
Temecula, CA 92590
Phone: 909-296-5757
www.westpakavocado.com
Avocados

WHITE WAVE, INC. *page 78*
1990 North 57th Court
Boulder, CO 80301
Phone: 303-443-3470
Fax: 303-443-3952
silkissoy.com
Silk Vanilla Soymilk

WILCOX FARMS *page 38*
40400 Harts Lake Valley Road
Roy, WA 98580
Phone: 360-458-7774
www.wilcoxfarms.com
Milk and eggs

WILSON BATIZ, LLC *page 120*
2225 Avenida Costa Este, Ste. 1100
San Diego, CA 92154
Phone: 619-661-5222
Fax: 619-661-8032
www.wilsonbatiz.com
Colored bell peppers, beefsteak tomatoes and English cucumbers

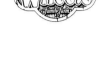

U.S. MEASUREMENTS & METRIC CONVERSIONS

| UNITED STATES | | | | INTERNATIONAL | | TEMPERATURE | |
tsp.	tbsp.	cups	fl. oz.	grams*	ml	F°	C°
1/4					1	100	40
1/2					2	125	50
3/4					4	150	65
1	1/3			5	5	175	80
1 1/2	1/2		1/4	7	6	200	95
2	2/3			10	10	225	110
3	1		1/2	14	15	250	120
	2		1	28	25	300	150
	3		1 1/2	43	45	325	165
	4	1/4	2	57	60	350	175
		1/3		76	75	375	190
	8	1/2	4	115	125	400	205
		3/4	6	172	175	425	225
		1	8	230	250	450	230
		1 1/2	12	375	375	475	245
		2 (1 lb.)	16	500	500	500	260
		4	32 (1 qt.)	1,000	1,000		

*Conversions have been rounded to the closest whole gram and may vary by ingredient.

F

interview with, 41–43

recipes from, 60–61, 73

Trapper's Creek smoked salmon, 19

Tree Top apple juice, 79

Trident Seafoods cod, 29

Trout, rainbow with

lime ginger sauce, roasted, 96

Tuna

albacore pasta primavera, 148

Creole, tomato ketchup, 174

Waldorf salad, 134

Turkey

pesto roll, 32

spring rolls, Thai-style, 90

turkey surprise, healthy multi-grain, 58

wine for, 153

Turnips

gratin, potato and, 145

soup, with maple syrup, 190

Tutka Bay Wilderness Lodge, 21

Tyson Foods, Inc., 101

soup, tortellini, 190

stew, game and garden, 34

stir-fry, crispy dumpling, 59

stir-fry, tangy imperial, 229

Velveeta Cheese, 93

Vie de France croissants, 182

Vol-au-vents, asparagus and red pepper, 206

Walkers Shortbread Cookies, 211

Wallace Farms potatoes, 16

Walnuts, endive salad and, 188

Water, 159

Webster, Alan, 100

Whipped cream, rugala with, 157

Whiskey, Irish coffee, 79

White, Jasper

interview with, 127–129

recipes from, 144–145

Wilcox eggs, 38

WilsonBatiz grapes, 120

Wine

apple dessert salad, 38

chicken, with mushrooms

and smoked ham, 33

chicken breasts, baked with Riesling,

spiced apples, cabbage and parsnips, 33

dessert types, 74–75

for fish and seafood, 172

for meats, 153

pears roasted with cinnamon and, 72

port and dried cranberry sauce, 68

for spicy food, 118

Winters, Charlie, 68, 69, 123, 177

Wraps

romaine hearts, 137

spinach, mushroom and mozzarella, 46

Yang, Jung-Min, 217

Yeh, Melissa, 230

Yogurt

on muffins grilled with fruit, 104

smoothie, apple strawberry banana, 79

smoothie, peach, 107

Yoshida's Gourmet Sauce, 147

Zamora Armenta, Gaspar, 203

Zespri Kiwifruit, 78

Zucchini, vegetable garden pot roast, 98

*Diana's Summer
Berry Tartlets
Page 35*

Acknowledgments

THERE ARE MANY, many hardworking people at Costco and elsewhere who have contributed to this book. In response to a request in *The Costco Connection*, Costco's magazine for Business and Executive Members, we received more than 1,000 recipes from seven countries. In addition, Costco employees responded with their own favorites. We thank you all.

Submissions were sorted into food categories and then 118 were selected for testing by a panel of Costco employees and members. We want to thank the following testers who had the enviable but demanding task of narrowing the selections to the 70 employee and member recipes that appear in the book: Ken Broman, Paula Broncheau, Carlene Canton, Heather Carey, Linda Carey, Jesper Chou, Gary Cornell, Rossie Cruz, Linda Dahl, Steve Franz, Dave Fuller, Jose Garcia, Blakely Hachiya, Brian Haupt, Hiroko Huntoon, Carol Ideta, Joseph Jiminez, Chitomi Kato, Jane Klein-Shucklin, Diane Larson, Hallie Larson, Jeff Marker, Sean McGriff, Aliw Moral, Anita Nichols, Mario Padilla, Betty Pien, Kimberly Reaume, Jillian Sanchez, Asako Santo, Yukako Sirota, Fransisca Soerjono, Toby Sugden, Anita Thompson, Yvonne Todd, Karen Tripson, Steve Trump, Gary Volchok, Pat Volchok, Vicki Watts, David Wight, Shelley Wilson, Doris Winters and Rhinee Yeung.

The taste-testing could not have happened without the expertise of our guest chefs. Jim McGuire, career counselor at the Art Institute of Seattle, and Chef John R. Fisher at Renton (Washington) Technical College helped us secure senior culinary students with a background in international cuisines. They were as follows: Mexico lead chef Gilbert Arangure, with assistants Juan Armando Rodriquez, Justin J. Kauer, Michael Watkins, Steven Saban Jr. and Charlie Skidmore; Korea lead chef Suna Johnson, with assistant Jihyun Kim; Japan lead chef Soma Mutsuko, with assistants Kim Moore and Andrew George; Taiwan, Canada and UK lead chef C. J. Houck, with assistant Kendrick Tippler; U.S. lead cook Linda Carey, with assistant Diane Larson.

Coordination and translation of the international recipes (as necessary) was handled with able assistance from the following employees in Costco's international offices: Stephanie Laberge, Canada; Veronica Hidalgo, Mexico; Pam Broadhurst, United Kingdom; Sungwon Hwang, Korea; Kyla White, Japan; and Melissa Yeh, Taiwan.

Special thanks go to Canadian food professionals Anne Desjardins, Marcy Goldman and Sandi Richard, as well as Diane Madill and Carol Lambourne for contributing their recipes. Also thanks to Frank Bordoni, food columnist for *The Costco Connection*'s UK edition.

Several Costco employees were instrumental in providing technical assistance, including Christine Summers and Sherry Anne Allen of the Quality Assurance department; Francine Weste in R & D International; Doug Holbrook, director of Fresh Meat U.S.; Alan Webster, catering manager; and Don Dvorak, deli manager. Also thanks to members of the Fresh Foods team who provided their expertise, including David Andrew, global wine director; Jeff Lyons, vice president/senior general merchandise manager of Fresh Foods/Corporate Foods; Sue McConnaha, vice president of bakery operations; Frank Padilla, assistant general merchandising manager, Fresh Foods; and Charlie Winters, vice president/director of meat operations.

We want to especially thank these employees of the vendors and suppliers who took part in the creation of the book: at Iridio Photography, Seattle, kitchen manager Linda Carey, food stylist assistants Diane Larson, Helen Kearny and Mary McKillop, and account coordinator Traci Joy; at Midas Printing, Jim Letzel and Erika West; and at AMS book distributors, Susan Latham and Adam Zoldan.

In the Publishing Department, special thanks go to Dorothy Strakele, Kathi Tipper-Holgersen and Bill Urlevich, who provided hands-on coordinating assistance, and to Tim Talevich and Lory Williams, who kept the regular work flow humming. Stephanie Ponder and Mark Stroder added their writing talents. Will Fifield, Tod Jones, Shana McNally, Stephanie Ponder, Mark Stroder, Tim Talevich and David Wight assisted with proofreading. Rossie Cruz coordinated shipping and distribution of the book, and Janet Burgess was business manager.

Other Costco employees also played key roles: Joel Benoliel, Dick DiCerchio, Pennie Clarke Ianiciello, Chris Eiche, Jodi Ellis, Sheri Flies, Stephanie Gardner, Jim Klauer, Dennis Knapp, Ronda Miller, Ginnie Roeglin, Tim Rose, and Wendi Wamboldt.

Photo credits

l. = left   r. = right   c. = center
a. = above   b. = below

All photographs by Iridio Photography, with the following exceptions:

©2003 E. Jane Armstrong, 7
France Freeman, 10-11
©2003 Mike Hipple/Hipphoto.com, 12 (chef portrait)
Linda Holt Ayriss/Artville, 12 t.l., 40 t.l., 86 t.l., 108 t.l.,
    160 t.l., 204 t.l., 226 t.l.,
Chip Porter/Getty Images, 12 t.r.
Photodisc, 13 t.l., 42 b.r., 80 t.l., 81 b.l., 126 t.l.,
    128 t.r., 184 t.l., 185 b.l., 194 t.l., 212 t.l., 218 t.l.
Bruce Forster/Getty Images, 13 c.l.
Peter Correz/Getty Images, 13 b.l.
Connie Coleman/Getty Images, 14 t.r.
Nick Gunderson.Getty Images, 14 b.r.
Alan Abramowitz/Getty Images, 15 t.l.
© Ariel Skelley/CORBIS, 15 c.
Global Fishing, 28 c.l.
Duell Fisher, 30 (chef portrait)
Starbucks, 39
© Tom Paiva, 40 (chef portrait)
Gerald French/Getty Images, 41 t.l.
Chris Cole/Getty Images, 41 c.l.
Burke/Triolo Productions/FoodPix/Getty Images,
    41 b.l. (grapes)
Luis Veiga/Getty Images, 42 t.r.
Anthony Johnson/Getty Images, 43 t.l.
V.C.L./Paul Viant/Getty Images, 43 b.l.
Sun World, 54 t.l.

Continental Mills, 74 b.l.
Douglas Peebles, 80 (chef portrait)
© Bob Krist/CORBIS, 81 t.l.
A. Witte-C. Mahaney/Getty Images 81 c.l.
Ernie Block, Kansas City, 86 (chef portrait)
Melissa Farlow/NATIONAL GEOGRAPHIC
    IMAGE COLLECTION/Getty Images 87 t.l.
© Little Blue Wolf Productions/CORBIS 87 c.l.
© CORBIS 87 b.l.
Rob Brimson/Getty Images 88 t.r.
David Hanson/Getty Images 88 b.r.
Paul Chesley/Getty Images 89 t.l., 213 b.l., 218 b.r.
Vcl/Spencer Rowell/Getty Images, 89 b.l.
Kraft Foods, 102 t.l.
Merisant, 105 t.r.
Ralph Lauer, 108 (chef portrait)
Richard H. Johnston/Getty Images, 109 t.l.
Gavin Hellier/PictureQuest, 109 c.l. (route 66 place)
Frank Siteman/PictureQuest, 109 b.l.
Harald Sund/Getty Images, 110 c.r.
Randa Bishop/PictureQuest, 110 b.r.
Walter Bibikow/PictureQuest, 111 t.l.
Reproduced with permission of
    Globe Newspaper Company, Inc., 126 (chef portrait)
Creatas, 127 t.l., 162 b.r., 226 b.r.
© Catherine Karnow/CORBIS, 127 c.l.
© Jonathan Blair/CORBIS, 127 b.l.
Leland Bobbe/Getty Images, 128 c.r.
© Richard Cummins/CORBIS, 128 b.r.
Donovan Reese/Getty Images, 129 t.l.
Digital Vision/Getty Images, 129 c.l., 161 b.l.
H.J. Heinz, 132 c.l.

Kelsenbisca, 157 t.r.
Lew Robertson/FoodPix/Getty Images, 159 t.r.
Peter Frank Edwards, 160 (chef portrait)
Wayne Eastep/Getty Images, 161 t.l.
Andy Sacks/Getty Images, 161 c.l.
Patrick Molnar/Getty Images, 162 t.r.
Tom Raymond/Getty Images, 163 c.l.
Hiroyuki Matsumoto/Getty Images, 163 b.l.
Ferrero, 181 t.r.
SuperStock, 184 t.r.
Stephan Poulin/SuperStock, 184 b.r.
© Alex Steedman/CORBIS, 185 t.l.
Michael P. Gadomski/SuperStock, 185 c.l.
Fisheries, 186 b.l.
Rosemary Calvert/Getty Images, 194 t.r.
Philippe Colombi/Getty Images, 194 c.r.
Paul Harris/Getty Images, 195 c.l., 212 t.r.
Robert Frerck/Getty Images, 195 b.l.
C Squared Studios/Getty Images, 204 t.r.
© Jacqui Hurst/CORBIS, 204 c.r., 205 b.l
© Annie Griffiths Belt/CORBIS, 204 b.r.
Neil Beer/Getty Images, 205 t.l.
Neil Farrin/Getty Images, 212 b.r.
Tim Bieber/Getty Images, 213 c.l.
Victoria Pearson/Getty Images, 218 t.r.
Ryan McVay/Getty Images, 219 t.l.
Photolink/Getty Images, 219 b.l.
Jean-Marc Truchet/Getty Images, 226 t.r.
Stone/Getty Image, t.l.
Simon Watson/Getty Images, c.l.

Writing credits

Anita Thompson/Buyer biographies, 10-11
Pat Volchok/All chapter introductions and chef interviews, 12-15, 40-43, 80-81, 86-89, 108-111, 126-129, 160-163, 184-185, 194-195, 204-205, 212-213, 218-219, 226-227
Mark E. Stroder/Frank's Mushroom Tips, 19; How to Properly Ripen Pears, 20; Selecting the Right Avocado, 50; Storing Fresh Cherries, 103; Keeping Salad Mix Fresh, 135
Karen Tripson/Unique Regional Fish Values, 29; Plank Cooking, 30; Using Leftover Ham, 31; Wilcox Almond Rice Pudding recipe, 38; Goodness Grapecious, 46; Sunny Cove Spicy Orange and Shrimp Kebabs recipe, 47; Nancy's Specialty Foods Top-and-Serve Ideas, 47; Balsamic—the Fine Wine of Vinegar, 52; Safe Seafood at Home, 65; Special Occasion Cuts, 69; Dessert Ideas for Kirkland Signature Macadamia Nut Cereal, 76; Make Soymilk Part of Your Day, 78; Spicy Granny Smith Potato Slaw recipe, 92; Hot Potatoes! Cold Potatoes!, 95;

Kirkland Signature Canned Salmon—Quick and Healthful, 96; Best Value Cuts of Beef, 97; Kirkland Signature Rotisserie Chicken ideas, 102; Best Value Pork Cuts, 123; Say Cheese, 133; General Mills Gorgonzola Squares recipe, 133; Serving Ideas for Sabatasso's Vegetable Lasagna, 143; Nonni's Biscotti Serving Ideas, 157; Facts About Water, 159; Tilapia Facts, 173; Best Cuts for Grilling, 177; Mexican Ingredients, 199; High Praise for Pozole, 202; Fresh Salmon Tips, 207; Anytime for Lamb, 209; Best Beef for Korean Cooking, 215; Miso, 220; Essential Japanese Flavorings, 222; Oils in Asian Cooking, 229
Stephanie E. Ponder/Artisan Breads, 58; Bagels, Bagels, Bagels, 138; Cheesecake Extras, 181
David Andrew/Wine with (or as) Dessert, 75; What to Drink with Spicy Food, 118; Marrying Meat and Wine, 153; Sipping Wine with Seafood, 172